Engaged Research and Practice

Additional titles in the **Engaged Research and Practice for Social Justice in Education** series:

Research, Actionable Knowledge, and Social Change
Reclaiming Social Responsibility Through Research Partnerships
Edward P. St. John
Foreword by Penny A. Pasque

Reflection in Action
A Guidebook for Student Affairs Professionals and Teaching Faculty
Edited by Kimberly A. Kline
Foreword by Edward P. St. John

Critical Action Research
A Guide for Students and Practitioners
Leticia Bustillos and Edlyn Peña

Intersectionality in Educational Research
Edited by Dannielle Joy Davis, Rachelle J. Brunn-Bevel, and James L. Olive
Foreword by Susan R. Jones

Using Action Inquiry in Engaged Research
An Organizing Guide
Edward P. St. John, Kim Callahan Lijana, and Glenda D. Musoba
Foreword by Timothy K. Eatman
Afterword by Rick Dalton

Engaged Research and Practice

Higher Education and the Pursuit of the Public Good

Edited by Betty Overton, Penny A. Pasque,

and John C. Burkhardt

Foreword by Tony Chambers
Series Foreword by Edward P. St. John

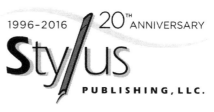

1996–2016 20TH ANNIVERSARY

Sty/us

PUBLISHING, LLC.

STERLING, VIRGINIA

Published by Stylus Publishing, LLC.
22883 Quicksilver Drive
Sterling, Virginia 20166-2102

Library of Congress Cataloging-in-Publication Data

Names: Overton, Betty, editor, author. |
Pasque, Penny A., editor, author. |
Burkhardt, John, editor, author.
Title: Engaged research and practice :
higher education and the pursuit of the public good /
edited by Betty Overton, Penny A. Pasque and John C. Burkhardt;
foreword, Tony Chambers.
Description: 1st ed. |
Sterling, Virginia : Stylus Publishing., LLC, 2016.
Identifiers: LCCN 2016013367 (print) |
LCCN 2016025330 (ebook) |
ISBN 9781620364406 (pbk. : alk. paper) |
ISBN 9781620364390 (cloth : alk. paper) |
ISBN 9781620364413 (library networkable e-edition) |
ISBN 9781620364420 (consumer e-edition) |
Subjects: LCSH: Action research in education--United States. |
Community and college--United States. |
Education, Higher--Aims and objectives--United States. |
Common good--United States.
Classification: LCC LB2326.3 .E65 2016 (print) |
LCC LB2326.3 (ebook) |
DDC 370.72--dc23
LC record available at https://lccn.loc.gov/2016013367

13-digit ISBN: 978-1-62036-4390 (cloth)
13-digit ISBN: 978-1-62036-4406 (paper)
13-digit ISBN: 978-1-62036-4413 (library networkable e-edition)
13-digit ISBN: 978-1-62036-4420 (consumer e-edition)

Printed in the United States of America

All first editions printed on acid-free paper
that meets the American National Standards Institute
Z39-48 Standard.

Bulk Purchases

Quantity discounts are available for use in workshops and for
staff development.
Call 1-800-232-0223

First Edition, 2017

10   9   8   7   6   5   4   3   2   1

We dedicate this book to all of the community partners, faculty, students, and administrators working toward engaged scholarship.

CONTENTS

Growing, Learning, and Bringing Back
    Amicia Gomez Bowman

Reflective Narrative   *268*
Undocumented Students
    Chengchen Zhu

PART FIVE   Concluding Thoughts on Engaged Research and Practice

12.   Reflections   *273*
      Lessons Learned and Next Steps
          Betty Overton

      Contributors   *281*

      Index   *291*

Series Foreword

U nfortunately, well-meaning higher education researchers have unintentionally contributed to structural inequality in state educational systems by focusing on narrowly framed problems and using traditional research approaches. *Engaged Research and Practice: Higher Education and the Pursuit of the Public Good*, edited by Betty Overton, Penny A. Pasque, and John C. Burkhardt, is an important book at a critical time. Congratulations to the editors and authors for raising the standard for research on the public good.

To illustrate the importance of this book, I share a few reflections about the revolution within the National Forum for the Public Good (National Forum) and the origins of the book and series. Even before I arrived at the University of Michigan (UM) in 2005, I was concerned about structural inequalities in the state education system (e.g., St. John & Chung, 2004). Inequalities in Michigan had been increased by reforms advocated for because of educational research meant to promote the public good.

When I came to UM, the National Forum was conducting studies for the Cherry Commission appointed by then-governor Jennifer Granholm. Like most research at the time, the studies being conducted used traditional methods to examine the correlation between high school courses and college access; they treated social conditions as background and failed to consider how financial inequalities influenced both preparation and the ability to pay for college. As I reflect back, it is evident these early studies at the National Forum systematically overlooked the social, cultural, and economic challenges facing families that remained in Detroit, Flint, and other Michigan communities, locales once called great American cities. This new book focuses explicitly on transforming social and cultural barriers that have entrenched inequality for so long. Sadly, the studies of the structural aspects of schooling (e.g., math courses completed in high school) resulted in policies that contributed to socioeconomic class divide in educational attainment in Michigan.

Nate Daun-Barnett coordinated quantitative studies for the National Forum. He and I began talking about the limitations of the studies, such as exclusion of financial aid variables, after I commented on a presentation he made at the Association for the Study of Higher Education in November

2004. Years later, I was honored to see how Nate reflected on these events and subsequent increases in inequality in Michigan higher education as part of a case study for our book (St. John, Daun-Barnett, & Moronski-Chapman, 2013). Nate's journey illustrates how the National Forum has functioned in a leadership role in Michigan education and that it is possible to reflect on experiences and learn from them. I am very happy to see Nate's chapter in this volume. He provides a mature, informed perspective on alignment of state policy and educational reform.

In 2005, Penny Pasque began working on her doctoral dissertation. She and I had also started talking about the problems with the narrow points of view being used in research on policy at UM (e.g., St. John, Hill, Wooden, & Pasque, 2015). In our earliest conversations, we shared the dream that social justice could become an integral part of research by scholars in the field of higher education. Both Penny and I had too frequently experienced the silencing of our voices when we raised issues related to inequality. Advocacy for social research and action that promotes justice as well as work on empowerment and inclusion were routinely disregarded. I decided to cochair Penny's dissertation so she would have an opportunity to address some of the core challenges facing higher education, rather than being forced to codify every bit information as either costs or benefits and as public or private good. Not everything falls into neatly constructed boxes.

The fact that Penny could approach her scholarship with an open mind was revolutionary in its results. Her bold study of the prevalent myopic discourses on the public good (Pasque, 2010) served as a wake-up call for some researchers at UM. She revealed how, in policy meetings, the voices of people who had too often been excluded from the policy table were met with silence. The presence of critics at these meetings did not change the ways social and educational problems were formulated and discussed. Commentaries on the inhumanity of the current conception of the "public good" were simply beyond that range of consideration among those who held power in these policy oriented conversations. Beneath the prevalent neoliberal stance so dominant at the time lurked the pain of people who had been harmed by those who sought to do good deeds through structural tinkering.

My joy in reading this volume is profound because it conveys compelling truths about educational and social change that were ignored for so long at UM, one of the highest-rated doctoral programs in our field. After much personal reflection, John C. Burkhardt took a step beyond his well-trodden organizing method. He engaged with graduate students in reflective conversations about critical issues in higher education, the problems beyond the margins of structural thinking in education.

John also advocated for bringing Betty Overton to the University of Michigan's Center for the Study of Higher and Postsecondary Education (the Center). It was a critical time in the history of the National Forum and the Center. When Betty Overton stepped into this complex environment—a place of high social aspirations that had a history of silencing voices that commented on the injustices created by the educational system—she saw a way through the problem. She encouraged students and her colleagues to engage with community groups to find new solutions to serious problems.

To break through the lingering implicit barriers of race and social class that limit reform, it remains necessary to do the following:

- Discover the ways knowledge is created and transmitted in families and communities in the inner cities,
- Focus our inquiry on challenges in the lives of people who are caught in the turbulence of educational, economic and social change in these communities, and
- Participate in the process of change not only to facilitate discovery of new pathways but to encourage navigation through barriers as an empowering practice.

More than all but a precious few other books, including some now being published by Stylus Publishing, this volume illuminates the importance of scholarship that engages communities in educational change. I sincerely congratulate Betty, John, and Penny for their outstanding work on this book, which is indeed an important contribution to the field. I am happy they included this new book in the Stylus series on engaged scholarship for social justice. I applaud Betty, Penny, and John for taking this important work forward. My hope is that they inspire more engaged scholarship in our field. The future of higher education hangs in the balance.

Edward P. St. John
Professor Emeritus
Center for the Study of Higher and Postsecondary Education
School of Education
University of Michigan

References

Pasque, P. A. (2010). *American higher education, leadership, and policy: Critical issues and the public good.* New York: Palgrave.

St. John, E. P., & Chung, C. G. (2004). Merit and equity: Rethinking award criteria in the Michigan scholarship program. In E. P. St. John & M. D. Parsons (Eds.), *Public funding of higher education: Changing contexts and new rationales* (pp. 124-140). Baltimore: Johns Hopkins University Press.

St. John, E. P., Daun-Barnett, N. J. & Moronski-Chapman, K. (2013). *Public policy and higher education.* New York: Routledge.

St. John, E. P., Hill, O. C., Wooden, O. S. & Pasque, P. A. (2015). Breaking through racial and gender barriers: Reflections on dissertation mentorship and peer support. In C. S. V. Turner & J. C. Gonzalez, *Modeling Mentoring Across Race/ Ethnicity and Gender.* Sterling, VA: Stylus Press.

Foreword

At a deeper level, I have this growing conviction that what's also needed is not just more programs, but a larger purpose, a larger sense of mission, a larger clarity of direction in the nation's life. . . . I'm convinced that ultimately, the scholarship of engagement also means creating a special climate in which the academic and civic cultures communicate more continuously and more creatively with each other, helping to enlarge what anthropologist Clifford Geetz describes as the universe of human discourse and enrich the quality of life for all of us.

(Boyer, 1996, pp. 19–20)

Fifteen years ago I was a part of the origins of the National Forum on Higher Education for the Public Good (National Forum) experiment. John C. Burkhardt, the visionary founder of the National Forum, invited me in as the associate director to contribute to the development of foundational thinking and work that marked the National Forum's beginning. I have remained a grateful and committed steward of the work we started and an unwavering supporter of the work that John and now Betty Overton and their colleagues have advanced since my departure from the National Forum 10 years ago. The fundamental principles guiding the formation of the National Forum have endured and been strengthened over the years. From early on, the basic principles included the following:

- Community involvement
- Collective and authentic discourse
- Support for critical inquiry and exploration
- Support for and sustaining of a community of intergenerational engaged scholars
- Dissemination of collective discovery
- Acknowledgment of the larger movement and the role played by the National Forum as a part of the movement
- Formative assessment of the National Forum's social and educational relevance and impact

Although there was a good bit of intentionality in the formation of the National Forum's work, there was yet a serendipitous nature that guided the work as well. The voices of diverse participants; social, community, and institutional forces that demanded attention (e.g., challenges to affirmative action and opportunity; the events of September 11, 2001; the economic downturn of 2008); the genius and generosity of brilliant young and senior scholars, community actors, and other partners; committed staff; and the trust in good intentions and tested instincts added to what became the "whole" of the National Forum.

The past 15 years have also reinforced the early work of organizations like the National Forum. No doubt there is a much longer way to go as global and local societies seem to be inching toward a much more neoliberal value for higher education . . . actually, for education generally. The emergent benefit of education has shifted significantly toward economic (i.e., labor force) and personal (i.e., lifetime income, wealth) gains and away from social (i.e., community sustainability, equity, justice, and empowerment) and civic (i.e., social participation, knowledge creation, engagement, and leadership) gains. Our cherished and world-revered higher education system struggles against a strong, conservative tide bent on naming the sole benefit of higher education as the preparation of graduates for the workforce.

From my direct engagement in international discussions and activities on higher education's public good obligations over the past couple of decades, I believe that there is a growing philosophical/ideological-turned-policy divide that demands full, balanced, and global examination. At least two competing sides of the divide dominate the debate. One side contends, "Strong societies depend on strong economies," and most or all resources should focus on advancing the economies in the areas of concern. The other side contends, "Strong economies depend on strong societies." When people are safe, secure, contributing, and participating in societies to their fullest capacities with respect and dignity, they produce and are committed to the economic growth of their societies. Further, this second argument contends that all sectors of strong societies should focus their resources toward strengthening the capacities of all individuals and systems in particular societies. As with most contentious debates, the reality is potentially somewhere in the middle of the two arguments presented.

The global discourse around the concept of the "public good" and higher education's role in advancing it has significantly shifted toward the economic contributions of higher education to local, regional, and national jurisdictions. Given the now expansive and intractable global knowledge economies, multination partnerships, and the growing influence of institutions within most sectors beyond their national borders, geopolitical and global economic dynamics have morphed considerably in the past several decades. Governments have deepened their rhetoric and support for higher education as a central driver of economic vitality in various regions. At the same time, several international and domestic initiatives have strengthened calls for elevating the leadership role of higher education in closing the gaps of inequality around the world, increasing broader democratic participatory engagement and preparing future generations of workers and citizens who are concerned about being good at what they do and doing good in the world. A broad and serious critical examination of these shifts in public perceptions and policies needs to occur if higher education is to maintain its role as the last sector in modern society that systematically researches and serves the broad complex public needs of society, as well as educates subsequent generations of leaders to address future needs and interests of societies.

To me, the essential issues are clear, but their interpretations are muddy. There are a growing number of moving parts. Of certainty is the responsibility of higher education in democratic society to seek truth—not "The Truth," but "truth" through discovery, preparation, and active engagement.

One path to discovery is research inspired by and conducted with communities and organizations that are grappling with local social challenges and the rapidly changing global landscape. This is the focus on engaged scholarship and engaged research as noted in this book's title.

What can and what should engaged scholarship do to right the course of the higher education and community social compact? How do we as a society of learners, discoverers, and social actors mobilize our considerable collective assets to transform our institutions, communities, and selves?

Driving Question

What is at stake in higher education's calling to serve the public good? This seems to be the question at the bedrock of this call to engagement. Is life and death a matter of central concern here? Is comfort or distress? Is the wholesale existence of a beloved, or necessary, institution at risk? Are the relevance of the democratic ideal and the place it holds in our nascent diverse society at stake? Are the deep and life-sustaining questions with their prolonged search for understanding at stake? Are imagination, creativity, and the will to be more as a community than our individualism will allow at stake?

The answer to it all, and then some, seems to be "yes." Less at stake are reputation, recycled knowledge, status, position, and a false sense of self-righteousness and of being the sole holder of the "correct" answers to society's big questions.

Engaged Scholarship

Although the definition of *engaged scholarship* and synonymous terms have been shaped by considerable reflection and practice, this book nonetheless raises a few concerns about how it might be framed within the emergent context of contemporary, intractable social issues. As I have mentioned in previous places (Chambers & Gopaul, 2010), there are definitional and practical distinctions that I think are worth making to ground readers of this text. The noted distinctions are among what I'd term the *scholarship of engagement*, the *scholarship on or about engagement*, and the *scholarship for engagement*.

The scholarship *of* engagement involves partnerships between researchers and communities that are designed and implemented to address social or community needs. The interaction among partners for some socially defined outcome itself is a form of scholarship. The scholarship is undertaken by those engaged in the partnership. The scholarship *on or about* engagement is the study of the processes of collaboration, decision-making, research, and action within this relationship between scholars and communities. The partnerships or engagement dynamics are the subjects of study. The scholarship is not necessarily undertaken by those involved in the partnerships. It may be undertaken by third parties not directly a part of the engaging partnerships. Finally, the scholarship *for* engagement has the sole purpose of preparing for and supporting engagement between higher education scholars and communities toward specific social actions, outcomes, and impact. The common framing of engaged scholarship implies the integration of the three distinct forms ("of," "on or about," and "for"). It is important to know the parameters and intent of involvement in engaged scholarship, and these distinctions provide a ground upon which discernments can be made by scholars and communities.

Engaged scholarship has been a relatively recent frame within to consider the work of faculty members in academic institutions. The term has its roots in the work of Ernest L. Boyer, who suggested a broader definition of *scholarship*. Boyer (1996) wrote that "the academy must become a more vigorous partner in the search for answers to our most pressing social, civic, economic and moral problems, and must affirm its historic commitment to . . . the scholarship of engagement" (p. 11). The traditional conception of scholarship is extremely important to the history of higher education and the disciplinary and professional guilds that constitute academe; however, Boyer's suggestion required reconceptualizing the work not only of academics but also the relationship of higher education to the larger society and the purposes of higher education.

Engaged scholarship presents a break from the "top-down" or "expert-driven" model of partnership between colleges, universities, scholars, and communities. Engaged scholarship seeks more than characterizations of service—it emphasizes collaboration and relationship. An important first step in distinguishing an engaged scholarship approach from the traditional research approach is to emphasize a bidirectional reciprocity between communities and scholars (Sandmann, 2007). Here the coconstructed and multidirectional nature of learning and instruction are highlighted and the notion of expertise is shared (Rice, 2002).

Read this book! The essential messages among the pages are not the first or final words regarding higher education's special relationship with the society that created and supports it. Sit with it. Put it down and pick it up again later. It shifts perspective kaleidoscopically; what you see depends on where you stand at any given moment. The messages encourage reflection, as all good work should do. Argue with the perspectives outlined in the following pages. Curse and correct the messages. But don't leave the messages and their reflections be. Doing so begins the end of engagement and signals the irrelevance of scholarship. Engaged scholarship begs for engagement. Not necessarily agreement or blind fidelity, but stringent and earnest engagement.

The familiar focus and questions raised in these pages are as important today as ever. Perhaps more so in more complex and far-reaching ways as social boundaries morph and tensions repeat in and across multiple, seemingly unconnected jurisdictions.

If nothing else, this collection calls higher education to question, again, its claims to relevance at a time in American society (nay, world society) when neoliberal and commercial objectives of higher education are winning out over the broader life-sustaining objectives of justice, knowledge, compassion, and community.

Tony Chambers
University of Toronto

References

Boyer, E. L. (1996). The scholarship of engagement. *Journal of Public Service and Outreach, 1*, 11–20.

Chambers, T. & Gopaul, B. (2010). Toward a social justice-centered engaged scholarship: A public and a private good. In H. E. Fitzgerald, C. Burack, & S. Siefer (Eds.), *Handbook of engaged scholarship: Contemporary landscapes, future directions: Volume I: Institutional change* (pp. 55–70). East Lansing: Michigan State University Press.

Rice, R. E. (2002). Beyond scholarship reconsidered: Toward an enlarged vision of the scholarly work of faculty members. *New Directions for Teaching and Learning, 90,* 7–17.

Sandmann, L. R. (2007). Conceptualization of the scholarship of engagement in higher education: A ten-year retrospective. In L. Servage & T. Fenwick (eds.) *Learning in Community,* (p. 547–552). Halifax, Nova Scotia: Mount St. Vincent University.

ACKNOWLEDGMENTS

This book reflects the contributions of many individuals, each of whom played important roles in its development. Lena M. Khader and Krystal Golding-Ross provided invaluable support and copyediting for this project in their roles as graduate assistants at the University of Oklahoma. Ilana Israel, administrative assistant at the National Forum, helped in keeping us organized and the book project moving. We were also assisted by administrative assistant Charlotte Ezzo and graduate student Demar Lewis at the National Center on Institutional Diversity at the University of Michigan. Michael Betzold and Jeffrey Grim were enlisted late in the writing process where they provided copyediting, helpful insights, and expert technical assistance. In addition, we would like to thank John von Knorring, Stylus president; Sarah Burrows, Stylus acquisitions editor; and Edward St. John, Estela Bensimon, and Shaun R. Harper, series editors, for their support throughout the envisioning and publishing process.

We extend our thanks to all the legendary musicians, a title bestowed on the many individuals who—over 15 years—helped make the work of the National Forum on Higher Education for the Public Good possible. This includes the numerous faculty, administrators, staff, graduate students, community partners, foundation representatives, legislators, professional colleagues, and personal friends we have collaborated with over the years. Although many financial supporters contributed to sustaining and encouraging the work of the National Forum, special appreciation is due to the W.K. Kellogg Foundation for its unique vision of higher education as a force for change in our society and around the world.

This is a book that focuses on the importance of, and untapped potential that may be derived from, closer engagement between higher education and the communities, people, and institutions it collaborates with/serves. In documenting a sustained effort to both study and enact commitments to that idea, we must acknowledge the work of the growing number of people committed to community-university partnerships and engaged scholarship. What is global is also local, and what we do in any given place has repercussions far beyond what any one of us may personally experience—a belief that is crucial if we are to sustain the continued work engaged in by so many on behalf of social change.

Part One

INTRODUCTION TO ENGAGED RESEARCH AND PRACTICE

1

ENGAGEMENT FOR THE COMMON GOOD
Situating the National Forum's Work
Betty Overton

This book examines efforts of engaged research, with hopes to inspire and support similar work. The term *engaged research*, though increasingly used in higher education, conveys a vague notion about researchers showing up in communities and doing "something" with the local community members. Even among scholars of higher education the meaning of engaged research can get murky. Is it "real research"? Is it practice? Is it advocacy? What value does it add to scholarship? Is it helpful for communities? Do faculty who use engaged research get penalized during tenure and promotion? How does it contribute and to whom? This book is part of the Stylus Publishing series Engaged Research and Practice for Social Justice in Education. The series itself may be testimony that some in the field believe this topic merits further investigation and discussion.

Engaged research is part of a broad concept that has become known as "engagement," "engaged scholarship," or "applied research." Over the last 20 years, scholars have encouraged universities to create engaged scholarship in order to create accessible research that directly impacts local, national, and international communities (Boyer, 1990; Calleson, Jordon, & Seifer, 2005; Ellison & Eatman, 2008; Petersen, 2009; Saltmarsh, Giles, Ward, & Buglione, 2009; Van de Ven, 2007). As research universities prepare young scholars to create cutting-edge scholarship and prepare for academic careers, institutions have also created models of work and reward systems (Ellison & Eatman, 2008) to support engaged scholarship. Efforts begun by Ernest Boyer (1990) were continued by Glassick, Huber, and Maeroff (1997); Driscoll and Lynton (1999); Sandmann, Foster-Fishman,

3

Lloyd, Rauhe, and Rosaen (2000); and many others. Their work highlights the importance of embedding the scholarship of engagement in reward structures in different types of institutions. The 2005 revision of the Carnegie Classification of Colleges and Universities included an elective category of "engaged institutions" and demonstrated that many are interested in revitalizing their service and civic commitments through research (Saltmarsh et al., 2009).

What has led to the shifting view of engaged research? How did this form of scholarship, which began with so little institutional value, grow to be viewed today as having intellectual power and promise for societal impact? Many indicators help explain the increased interest, whether it is the many pressures, both inside and outside of higher education, to view academic quality as not just theoretical, but practical, or the increased desire from politicians for institutions to be more integral and involved in their communities. Certainly significant in altering views is the shift in the traditional role of universities as the primary generators and transmitters of knowledge, and institutions are of necessity learning to behave as participants, not owners, of increasingly complex new learning environments.

At the National Forum on Higher Education for the Public Good, we felt we had something to offer to this changing conversation about engaged research, and we intend for this book to contribute to a wider discussion and begin to answer questions about the nature and usefulness of engaged scholarship. Our particular contribution has been a variety of projects over a 15-year period—from the National Forum and from engaged research two to three degrees of separation from it—which attempt to apply scholarship to issues we identified as a "public good" and which we have framed within definitions we call "engaged research." We have embraced the engaged research model and the associated terminology for several reasons. First, there is a growing need for this socially focused research. In his book, *Research, Actionable Knowledge, and Social Change*, Edward St. John (2013) notes,

> Research conducted in partnership with schools, colleges, community-based organizations, and other educational service organizations provides a means of sharing responsibility in solving critical social problems in local contexts. It may be an impossible dream to think there is a universal solution to any particular recurrent social or educational problem. Not only must such a solution be conceptualized and tested, it would also have to be mandated through policy decisions and disseminated in ways that would be needed to fit diverse contexts and circumstances. (p. 25)

Second, research pursued by those associated with the National Forum has an underlying focus on contributing solutions to social problems and is conducted in ways that engage individuals, communities, and organizations in shared learning. Third, we believe our work is consistent as representative of an increasing field of practice. We have pursued our own interests but also gathered examples of practice beyond the National Forum that might generate a welcomed conversation among peers. In the resultant give-and-take of such a dialogue, we can grow, improve our efforts, and support others in their practice.

The Scholarship of Engagement as a Contextual Lens

The National Forum on Higher Education for the Public Good (National Forum) grew out of the work of the W.K. Kellogg Foundation during a period when the foundation was fully engaged with higher education in highlighting the academy's role in service to society. "In service to" was the operant idea. For Kellogg, higher education was seen as having a responsibility to society—a responsibility to use the academy's human and other resources to support problem-solving in neighborhoods and communities, in both rural and urban settings. With founder W.K. Kellogg's clear belief that "education is the only way to improve one generation over the next," the philanthropic imperative was to support institutions and programs that understood this role and were willing to vigorously pursue it. In other words, the foundation sought to support institutions that would "engage" with their communities in the various processes necessary to realize a vision attributed to the founder of the foundation, W.K. Kellogg, that saw benefits derived through education to improve one generation over another. At Kellogg, engagement took many forms: efforts to decrease health disparities in major cities, programs to strengthen leadership at minority-serving colleges, development of a cadre of new leaders within various communities, programs to improve the food systems within the nation, and the like. The one constant was the focus on getting new learning and improved services as close to people's lives as possible.

Although the foundation used many organizations and approaches to accomplish its goals, higher education was always a partner in this effort, almost from the inception of the foundation. Gail McClure, former vice president for programs at the Kellogg Foundation, described the foundation's hopes for "a new sense of commitment to the public service mission of American higher education" and added that "such a renewal of our covenant with society would reshape public policy, reshape institutional practices, reshape the expectations and experiences for our students, reshape our communities, and ultimately revitalize and secure democracy" (London, 2003, p. 16). These were lofty ambitions laid out for the higher education community.

Consistent with this vision were the foundation's support for the report of the Commission on Community Engagement Scholarship in the Health Professions (Calleson et al., 2005) and, in 2000, *Returning to Our Roots*, a report of the Kellogg Commission on the Future of State and Land-Grant Universities. Both reports call for more involvement and partnerships between institutions (health care and education) and communities. In *Returning to Our Roots, engaged institutions* were defined as those that "designed their teaching, research and extension and service functions to become more sympathetically and productively involved with their communities, however community may be defined" (p. 27).

Kellogg aligned itself with the historic service focus of the academy and with an emerging academic conversation spurred by the 1990 publication of Ernest Boyer's *Scholarship Reconsidered*. Boyer was not the first to articulate the role of higher education in service to society, but his contemporary framing of the commitment and his conceptualization of the academic framework for faculty involvement caught the attention of his higher education colleagues. Boyer's initial categories of new domains for thinking about academic scholarship focused on four types of scholarship: discovery, integration, application, and teaching. The scholarship of application was Boyer's acknowledgment of the role of higher education in not just discovering or teaching knowledge but applying it within society. He asked, "How can knowledge be responsibly applied to consequential problems?" (Boyer, 1990, p. 21). His response to that question was to call on the higher education community to do a better job of fusing theory and practice such that issues of society were also the work of the academy. But the "scholarship of application" designation did not go far enough for him. In a speech in 1995, he expanded his categories and added the concept of the "scholarship of engagement." Boyer announced, "[T]he academy must become a more vigorous partner in the search for answers to our most pressing social, civic, economic, and moral problems, and must reaffirm its historic commitment to what I call the scholarship of engagement" (cited in Boyer, 1997, p. 30). In that presentation he coined a new phrase and threw down a challenge to the academic enterprise. He identified engagement as "a way for scholarship to flourish" (cited in Boyer, 1997, p. 32). The work of the National Forum is situated in that intellectual context of engagement.

Further, Braxton, Luckey, and Helland (2002) point out that the essential differences between Boyer's scholarship of engagement and the scholarship of application are types of problems being addressed and the beneficiaries of the scholarship. Boyer expected colleges and universities to use their resources and authority not only for research but also to help engage society in applying knowledge. The scholarship of application and the scholarship of engagement are complementary but call for different approaches to scholarly efforts and to work in the community. Application tends to be a one-way approach, with scholars applying their research and knowledge on issues that belong to someone else. While the persons or organizations involved may benefit, the primary intent of the interactions is for researchers to focus on using research or supporting the use of it by others. Engagement, on the other hand, implies at least some level of reciprocity in interactions between the institution and those it works not just for, but with. The level of involvement can vary, but involvment is an essential component of the work. More than just service, the work begins with scholarship and is grounded in pushing the boundaries of current knowledge. In the type of engagement Boyer envisioned, scholarship benefits a community, a neighborhood, a school, or an organization as much as the researcher. The scholarship is intentionally "in service to" others.

Barker (2004) notes that Boyer's use of the term *scholarship* was expansive. It cut across prevailing definitions, but so did Boyer's use of *engagement*. Coupling the two ideas, Boyer evoked the traditions and prestige of higher education's academic responsibilities to tie them concretely to increasingly important civic and social responsibilities. Although Boyer did not use the term *public good*, this was clearly a mandate. Varied attempts at definition illustrate how this type of scholarship can be conceived. Barker suggests that the scholarship of engagement "consists of (1) research, teaching, integration, and application scholarship that (2) incorporate reciprocal practices of civic engagement into the production of knowledge" (p. 65), pointing out how the types of scholarship may be used for engagements. Barbara Holland (2005) describes this as

> a specific conception of faculty work that connects the intellectual assets of the institution (i.e., faculty and student expertise) to public issues such as community, social, cultural, human, and economic development. . . . Faculty apply their academic expertise to public purposes as a way of contributing to the fulfillment of the core mission of the institution. (p. 11)

Holland's definition centers the concept in faculty work, an important part of what scholars do with their knowledge. This normalization is important especially for faculty at elite institutions where traditional research and teaching are the coin of the realm. Understanding the need to place engagement into the structural frame of the academy's recognized work, the Committee on Institutional Cooperation (CIC—the Big Ten and the University of Chicago) (2005) issued its definition:

> Engagement is the partnership of university knowledge and resources with those of the public and private sectors to enrich scholarship, research, and creative activity; enhance curriculum, teaching, and learning; prepare educated, engaged citizens; strengthen democratic values and civic responsibility; address critical societal issues; and contribute to the public good. (p. 143)

In this way, the CIC expanded the possibility of engagement from the exclusive domain of the faculty to the possibility that engagement is also an institutional responsibility (the "engaged campus").

Boyer's work allowed the academy's concept of scholarship to expand, and he gave new impetus to what was already a sporadic movement in the direction of engagement, with antecedents going back to John Dewey, who had pushed education in this direction in *The Public and Its Problems* published at about the time of his arrival at the University of Michigan in 1884 (Dewey, 1927/1991). Dewey's work, when read today, has an impressive relevance; he posits that some problems can only be solved through collective knowledge and action, and he calls for social contracts among institutions that promote a vibrant democratic state. Further, the history of land-grant colleges and their extension service created models for the application of scholarship.

Admittedly, some colleges and universities have always been connected and committed to their communities and society (Bender, 1988). As president of the prestigious Carnegie Foundation for the Advancement of Teaching, Boyer sparked a new national conversation and reframed both the language (e.g., "outreach," "service") and the relational models for that conversation. Boyer's insights about engagement have been extended and elaborated upon for more than 25 years. His concept has increasingly caught the imagination of the higher education community and has become the way we now describe many aspects of our work. There are engaged institutions, engaged faculty, engaged teaching, engaged research, engaged students; there are community engagement, global engagement, and other ways of modifying the many aspects of higher education to link the work of the academy to societal issues and what we identify as "the common good."

Because the term *engagement* covers such a wide variety of activities, it is not surprising that there are some areas of definitional muddiness. In fact, Van de Ven (2007) notes that a 2006 Google.com search returned more than 35,000 entries on *engaged scholarship*. However, there have been enough studies of the practices and outcomes involved (e.g., Fogel & Cook, 2006; Holland, 2005; Moxley, 2004; St. John, 2013) in these various usages to forge a "family of practices" identified by shared intent and work.

It is clear from his writings that Boyer intended to extend the idea of scholarship to have a broader purpose. His message clearly set forth the idea that scholarship could no longer be envisioned as the sole domain of bench scientists or walled-off academics speaking strange languages to one another. Some forms of research may be appropriated by nonacademics to explore topics that the academy has not explored, while also providing space for academics and non-academics to use shared processes to engage shared questions. As such, people in communities might actually do research, with academics or independently, leading to the popularity of new methodologies such as participatory action research (McIntyre, 2007; Whyte, 1991). Barker (2004) suggests that in adding "engagement" to the options for scholarship, Boyer was creating the possibility for a host of practices to cut across disciplinary boundaries, and these new practices allow scholars and others to work in more integrative ways. It is within this new framing of scholarship that the National Forum began working 10 years after the publication of Boyer's seminal work.

Situating the National Forum's Work in the Context of Engaged Scholarship

An earlier reference to the National Forum's origins situates the work of engagement in its Kellogg roots. However, while the roots may have been germinated in the soil of service, they were watered by an understanding that those perspectives on service would grow best if colleges and universities grounded this work for themselves and the communities they served with strong research. Thus, the National Forum was planted in the organizational soil of one of the richest research environments in the country, the University of Michigan–Ann Arbor. This selection of an academic home ensured that the National Forum's outlook would be research focused. The strong tradition of methodologically sound research of the Center for the Study of Higher and Postsecondary Education, the National Forum's departmental affiliation at Michigan, provided the scholarly base for its research efforts, while providing an abundant supply of graduate students with new ideas and research skills. These elements proved to be the right mix to kick-start many of the efforts described in this book.

At the core of this work were the passion, vision, and intellect of John Burkhardt, the founding director, who was committed to making the National Forum a place where the public good would be both model and mandate. For example, Burkhardt, Pasque, Bowman, and Martinez (2009) in their introduction to *Critical Issues in Higher Education for the Public Good: Qualitative, Quantitative, & Historical Research Perspectives,* stated:

> The concept of higher education's place in society and the assertion that colleges and universities are responsible for more than what is currently expected of them—more than they are giving for sure—is one that is central to our work at the National Forum for the Study of the Public Good. (p. 32)

This focus on broadening and deepening the possibilities of engagement with the issues of society characterizes much of the work of the National Forum. Consistent with the scholarship of engagement, the issues tackled by the Forum National do not fit neatly into a single disciplinary package. A common thread among the issues the National Forum took on was the response to higher education needs articulated most often by external constituents and voices. The National Forum has over the last 15 years acted as a place willing to entertain others' questions and then to apply research and scholarship to putting forth possible responses.

A few examples of external questions are: In what ways do people in Michigan understand the needs for college education? What are the varying ways in which state policies address college admissions for undocumented students? How do low-income communities build social capital and a sense of agency to foster a college-going culture for their young people? How do high school counselors and college admissions staff create shared understanding and working practices to serve undocumented students? How did minority-serving institutions fare in the recession? These are questions that find their ways to the National Forum's door, because they require not only good scholarship but also the involvement of people who are living with the issues to work with researchers in a search for solutions.

The National Forum's approach to engagement has taken many forms. In situating the National Forum's work within the scholarship of engagement, Barker's (2004) taxonomy of engagement provides a useful framework for categorizing the work and outlining the elements involved. Barker identifies five emerging practices of engagement: public scholarship, participatory research, community partnerships, public information networks, and civic literacy scholarship. He suggests that each offers its own methodology in response to particular issues. However, the practices overlap, and more than one may be used in a specific environment. Table 1.1 provides categories of types of engagement that have emerged in the field.

TABLE 1.1
Barker's Taxonomy Based on Five Practices of Engaged Scholarship

Engagement Practice	Practice Description	Problems Addressed	Methods
Public Scholarship	Academic work that incorporates deliberative practices, such as forums and town meetings, as opportunities to apply scholarship to public problems	Complex "public" problems requiring deliberation	Face-to-face, open forums, dialogues
Participatory Research (Action Research)	Involvement of people from communities or organizations, not as subjects of research, but in the production of academic knowledge; especially reaching out to marginalized or previously excluded groups to learn and be part of the research process	Inclusion of specific groups	Face-to-face collaboration with specific members of the public
Community Partnerships	Creation of formal and/or informal relationships with community groups or other organizations to foster the social interactions and reciprocal transformations that can emerge from shared work	Social change, structural transformation	Collaboration with intermediary groups
Public Information Networks	Networks or networked resources providing asset information and linkages	Problems of networking, communication	Database of public information
Civic Literacy Scholarship	Public knowledge and skills aimed at reducing the separation between academic experts and community knowledge	Enhancing public discourse	Communication with the general public

The National Forum's work—and the work as a ripple effect beyond the National Forum—illustrated in this book falls into at least four of these categories: *public scholarship* (see Chapter 11: Linking State Priorities With Local Strategies and Chapter 6: Challenges to Diversity:); *participatory action research* (see Chapter 4: Community Agency and College-Going Culture and Chapter 3: Conflating Community Means With Organizational Ends); *public information networks* (see Chapter 11: Linking State Priorities With Local Strategies); and, in almost all of the projects presented here, there is some aspect of *community partnership*. Further, though *civic literacy scholarship* is not the focus of particular projects, the National Forum's interest in the deliberative dialogue process and strong dissemination efforts demonstrates a commitment to growth in public knowledge that reduces the separation between academic experts and community knowledge.

In the next chapter, John C. Burkhardt, the National Forum's founding director, provides an in-depth discussion of the historical framing and vision of the National Forum that began to incorporate these practices, and we offer this as a way to, hopefully, be useful to scholar-practitioners interested in these concepts. The National Forum did not begin with Barker's taxonomy in mind; in fact, we did not discover it until our work was well under way. But, it has provided a way for us to begin organizing how we look at what we have been doing.

Engaged Research: Definitional Considerations

The work covered in this book is situated in the larger context of the scholarship of engagement. Although falling in the Boyer frame of the scholarship of engagement, the work is specifically "engaged research." There are many terms for what we have called *engaged research*. Holland (2005) suggests,

> Today, we understand more clearly that applied research has many dimensions and methodological approaches. Community based research, action research, participatory action research, engaged research, and other terms represent only a few of the permutations of applied research that bring Boyer's integrative view of scholarship to life and reveal the intellectual power inherent in applied research. The scholarship of engagement, in its many forms, demonstrates that knowledge can have a public purpose when it is applied to local problems or opportunities. Indeed, the growing sphere of institutions that embrace engaged scholarship demonstrate its capacity to bring coherence to curricula and strengthen research productivity while also connecting research to a community's quality of life through knowledge exchange relationships with external partners. (p. 44)

Although many of the terms used to describe this new type of community-focused research overlap in their meaning, there are also distinctions. In describing our work, we have used what we consider one of the broader terms—*engaged research*—because it allows us greater flexibility and is consistent with the ways many scholars are beginning to conceptualize these new research approaches as problem centered, interdisciplinary or transdisciplinary, heterogeneous, hybrid, demand driven, networked, and focused on outcomes (Gibbons et al., 1994). These more integrative models of research often require collaboration across partnering groups, and these relationships growing out of the engaged models make it possible to solve increasingly complex problems.

Engaged research as a strand of the scholarship of engagement utilizes the long-tested tools of the research community. As such, the efforts described in this book will be familiar to research scholars. The chapters in the book employ the tools and methods of social science research such that the results are credible to other academics and reliable to policymakers. But just as important, they give back to those most needing the information and provide better ways of addressing current issues and asking new questions. This is "real" research grounded in the triple roles of the academy: teaching, research, and service. The old models and methods of research are not jettisoned because of our interest in social impact. The lessons learned from bench science and traditional research are still needed and underpin our work. However, the refocusing of research (applied research, action research, actionable research, participatory action research, engaged research) and the work that reframing allows permit us to take well-established models and methods and apply them in new ways. Scientific tests and social science theoretical applications ground and strengthen research applied to these social issues, and new applications used in conjunction with existing approaches are complementary ways to reach new understandings of social justice concerns.

The emerging new applications of research give evidence that the scholarly community understands the role research can play in moving society toward long-term solutions to difficult issues. We need to use every tool in our arsenals and look for ways to open up dialogue, create new alliances, and promote action-based initiatives. As some of the projects highlighted in this book illustrate, research may often be most helpful to communities when it is produced and delivered with the involved communities rather than from the safety of our ivory towers. Objectivity is still a value, but as St. John (2013) points out, "Rather than argue for a return to decentralized local control, it is crucial to reconstruct theory, policy, and practice to encourage professional action that fosters innovation and fairness at all levels in public systems" (p. 39).

Further, St. John introduces the concept of "stance" as another way of thinking about the ways we can approach research that points toward social change.

> We can use the concept of stance as a way of building shared understandings of problem situations even when there are differences in ideological beliefs if there is a willingness to test assumptions in action and to use evidence widely. Taking a stance that is made up of value-centered and testable assumptions makes it possible to engage in the review, development, and use of evidence to inform action. . . . Research focusing on problems that emerge in practice that evolve as a consequence of new policies provides an evidence-based approach for using theory and methods from the social sciences in partnerships formed of advocates for social justice and fairness. Research about critical challenges and the evaluation of interventions can inform exchanges among people taking neoliberal and neoconservative stances about public policy and economic development, but it is necessary to focus on problem solving rather than ideology. (p. xvi)

National Forum projects situated at Marygrove College, the Hope Village community in Detroit, and in our work with policy issues related to undocumented students—and decisions about program models, resource mapping, and tuition policy—happened in conjunction with an ongoing research process, not after the research was completed and reported. For example, Magdalena Martinez's work with undocumented Latino college students grew out of the concerns of communities and attempts to provide alternative portrayals of the aspirations and cultural resources of these students. Rather than just providing information for decision-making, these engaged processes facilitated a shared sense of commitment to and stance toward issues, so the framework of community partnership was not just a contractual arrangement but a collective mentality that created a new kind of "insider" role for researchers.

Engaged research, and its cousins by other names, may mean a type of intellectual involvement encapsulated by the "in service to" concept and generating a sense of responsiveness to the immediacy of issues as well as their long-term outcomes. Our work with the BOLD (Building Our Leadership in Detroit) Project at Marygrove is a good example. While our team worked as paid consultants, we were also "in community" with the work of building a model of leadership development for Detroit. We were in faculty meetings, maintaining a campus office to be present and available, on committees, and at retreats. Being seen as part of the community was important to the authenticity of our work.

So what happens to the aloof, objective scholar, interested in the truth and nothing but the truth? We have known for years that the idealized objectivity is not real and perhaps not even desirable. Engaged research is not a code word for sloppy research. Indeed, the deep commitment to issues is cause for a more rigorous sense of dedication to truth, as a part of the "in service to" process.

Consistent with our understanding of Boyer, our engaged research has meant our ability to reach beyond our campuses and to couple our knowledge and resources to enrich scholarship and creative activities with the idea of a "public good." This work, though often addressing specific community issues, also enhanced curriculum, teaching, and learning; prepared educated, engaged citizens; strengthened democratic values and civic responsibility; addressed critical societal issues; and contributed to the public good (Committee on Institutional Cooperation, 2005).

This Book: *Engaged Research in Practice*

Part One: *Introduction to Engaged Research and Practice*

Part One serves as the introduction to this five-part book and presents the historical and theoretical backdrop for the chapters to follow. The first chapter places the work presented in a context that allows readers to understand the overarching metaphor for the work. The second chapter provides a more historical sense of the development of the work over time. The founding director of the National Forum, John C. Burkhardt, walks us through his own insights into the evolution of the National Forum's work and its creation of a unique mode of thinking and practice.

Part Two: *Engaging the Community Level*

Part Two focuses on community-engagement research projects. All of the projects directly involve community partnerships, and the contributors capture the importance and the challenges of such research efforts. The researchers share an interest in serving as partners targeting community concerns, lending support, using scholarly and methodological tools, and borrowing the wisdom and approaches of the community.

In Chapter 3, for example, "Conflating Community Means With Organizational Ends," Elizabeth Hudson shares the experience of the National Forum working with a Detroit community on a project to improve educational opportunity. But the project is more than that; the National Forum became part of a multisector coalition with varied partners. The National Forum's role has shifted over time as it has learned to adjust to the needs of the community. The chapter examines the most appropriate roles for higher education in community partnerships. Can we be direct service providers given that our workforce may include streams of transient students? Hudson also speaks to the distrust of higher education institutions that many community members have and the efforts we, as researchers and scholars, make to explain the motivations of institutions working in community.

Like the work Hudson describes, Esmeralda Hernandez-Hamed's Chapter 4, "Community Agency and College-Going Culture," is situated in Detroit and describes a National Forum community dialogue project completed with support from the Kettering Foundation. This chapter examines our use of participatory action research, a process engaging community participants as our research peers. The chapter raises questions about the role of colleges and universities as facilitators for community dialogue.

In Chapter 5, "Collaborative Approaches to Community Change," Penny A. Pasque focuses on the perspectives shared by community partners in community-university partner relationships throughout the United States. She focuses on an aspect of a larger research project as she evokes a community partner's words when he described community-university partnerships as "dog and pony shows." Pasque urges us to interrupt this cycle of academic socialization in order to make a concerted effort toward social change. Further, she explores the complexities of power within community-university relationships; the importance of sincere collaboration with a foundation of trust; and the intentional ways university faculty, administrators, and students may work toward social change through engaged research and practice.

Part Three: Engaging the Institutional Level

Part Three introduces projects we and our colleagues have pursued with various higher education institutions as partners working on efforts that involve institutional change. Chapter 6, "Challenges to Diversity," by Cassie L. Barnhardt, examines the potential pathways and processes that would allow higher education institutions (and their leaders) to become more eager to actively engage with social issues that evoked a particularly high level of dissensus in the public domain. The chapter provides insight into a multicampus project, including the National Forum and supported by the Carnegie Corporation of New York. The project activities were prefaced on what is known about university engagement as an administrative process and idealized models of instances where higher education contributed substantially to social change. These insights help to focus attention on the work of a small set of senior leaders in clearly defined roles (campus public relations leaders, general/legal counsel, and chief diversity officers) to better enable them to approach contentious matters of diversity.

In Chapter 7, "Access Points to the American Dream," Kyle Southern, a graduate student with the National Forum, along with Teresita Wisell and

Jill Casner-Lotto, two community partners from Westchester Community College and the Community College Consortium for Immigrant Education, present the work of a national consortium of community colleges as an example of engaged scholarship. The authors discuss the vital and ongoing role of community colleges as facilitators of empowerment and advancement for students in American higher education and the workforce. In particular, they focus on the population of immigrant students who pursue postsecondary opportunities through community colleges, including students who lack documentation of legal residency in the United States. Professional educators who work in or with the two-year sector may draw insights on how these institutions may support the educational success of immigrant students.

Lara Kovacheff-Badke, in Chapter 8, "Organizational Transformation for Catalytic Social Change," shares the National Forum's involvement with Marygrove College in Detroit. As an urban, Catholic, predominantly Black institution, Marygrove has a unique place in Detroit. Its BOLD project is an example of an institutional transformation effort embedded in community. The National Forum's partnership with Marygrove is an example of how institutions may engage with each other on collaborative research work focused on social justice issues.

Part Four: Engaging Policy Discussions at the State and National Levels

Part Four showcases some of the policy-level work on state and national issues. In Chapter 9 on "Undocumented Student Access to Higher Education," Kimberly A. Reyes, Aurora Kamimura, and Kyle Southern provide insight into the efforts of institutions in order to provide access to undocumented students despite ambiguous legislation and misinformation. This work illuminates some of the 10 years of work that the National Forum has done in this area. In a related vein, Magdalena Martinez focuses on research with Hispanic-serving institutions with four of the seven public postsecondary institutions in the state of Nevada in Chapter 10, "'The Problem With Our Students. . . Is That Their Families Don't Value Education.'" This research illuminates the difficult, yet needed, facilitation of deep conversations about race, ethnicity, and gender. The study presented showcases an approach to examining institutional data in a way that engages postsecondary leaders and allows them to find solutions that work in their spheres of influence. Martinez emphasizes that engaged research needs to incorporate multiple levels of critical analysis in order to challenge embedded assumptions. In Chapter 11, "Linking State Priorities With Local Strategies," Nathan J. Daun-Barnett examines the development of the community-based college access strategy in Michigan from the work of the Statewide Commission on Higher Education and Economic Growth in 2004 through the announcement of the Kalamazoo Promise to the proliferation of local college access networks (LCANs) and Promise Zones through the second decade of the twenty-first century. Michigan is not the only state to connect local assets and initiatives (grassroots) with state-level policies and priorities (grasstops), but it is the first to elevate communities to such a prominent role in postsecondary access. The seeds of innovation from Michigan are beginning to take root in other states, and their experience is instructive for others.

Part Five: Concluding Thoughts on Engaged Research and Practice

Part Five offers a cumulative view of engaged research in Chapter 12, "Reflections" by Betty Overton. As director of the National Forum I attempt to sum up the various perspectives, experiences, and outcomes from the various engaged research and practice initiatives. My intent is to highlight the lessons we have learned and how they add to the pool of knowledge about engaged research. In keeping with the National Forum's focus on "public good," the final chapter of this book posits that these "engagements" we describe with communities, with institutions, with policy issues, and with students—our own and others—are about that "good." Ultimately, those involved in the development of this volume hope it will be used by faculty researchers to spur their work, by administrators to help shape the forms of their support, by policymakers to imagine how they can influence more engagement, and by community leaders to better understand how institutions might work with them.

Reflective Narratives at the End of Parts Two, Three, and Four

At the end of the middle sections, student research partners share their reflective narratives about involvement in engaged research. The student reflections are important as they share their thoughts about the connection between research and practice. They are the voices of the future and the hope for continuation of this work. The narratives allow readers to sense the impact of community engagement on the students and see the work through their eyes—whether they are engaged from the vantage point of the University of Michigan, University of Oklahoma, University of California–Berkeley, high schools, community colleges, or in local communities.

References

Barker, D. (2004). The scholarship of engagement: A taxonomy of five emerging practices. *Journal of Higher Education Outreach and Engagement, 9*(2), 123–137.

Bender, T. (1988). Introduction. In T. Bender (Ed.), *The university and the city: From medieval origins to present* (pp. 3–12). New York, NY: Oxford University Press.

Boyer, E. L. (1990). *Scholarship reconsidered: Priorities of the professoriate.* Princeton, NJ: Carnegie Foundation for the Advancement of Teaching.

Boyer, E. L. (1997). *Ernest L. Boyer: Selected Speeches, 1979–1995.* San Francisco, CA: Jossey-Bass.

Braxton, J. M., Luckey, W., & Helland, P. (2002). *Institutionalizing a broader view of scholarship through Boyer's four domains. ASHE-ERIC Higher Education Report, 29*(2). San Francisco, CA: Jossey-Bass.

Burkhardt, J. C., Pasque, P. A., Bowman, N. A., & Martinez, M. (2009). Higher education for the public good: Exploring new perspectives. In P. A. Pasque, N. A. Bowman, & M. Martinez (Eds.), *Critical issues in higher education for the public good: Qualitative, quantitative, & historical research perspectives* (pp. xiii–xx). Kennesaw, GA: Kennesaw State University Press.

Burkhardt, J., Kezar, A. J., Chambers, A. (2005). *Higher education for the public good: Emerging voices from a national movement.* San Francisco, CA: Jossey-Bass.

Calleson, D., Jordon, C., &. Seifer, S. D. (2005). Community-engaged scholarship: Is faculty work in communities a true academic enterprise? *Academic Medicine. 8*(4), 317–321.

Calleson, D., Kauper-Brown, J., & Seifer, S. (2005). *Community-engaged scholarship for health collaborative toolkit.* Retrieved from www.communityengagedscholarship .info

Committee on Institutional Cooperation Committee on Engagement. (2005). *Engaged scholarship: A resource guide and recommendation for defining and benchmarking engagement.* Committee on Institutional Cooperation. Champaign, IL: Author. Retrieved from www.cic.uiuc.edu/groups/CommitteeOnEngagement

Dewey, J. (1927/1991). *The public and its problems.* Athens, OH: Swallow Press.

Driscoll, A., & Lynton, E. (1999). *Making outreach visible: A workbook on documenting professional service and outreach.* Washington, DC: American Association for Higher Education.

Ellison, J. & Eatman, J. K. (2008). *Scholarship in public: Knowledge creation and tenure policy in the engaged university.* Syracuse, NY: Imagining America. Retrieved from http://imaginingamerica.org/fg-item/full-participation-building-the-architecture-for-diversity-and-community-engagement-in-higher-education/?parent=442

Fogel, S. J., & Cook, J. R. (2006). Considerations on the scholarship of engagement as an area of specialization for faculty. *Journal of Social Work Education, 42*(3), 595–606.

Gibbons, M., Limoges, C., Nowotny, H., Scwartzman, S., Scott, P., & Trow, M. (1994). *The new production of knowledge: The dynamics of science and research in contemporary societies.* London, UK: SAGE.

Glassick, C. E., Huber, M. T., & Maeroff, G. I. (1997). *Scholarship assessed: Evaluation of the professoriate.* San Francisco, CA: Jossey-Bass.

Holland, B. A. (2005, May 18). *Community engagement and community-engaged scholarship: Clarifying our meaning when using these terms.* Retrieved from http://

www.learningace.com/doc/2687977/cd682dc43de7ec7f75648e722b1d254b/
hollandfipse-5-18-teleconf

Kellogg Commission on the Future of State and Land-Grant Universities. (2000). *Returning to our roots.* Washington, DC: National Association of State Universities and Land-Grant Colleges.

London, S. (2003). *Higher education for the public good a report from the national leadership dialogues.* Anne Arbor, MI: National Forum on Higher Education for the Public Good.

McIntyre, A. (2007). *Participatory action research.* Thousand Oaks, CA: SAGE.

Moxley, D. P. (2004). Engaged research in higher education and civic responsibility reconsidered: A reflective essay. *Journal of Community Practice, 12*(3–4), 235–242.

Peterson, T. H. (2009). Engaged scholarship: Reflections and research on the pedagogy of social change. *Teaching in Higher Education, 14*(5), 541–552.

Saltmarsh, J., Giles, D. E., Ward, E., & Buglione, S. M. (2009). Rewarding community-engaged scholarship. *New Directions for Higher Education, 147,* 25–35.

Sandmann, L., Foster-Fishman, P., Lloyd, J., Rauhe, W., & Rosaen, C. (2000). Managing critical tensions: How to strengthen the scholarship component of outreach. *Change, 32*(1), 44–58.

St. John, E. P. (2013). *Research, actionable knowledge, and social change: Reclaiming social responsibility through research partnerships.* Sterling, VA: Stylus.

Van de Ven, A. H. (2007). *Engaged scholarship: A guide for organizational and social research.* Oxford, England: Oxford University Press.

Whyte, W. F. E. (1991). *Participatory action research.* Thousand Oaks, CA: SAGE.

2

SCHOLARSHIP AND ACTIVISM ON BEHALF OF HIGHER EDUCATION'S PUBLIC GOOD MISSION

An Organizational Context

John C. Burkhardt

My father and grandfather were bookbinders, working mostly with leather. In pursuing their work they took care to ensure that the most obvious task of the binder was fulfilled by making sure that the book held its form and the pages stayed in place when handled. Because they intended their binding to be strong and lasting, they checked carefully to make sure that the specific sections that belonged in a particular book were all included and in the proper order. This also required that they verified that any material meant for some other project, perhaps one being assembled elsewhere in the factory, had not become inadvertently incorporated. Again, no matter the subject described in its pages or its fleeting or enduring interest (and because leather was expensive), my father and grandfather took special pride in their contribution to turning a manuscript into a book. For them the decisive crush of the press was definitive and final.

Careful gathering and strong binding of well-chosen materials was expected of all bookbinders. But my grandfather and father made their most satisfying contributions and gave the truest expression of their art in showing care in the thoughtful choice of leather, how it was crafted and tooled, and its resulting feel and appearance. They believed that a book *could* be judged by its cover when the text and its context related in ways that integrated and announced a book and its particular contents. In editing this volume and introducing the organizational context in which the thinking that guided it was shaped, I am following their example. While it is our work

21

as editors to make sure that the book takes form, that it holds together, that it includes what is necessary and only what belongs, and that the reader is prepared for what may be found within, it is my hope in writing this chapter that I might inspire the reader's interest.

It is more than a metaphor to suggest that this is a book that reflects a long process of gathering and binding. The scholarship included here represents the work of individuals who enjoyed an organizational affiliation, a set of commitments, and a shared history. In becoming the scholars they now are, they were influenced in their choice of professional priorities and their approaches to scholarship by their connections to one another, even though they may not have worked side by side at any given time. The common thread that ties these chapters together is that each was written by someone who spent some part of his or her formation as a scholar examining and advocating for changes in the ways in which higher education served society, either through the work of the National Forum on Higher Education for the Public Good (National Forum) or with two or three degrees of separation. This commonality created and sustained the work of the National Forum at the University of Michigan, where most authors worked for some period of time between 2000 and 2015. In their individual and combined efforts, they challenged one another and built on each other's experiences. Wonderfully, although they shared something they valued in common, they adopted different perspectives, different approaches, and different professional identities, as this book effectively demonstrates.

This chapter examines the particular organizational setting that, although it has evolved in many ways from its inception to now, became closely related to the scholarship that is represented in this volume. In juxtaposing the context, its culture, and the work emanating from it, we are given further evidence of the deep connections among place, time, people, and the creative process.

A Unique Organizational Context and Its Influence on the Scholarship It Inspired

The National Forum was established at the University of Michigan in 2000. From its inception, it was closely affiliated in direct ways with the Center for the Study of Higher and Postsecondary Education (CSHPE). Located in the same building, drawing on some of the same graduate students, and often sharing faculty resources, the National Forum nonetheless was something of a noisy, even disruptive, neighbor. CSHPE was established in 1957 as one of the nation's first centers to focus on scholarship and teaching about higher education. Just prior to the celebration of CSHPE's Diamond Jubilee, in moved an organization whose work seemed to test many of the underlying assumptions associated with higher education scholarship. The differences in approach reflected a difference in goals—as is elaborated in this chapter—and often introduced a productive tension. Sustained mutual goodwill and many complementarities were found between CSHPE and the National Forum, and these shared relations resulted in the development and encouragement of hundreds of scholars who emerged from their experiences with not only graduate degrees but also a passion to make a difference through their future professional commitments.

As noted previously, the National Forum was founded with support from the W.K. Kellogg Foundation as part of an effort to secure greater contributions from U.S. colleges and universities for addressing society's challenges. This goal was pursued through many of the foundation's other grant-making and programmatic strategies, but the specific strategy that led to the investment in the National Forum was grounded in a foundation goal of redirecting scholarship about higher education toward better informed efforts to *change* what had already been quite adequately described in years of educational research. The National Forum, in fact, evolved from a collaboration of scholars and higher education practitioners that had been organized and coordinated in-house, the Kellogg Forum for Higher Education Transformation (KFHET), and had operated from 1997 through 2000 (Peterson, 2005). In the sense of the Kellogg Foundation, further description of the problems faced at the intersection of higher education and society was not going to result in changing the conditions that had been already very well documented. There was a special interest at the foundation to use acquired knowledge to guide strategies that might eliminate barriers to access, systematic inequity, problems associated with increasing corporatization, and declining public support for education.

The way that the foundation approached its own work influenced the adoption of a social movement orientation for the National Forum's work. This was an overriding orientation reflected in the ways that the foundation viewed the challenges it faced in health, education, food systems security, volunteerism, and institutional transformation (W.K. Kellogg Foundation, 2003). This broad-scale view of "how things change" shaped the foundation's approach to leadership development as well. This view was not only a way of making sense of the foundation's work across many fields but also a sense-making framework for the National Forum. It affected the choice of our research activities in very direct ways, placing our attention on how policy debates were framed, the ways that the public understood the roles and purposes of education, the attitudes and behaviors of individuals and groups within the academy itself, and especially what these factors revealed about how the very work associated with higher education was understood and justified by different stakeholders.

From design to execution, the ultimate goals of promoting better understanding while trying to influence higher education's role in U.S. society guided a wide range of research studies and influenced the training and early work of dozens of scholars over 15 years. The interaction between "what we do" and "how we do it" not only shaped the work of the National Forum as an organization but also influenced how its work was received in the field. It also had an effect on what kinds of scholars and graduate students chose to affiliate with the National Forum, and it determined how patterns of funding were established to support its development. These several interdependent influences are examined in the first half of this chapter and complemented with some thoughts about how and why this retrospective analysis can be of assistance to practitioners and scholars.

Adopting a Research Framework to Fit the Mission of the National Forum

The relationship between ontology and phenotype—how things begin and the shape they take—is one that has been examined in many different disciplines and applied to everything from bugs to bureaucracies. The many factors and circumstances that combined in the establishment of the National Forum influenced the evolution of its work and can be seen in the scholarship that forms the core of this volume. Among these many influences, three stand out as being pronounced and persistent in their effects. These became defining challenges of a sort:

1. Balancing activism directed toward an articulated goal—"the public good"—within traditional expectations of objectivity in higher education scholarship
2. Appropriately respecting the important role of philanthropy in the work of the National Forum
3. Adopting a suitable research paradigm for the National Forum's work

Examining these influences and the questions that they raised is important in framing the research in the chapters that follow. Rather than three independent influences with independent responses, they combined and were interrelated. Consequently, although any of the three influences could be selected as the axis for examination, the fact that this chapter introduces work that represents how we responded to the third of these influences suggests that I briefly describe the first two conditions and show how they shaped our choices regarding the topics for scholarship that are illustrated in this volume and the ways this body of scholarly work was addressed.

New deviations from traditional research paradigms invite skepticism, and they probably should. This problem is familiar to scholars and their students who have experienced the challenges to qualitative studies, feminist perspectives, and phenomenology (to name a few), or even more recently the effective and appropriate use of big data in research. In finding a suitable approach to scholarship that could support the mission and goals of the National Forum, we were not required to set out on our own or invent something new. But we did need to reflect on the specific limitations and the different opportunities associated with several emerging research frameworks and, in some cases, question the assumptions that were associated with them.

At the time of our appearance, there was still considerable discussion in the scholarly community about the concept of engaged scholarship sparked by the influential essay written by Ernest Boyer (1990) of the Carnegie Foundation. His ideas have now become increasingly integrated into the expectations and the value systems that shape research about higher education. In reaching this point, the field has had to wrestle not only with questions about the topics worthy of study but also with the methods by which they would be approached. Each of these concerns, still very much afoot in 2000 (and not entirely resolved today), brought different challenges. The second of them, in particular, has been the focus of the current series of books into which this volume has been included.

The increasing importance placed on engaged scholarship in the field of higher education has revealed an additional consideration, one that may even be more fundamentally related to the traditional way in which *research* has been defined in the academy. That question revolves around the assumptions of objectivity and the merits of detachment that we associate with a positivist orientation to the world, a perspective closely associated with methods of inquiry and proofs of truth derived largely from work in other academic disciplines. Although most of us realize that the expectations placed on research by distancing ourselves from the object of our study have limiting consequences and may not even reflect the contexts or the fundamental realities of what we observe and report, the pressure to remain aloof from our interests and indifferent as to our findings—though acknowledged as something of an artifice—is still very powerful.

There was—and remains—another problem in educational research that follows from the pretension of objectivity. In order to make clearer, more definitive, and more confident statements about what we study, we focus our examination and limit our observations to smaller and smaller aspects of the environment we are attempting to describe. In effect, the tighter the field of vision, the more we can turn up the power of our lights and lenses. Although this results in more focused studies and limits overgeneralizations, it also means that we are frequently looking at only parts of complicated structures, often at the expense of understanding and even forgetting the whole of what concerns us.

Finally, in considering the platforms and assumptions undergirding research in education, at least as interpreted as recently as 20 years ago when the work described in this book was first conceived, we have the challenge of accurately characterizing things that move, especially when both subject and observer move in separate ways. Objects that move have so influenced the structures of science that, from Galileo onward, we have had to specify movement as a variable in everything we study. Even though the problems of observing and describing anything that moves have been adequately managed in fields as widely spaced as physics and child development, we remain unsure of how to deal with the added complication of the researcher moving the table during the experiment. That is a real challenge to scholarly activism (or activist scholarship) and it has long been acknowledged.

Certainly there are legitimate approaches to scholarship that take these problems into account (Pasque, Bowman, & Martinez, 2009; Pasque, Carducci, Kuntz, & Gildersleeve, 2012; Weber, 1978), but the research described in this book goes beyond simply better clarifying the relationship of the reflective and stable researcher to the subject. This is a book about scholarship that is grounded in points of reference that sometimes move together, sometimes independently, and sometimes randomly. It might be analogous to reporting on different experiences related by individuals taking notes while fighting fires within windstorms. It raises and attempts to address questions that are common to practitioners as well as scholars, but also to the woman or man simply trying to understand and address difficult problems. Often those questions begin with one that is the most obvious in the analogy: Where's the fire? (Weick, 1993).

The challenges of scholarship related to issues of equity, diversity, and inclusion within a dynamic, changing society, and as observed through institutional structures, have been explored in excellent recent work, some reported in the series of books of which this volume is a part. These studies reflect the increasing application and growing sophistication of qualitative research methods in conducting research about diversity and equity in higher education. This volume reports work that falls into this general category (although it includes both qualitative and quantitative research) and that bears the unique distinction of having been conducted over many years within a specific scholarly environment. This setting brought together and forged affiliations among young scholars who not only acknowledged the challenges described previously and debated their implications, but also attempted to deal with these challenges while vigorously pursuing a public agenda in a public manner.

When describing an approach that differs from what is normal or expected in a given field, it is important to relate innovation to the standards operating in the environment, even if some of those tests of validation are not assumed in the work. To be useful, the scholarship conducted at the National Forum obviously could not incorporate bias nor be sloppily conducted. This was important not only because of the inherent skepticism our known positions on issues could invite, but also because the doctoral students were being trained and evaluated in two traditions simultaneously. We needed really good scholarship to guide and refine our strategic commitments. The last people we wanted to mislead were ourselves.

Consequently, the distinctive approach that forms the central axis for the research reported in this volume is much more than an attempt to deal with limitations by ignoring them. The circumstances surrounding its development strengthened it immeasurably, gave it a sense of vitality, and created a high standard for its rigor and application. These same circumstances (including the fact that the organization itself was funded almost entirely on foundation grants) led to an ongoing evolution in the topics we studied.

How the Research Reported in This Volume Evolved Concurrently With the Development of the National Forum as an Organizational Form

Our initial guiding research for the National Forum was practically related to our organizational mission. We sought to determine how higher education was regarded by the public, how this was reflected in public behavior, and how it resonated in public policy. We adopted an a priori commitment to advancing "higher education as a public good," but for reasons we thought were sound, we steadfastly avoided offering a specific definition of what constituted *public good* except in general terms. The decision we took to avoid defining the public good for others was based on several observations. We acknowledged the privilege (and the potential for bias) that was associated with our place inside the academy. To define the public benefit outside the reference of a broad public discourse seemed presumptuous. Consistent with that point, we were hoping to foster a discussion about the public benefits of higher education among the widest possible range of parties. If we were to preempt that discussion with a fixed idea, all other suggestions would be reactive to what we posited.

The early research we conducted examined the ways in which attitudes, statements, practices, and policies interacted to constitute the changing relationship between higher education and a changing, increasingly diverse democratic society (Kezar, Chambers, & Burkhardt, 2005). Some of the chapters of this book shed light on the questions that arose from that fundamental curiosity. In the early years of our efforts, we directed our attention to the attitudes held by educators themselves, especially those who held key leadership positions with colleges and universities or their affiliated national associations. We commissioned research on public attitudes and convened structured discussions among leaders to examine what those attitudes might mean for higher education and its future. We gathered groups of scholars to more deeply examine the implications of a changing perspective on education from a democratic right to an economic investment, and we encouraged further research (beyond our own) with the goal of establishing a framework that could inspire and guide conversations beyond the academy itself (London, 2003).

Within a relatively short time, we came to see that this approach had won us a place in a conversation among scholars and policymakers, but it would have little effect beyond groups that already had a constituency interest in knowing how higher education "should" relate to the public and to society. We girded ourselves for a conversation that took us outside the boundaries of our own perspectives and actively engaged individuals and groups within communities around the question "Who is college for?" This question and the invaluable assistance we received from the Kettering Foundation in framing it for public deliberation made it clear that there was more to understanding higher education and its public benefits than could be gathered without deeper consideration of beliefs and assumptions held within families, neighborhoods, and communities (Mathews, 2005).

This realization ushered in two closely related areas of inquiry and engagement. For many years we directed attention to better understanding community attitudes about higher education generally and the importance of college for individuals. This work, generously supported by the Lumina Foundation for Education, among others, placed us in the position of disciplined listeners and eventually inspired efforts to try to build upon community dynamics as a way of encouraging support for higher levels of educational attainment. Ultimately, the research we conducted in this area, incorporating both community attitudes about higher education, also shed light on the process of community coalition building (National Forum on Higher Education for the Public Good, 2007, 2008). This work eventually came to have some influence on both state and national policy, which can be seen in the creation of local college access networks in many communities across the country.

A few examples of the research conducted during this period will offer a sense of its range and importance. We conducted structured discussions in selected Michigan communities, involving thousands of people during an 18-month period. Adapting an approach refined by the Kettering Foundation and structured around the question "Who is college for?", these conversations allowed us to analyze common and differing perspectives held across communities in urban, rural, suburban, wealthy, and economically challenged communities (Dedrick, Grattan, & Dienstfrey, 2008). We also could examine differences in perspective held between groups that were identified with specific venues in which the forums were conducted. We were not able to track differences in individual viewpoints, but that was not our real goal. We wanted to see if community or group affiliation affected attitudes about college and how understanding these patterns might allow us to work at the neighborhood and community level to foster greater opportunities and commitments for college participation.

We learned a great deal from these dialogues, which is reflected in a few of the chapters of this book. In addition, we also discovered that words and phrases such as *hard work, qualification, merit,* and *ability* were understood and used quite differently in some communities and groups. We also found that when communities came together to discuss the role of college in their lives, their sense of power to change existing participation patterns shifted from external factors to personal and local factors. This finding, in particular, led the way for further investment in community organizing and coalition building at local levels across the state.

At about the same time, we were invited to provide research support for a statewide commission, appointed by the governor, that focused on the future of higher education. This work occasioned several new studies, introduced our work in other states, and led indirectly to contracts that examined factors shaping educational attainment at the regional level. Through research to support this important policy initiative, we learned that the general level of aspiration held across families in our state was higher than many had previously described. There was an entering assumption expressed by many of the commissioners that Michigan suffered from a culture of low educational aspiration. However this was not borne out in the surveys we reviewed—nor could it be reconciled with our previous work at the community level. The belief that Michigan residents were suffering under the "hangover" of easy jobs with low training demands was very hard to unseat, but our research was eventually influential in refuting—or at least quieting—this assertion (Lt. Governor's Commission on Higher Education and Economic Growth, 2004).

Throughout all of the work of the National Forum, dating back to its first years of formation, there could be found a sustained interest in the role and importance of minority-serving institutions. This preoccupation was rooted in several concerns that paralleled the long-term interest given to this subject by the Kellogg Foundation. These special institutions were important to not only educating otherwise underserved students, but they also offering valuable lessons about how culture and community could advance educational goals both for individuals and for groups. The preparation of leaders for these unique institutions merited particular attention, and we became involved in a number of studies to explore how various cultural groups might benefit from thoughtfully constructed leadership programs. The concern for strengthening leadership development has remained an important component of the National Forum's work to the present and has been central to the commitment to serve vulnerable communities and populations—and an essential insight into the way we think about the public good. After an initial evaluation of an ambitious philanthropic effort in this area (an effort funded by the Kellogg Foundation) we continued our relationships with minority-serving institutions through programs of research and advocacy. Currently, the National Forum is studying the effects of a leadership investment made 10 years ago with the goal of preparing provosts and presidents for these schools. It is a rare opportunity to follow cohorts of participants for such long periods of their careers.

Our work with minority-focused institutions indirectly led to involvement in the issue of access to education for undocumented students. This challenge, initiated in 2007 and still very much a part of the National Forum's work, stimulated several interesting studies. With support from the American Association of Hispanics in Higher Education, Noe Ortega (2011) conducted a study that provided new insights into the ways in which national associations influence the policy positions of their member institutions. Texas Guarantee philanthropies funded a national study of institutional practices related to undocumented students, which was greatly aided by partnerships with the National Association of Student Financial Aid Administrators and the Association of Collegiate Registrars and Admissions Officers. During this time, we also prepared policy briefs for foundations and several national agencies and hosted meetings with leaders across the country.

Lessons Learned From Combining Research and Advocacy to Advance Higher Education's Role in Serving the "Public Good"

In a book published to describe the overall work of the National Forum (Kezar et al., 2005), we suggested that advancing a commitment to higher education's role in serving the public good would require the mobilization of a social and professional movement. Writing at that time, Tony Chambers, the charismatic associated director of the National Forum during its formative period (who also wrote the foreword for this book), suggested that the rigors of such an approach placed responsibilities on individuals with differing roles and skills to work toward change over an extended period, combining, complementing, and reinforcing each other's work in different ways. This current volume continues in that spirit as it brings forward scholarship about higher education's changing place in society, describes specific friction points where the concept of a public good can be interrogated and argued, and provides a basis for professional practice that is grounded in a strong empirical foundation.

With that in mind, the chapters included in this volume were chosen to give practitioners an overview of some of the challenges faced across the field when institutional, system, and societal issues intersect. The depth of research presented here also offers valuable insight into the complexity of issues that coincide (and often collide) at these boundary points. Whether the findings of these authors translate into a basis for advocacy is a determination that has to be made by professionals operating within their own contexts and in light of the personal and institutional commitments they hold. But by using tools of scholarship to clarify, probe, and push questions from the desk of the researcher to the agenda of the professional leader, we hope this book makes an important and timely contribution to the field.

Moreover, as this particular chapter suggests, there was an unusually close bond between the organizational context that spawned the scholarship represented here, how it eventually took shape, and the impact it had in refining the research priorities of those who shared an affiliation with the National Forum. In reflecting on the interrelationships among context, people, and outcomes at the National Forum there are several observations that might be offered to explain how and why this happened. As is the case with many emerging organizations, the National Forum came to be known for its products along with its capacities to produce them. Many of our student employees were pursuing doctorates in higher education through a program that was known for its rigor and high standards. It was not by accident that the excellent training they received in the classroom found ready application in the assignments they took on at the National Forum. The emphasis on original scholarship that focused on contemporary issues and the eagerness shown by early career scholars to present their work in publications and presentations meant that the National Forum was frequently represented at national conferences and meetings.

The legitimacy gained from foundation support—originally through the Kellogg Foundation but later by Lumina, Ford, Carnegie, and many others—offered a distinct credibility and brought resources for expanding our staff capacity and for taking on new projects. The fact that the National Forum was funded almost exclusively by external resources (approximately $7 million over a decade) meant that our work was subjected to a specialized and incisive form of review: It had to pass a test of quality in terms of its scholarly merit, but it also had to be continually judged by foundations to be relevant and capable of prompting action on the part of educators, policymakers, or community members.

Finally, and this cannot be overlooked, the obvious passion expressed for the work in which they were engaged made our graduate students stand out as especially promising and highly determined. Their commitment to the various initiatives they led at the National Forum may have added months or even a year or two to the completion of a few of their dissertations, but when they completed their graduate study they emerged with a strong sense of purpose and the tools to articulate the social and educational implications of their scholarship with conviction and sophistication. Not a few of them also turned out to be excellent grant writers.

Talent often attracts talent, and the National Forum was situated in a deep river through which flowed a remarkable and steady stream of gifted young people. The affiliation with CSHPE and the University of Michigan School of Education meant that eager novitiates arrived year after year, often recruited by advanced students who sat on admissions committees or hosted program applicants during their visits to campus. The University of Michigan also offered a bounty of bright graduate students looking for meaningful work in a dynamic environment. Over the first 10 years of the National Forum's development we employed students from the Schools of Law, Business, Policy, Public Health, and Music.

There were other measures of diversity as well that appealed to faculty, staff, and students and helped to further distinguish and enrich the organizational climate. Among the earliest recruits to the National Forum were several extraordinarily bright African American women who went on to roles as faculty members or took positions in major foundations. We welcomed international students and hosted several research fellows who brought special personal backgrounds to the organization. The National Forum also adopted an intergenerational orientation with undergraduate, master's, and doctoral students, staff, and faculty sharing a rather constrained suite of offices. Our revered bookkeeper, Jenny Mosseri, had experienced life as a young girl in a German concentration camp. She inspired tremendous respect and played a regular role in the orientation of every new employee.

The National Forum frequently operated on a shoestring budget and took on something of a shoeless culture. It was expected that students, staff, and faculty would eat lunch together in the conference room. It invited grumbling and even indignation when a meeting was scheduled in that room between noon and one o'clock. The offices were quiet in the morning when students were in class, giving way to a din from midafternoon through late into the evening. Shoeless? Flip-flops were considered dress attire by many.

It was by intention that we created an organizational environment that was different from most others in the school and different from those that our graduates might expect to inherit when they took up places in their professions. We wanted to experiment with a culture that was as diverse, as expansive in age and experience, and as open to change as we could make it without losing a sense of continuity and order. Because we spoke and wrote about a vision of higher education where many different personality types, orientations, and experiences could come together, pursue shared purposes, and fully benefit from their differences, we chose to see if something of that sort could become a springboard for high achievement and continuous learning. We hoped that success in this endeavor might offer an insight into ways in which individual growth and success could enhance collective benefits and, going beyond the boundaries of the organization itself, actively promote something like a "public good." We felt that if we could demonstrate it, experience it, and sustain it, maybe the concept could be more than a dream.

References

Boyer, E. (1990). *Scholarship reconsidered: Priorities of the professoriate.* Princeton, NJ: Carnegie Foundation for the Advancement of Teaching.

Dedrick, J., Grattan, L., & Dienstfrey, H. (2008). *Deliberation and the work of higher education: Innovations for the classroom, the campus, and the community.* Kettering, OH: Kettering Foundation.

Kezar, A. J., Chambers, T. C., & Burkhardt, J. C. (Eds.). (2005). *Higher education for the public good: Emerging voices from a national movement.* San Francisco, CA: Jossey-Bass.

London, S. (2003). *Higher education for the public good: A report from the national leadership dialogues.* Ann Arbor, MI: National Forum on Higher Education for the Public Good.

Lt. Governor's Commission on Higher Education and Economic Growth. (2004). *Final report of the Lt. Governor's Commission on Higher Education and Economic Growth.* Retrieved from http://www.cherrycommission.org/docs/finalReport/CherryReport.pdf

Mathews, D. (2005). Listening to the public: A new agenda for higher education. In A. J. Kezar, T. C. Chambers, & J. C. Burkhardt (Eds.), *Higher education for the public good: Emerging voices from a national movement* (pp. 71–86). San Francisco, CA: Jossey-Bass.

National Forum on Higher Education for the Public Good. (2007, April). *Research on community deliberative dialogues to inform educational attainment.* Ann Arbor, MI: Prepared for The Charles F. Kettering Foundation.

National Forum on Higher Education for the Public Good. (2008, February). *Access to democracy: Summary report of findings and recommendations.* Ann Arbor, MI: Prepared for the Lumina Foundation for Education.

Ortega, N. (2011). The role of higher education associations in shaping policy that connects immigration to educational opportunity: A social capital framework. *Journal of Hispanic Higher Education, 10*(1), 41–65.

Pasque, P. A., Bowman, N. A., & Martinez, M. (Eds.). (2009). *Critical issues in higher education for the public good: Qualitative, quantitative & historical research Perspectives.* Kennesaw, GA: Kennesaw State University Press.

Pasque, P., Carducci, R., Kuntz, A. K., & Gildersleeve, R. E. (2012). *Qualitative inquiry for equity in higher education: Methodological innovations, implications, and interventions. ASHE Higher Education Report, 37*(6). San Francisco, CA: Jossey-Bass.

Peterson, M. (2005). A serendipitous search for a career in higher education. In J. C. Smart (Ed.), *Higher education: Handbook of theory and research* (p. 20). Norwell, MA: Springer.

Weber, M. (1978). *Max Weber: Selections in translation.* Cambridge, England: Cambridge University Press.

Weick, K. E. (1993). The collapse of sensemaking in organizations: The Mann Gulchdisaster. *Administrative Science Quarterly, 38*(4), 628–652.

W. K. Kellogg Foundation. (2003). *The vision of one, the power of many: Annual report of the W. K. Kellogg Foundation.* Battle Creek, MI: Author.

Part Two

ENGAGING THE COMMUNITY LEVEL

3

CONFLATING COMMUNITY MEANS WITH ORGANIZATIONAL ENDS
Strengthening Reciprocity in a Multisector Higher Education Access Partnership

Elizabeth Hudson

Understanding the role of higher education institutions in community partnership is more important now than ever as these institutions increasingly support complex, multisector community initiatives to determine and address community needs. These efforts are collaborations among diverse community and institutional partners, including public, private, and for-profit organizations. A guiding rationale for these complex partnerships is that if organizations collaborate, they can bring new resources to bear on public problems in communities. Community-based coalitions have been addressing public health needs for decades, but in recent years coalitions have been promoted across the country to improve educational opportunity in the nation's most distressed neighborhoods, as is the case with the federal Promise Neighborhood program. This chapter assists engaged leaders by developing deeper understandings of partnership equity that embrace the multiple and sometimes competing conceptualizations of the public good evident in community-based coalitions for education reform.

Higher education institutions can be essential partners in community-based problem-solving efforts, especially when the problem being addressed is educational opportunity (Corrigan, 2001; Hudson, 2013). To understand the relationship between two partners, a two-way street, or the concept of reciprocity, is a helpful guideline; however, as the complexity increases through coalition partnerships, the guidelines for practice need to grow in sophistication.

Serving—or even explicitly describing—the public good through partnership is easier said than done. In this chapter, I attempt to capture the complexity of defining and embracing the public good in a diverse, community-based multisector coalition. A constructivist framework enhances understanding of partnership building by attending closely to the expectations and communication processes among partners (Weerts & Sandmann, 2008). The construction of partnership through communication has implications for mutuality and reciprocity. The term *community* took on various meanings by partners from higher education institutions, regional organizations, and neighborhood organizations. Partnerships are created, logically, through the interactions of individuals and groups as they seek reciprocal and mutually beneficial ends. This is true in relatively simple and more complex contexts and holds true in this situation as well. However, in more complicated networked partnerships with many different interests to balance, attending to relationships may be even more important so that resident voices and concerns are not lost. The National Forum on Higher Education for the Public Good's (National Forum's) work with the Walnut Hills Education Network (WHEN) provides the context for this analysis.

Case: Walnut Hills Education Network

The subject of this chapter is the case of WHEN, and the hope is that this analysis will be useful for people developing or involved in complex university partnerships that enhance educational outcomes in communities. Except for the National Forum, organizations and individuals are referred to with pseudonyms to protect participants who wished to remain anonymous. Individuals were given pseudonyms that reflected how they were addressed within the partnership. This explains the variance between addressing people by title or first name.

WHEN is located in Walnut Hills, a neighborhood with approximately 13,000 residents in Detroit, Michigan. Since 2000, the population of the area decreased more than 30%. In tandem with Walnut Hills's shrinking population, the educational environment shifted, with city claims of shrinking enrollment leading to public school closures. Despite these challenges, the neighborhood was activating significant organizational assets to help reverse trends that limited opportunity. For example, in 2000 the Walnut Hills Coalition (WHC), consisting of neighborhood-serving organizations, was established to promote educational and social development. A pastor's committee formed a few years later to develop a neighborhood-wide, holistic vision for change, and a youth council was created to inform community programming. These activities attracted external attention through regional philanthropic investment, and higher education institutions from across the state became involved in the community.

The overarching goal of WHEN was to improve opportunity for Walnut Hills' youth to reach their educational goals. Part of the big vision involved having an "ongoing network of students" from the neighborhood prepared to enroll in the education partner institutions. The partnership aimed to create seamless access between educational institutions and the community. As graduates eventually came back into the neighborhood to work and live as role models, the conditions in the area would improve. That was the vision. This optimistic goal was shared by many in the partnership, both National Forum staff and Walnut Hills' community partners, who advocated for a system of education that could serve young people and bring them back to the community as champions of educational opportunity for future generations.

The partnership that became WHEN formed in 2006 to stem the tide of urban decline; its specific goals were to increase college access and to address other community needs. It formed out of close professional relationships between the National Forum leadership and leaders in the Walnut Hills community. The National Forum did not solicit this partnership, but the desire to explore educational opportunity solutions for urban youth provided a rich context to meet the organization's mission of closing the gap between research and practice. WHEN started with community leadership from a church and housing developer in Walnut Hills who reached out to the National Forum leadership to discuss university support for educational improvement once the neighborhood's public high school had closed. The discussions continued for several years, and the partnership expanded to include representatives from faith-based organizations, schools, other youth-serving organizations, and the local neighborhood association (see Table 3.1 for a list of key, sustaining partners). In total, more than 12 regional and neighborhood organizations were involved in WHEN, including four different higher education departments and institutions.

In 2010, partners secured funding from a state-administered program to improve higher education access. I supported WHEN as a researcher and administrative partner from the National Forum during most of the five years represented in this analysis. This chapter details an analysis of our shared work and work that eventually formed my research agenda in equitable partnership building in higher education.

TABLE 3.1
Selected Community-Based Organizations in WHEN

Community-Based Partners	Description
Walnut Hills Coalition (WHC)	A neighborhood coalition, WHC consists of member organizations throughout the neighborhood of Walnut Hills.
Walnut Hills Development	A Walnut Hills housing developer that aimed to provide affordable housing in the area surrounding the neighborhood. Financial challenges and the declining need for housing expanded its mission to include greenway projects and block development.
Walnut Community School (WCS)	WCS, a charter school on the border between Walnut Hills and another neighborhood to its immediate south, emphasized experiential learning through, for example, workshops. It opened in the mid-1990s for kindergarten through middle school, and expanded to a K–12 school around the time that the neighborhood public high school closed in 2007.
Walnut Baptist Church (WHBC)	The pastor of WHBC (Rev. Windsor) was an active partner in the WHC and was also director of the Walnut Hills Community Development Center out of the church. The church aimed to promote job opportunities for Walnut Hills' youth.
The Carpenter Foundation	The Carpenter Foundation has been a regional grant-maker for more than 50 years with annual city investments of tens of millions.
Midwest University	Midwest University is a major research university located approximately 45 miles from the WHEN Community. It has a number of activities in the area and operates a downtown campus in the Detroit area.
National Forum	An applied research center at Midwest University, the National Forum is engaged in a number of community engagement projects.

Methods

This study employed qualitative methods to understand partnership building within and around WHEN and utilized data collected during a five-year relationship development period from 2006 to 2011. Rich data sources were available for this analysis because of the trust established through the long-term relationships among National Forum and Walnut Hills partners. Of the more than a dozen members, 11 university and community partners participated in interviews in order to explore the experiences of the partners in collaborating on education improvement in Walnut Hills. The overall data set included transcripts from 16 semistructured interviews of approximately one-hour duration that were conducted by university students in 2008 and 2010. The data sources also included minutes from 24 meetings, video from a meeting, e-mails sent to a group list over several years, some internal National Forum communications, partnership evaluations, and accepted and rejected grant proposals.

The analysis was influenced by principles of thematic analysis and started by aiming to explain "what is going on" in the data set (Rubin & Rubin, 2011). The research process is similar to the constant comparative method outlined by Corbin and Strauss (2008), where the researcher constantly refines the classification scheme as the analysis continues. Braun and Clarke (2006) also inform this analysis with their work in thematic analysis. They frame the salience of a theme as the recurrence, repetition, and forcefulness of concepts in the data. Thematic analysis allowed for exploration of the "commonalities, differences, and relationships" (Jones, Torres, & Arminio, 2013, p. 90) among participants' responses. As the analysis progressed, "competing concepts of community" became a salient theme in the commonalities, differences, and relationships among WHEN participants. These concepts elucidated layers in how participants constructed their partnerships and had implications for encouraging equitable work with WHEN.

Findings

Throughout this complex, multisectoral partnership, both the community and the university members left many concepts undefined as they used them to describe their individual or collaborative work. The term *community* was complex in WHEN, and its different and similar usages came from higher education institutions, regional organizations, and neighborhood organizations. As a result, partners often assumed that they were working in one another's shared interest without explicitly negotiating their goals. The different uses of the term *community* have implications for the process of building an equitable partnership and creating educational improvement outcomes that can be recognized by residents and organizations in Walnut Hills. These varying understandings of community included community need as a process, reach to residents, and community as organizations (see Table 3.2). I outline their distinctions and implications in the next few sections.

TABLE 3.2

The Term *Community* **and Its Contested Constructs**

Community Need as a Process	Inclusive Community	Community as Organizations
Identifies needs through an inclusive and dynamic process	Addresses needs as outcomes that enhance the lives of a region's residents	Addresses needs as outcomes of organizations within the partnership or outcomes of the network itself

First Contested Construct of Community: Community Need as a Process

In this section, I outline how WHEN collaborators constructed the idea of *community* in relation to the process of determining community need. At times, WHEN partners framed community as dynamic, which meant the continual revisiting of defined needs. The Walnut Hills' partnership needed to be inclusive and responsive to the community, and only in alignment with those principles would the partnership be recognized as meeting community needs. Here, I describe how Walnut Hills and university partners constructed the ideas of inclusivity and responsiveness and highlight moments when these ideas showed tension among partners.

Inclusive Community Need

Throughout the process of forming partnerships in Walnut Hills, community-based partners expressed the importance of defining *need* inclusively. Listening has been discussed as an important concept in the engagement literature (Dempsey, 2009; Grabill, 2001; Nicotera, Cutforth, Fretz, & Thompson, 2011; Strand, Marullo, Cutforth, Stoecker, & Donahue, 2003), and this analysis supports these findings. Determining representation within a community is often difficult, and, although convenient, partners should never be the only community representation; knowing how to gauge the authenticity of a community representative is hard at the start for an external partner. As an outsider looking in, it takes time to understand the limits of an organizational partner's claim on community representation as well as to build trust and establish strong enough relationships to interrogate any given internal partner's claim on community representation.

Even within Walnut Hills, the idea of the "community" was not settled, though partners gave insight into how they understood the idea. The pastor at WHBC considered Walnut Hills' representatives to be "those who have been living and working and doing business in our community" and that without their "preeminent voice" in a Walnut Hills' effort, a partnership could not meaningfully support community needs. As such, being inclusive of all members in the partnership was essential, but it also proved to be difficult. Community need was recognized as diverse and segmented among WHEN partners. In a 2008 partnership grant proposal seeking university funds to build a collaborative research agenda for education reform, WHEN partners argued that a partnership required "multiple invested groups to form sustained commitment" to be successful, but partners knew community representation was complicated in a coalition-building process.

A housing developer in Walnut Hills put this community-university partnership challenge in a different way, noting how the absence of an inclusive process could build mistrust, saying, "Failing to reach out to some community partners could contribute to distance and mistrust of the partnership." There were multiple organizations and community leaders that came with goals and prior relationships, which brought a rich, diverse perspective, yet required strong consensus building and consistent check-ins to ensure members of the coalition were comfortable moving forward and not resentful of evolving group membership and direction. A youth program director highlighted the importance and difficulty of coalition building best by noting, "No matter what you do, I think you're going to get criticism, sometimes constructive . . . but not always."

Both partners, though, found communication as a solution to the representation challenges. Open discussions about participation in WHEN could counter at least some of the inevitable criticism of community representation. As the housing development partner mentioned, WHEN should just do its best by creating "an effort to keep everything as transparent as possible so that there's not that sense of a few people benefiting from the process moving quickly or something." It is important to define *need* and the ways in which one helps alleviate that need in a slow and deliberate manner; moving too quickly to decision or action could give a sense that some partners were deliberately excluded. In practice, *community need* was not always defined through inclusive conversation with residents or local organizations.

At times, an understanding of community need was attempted through a slow information-gathering process among partners or through survey data from regional organizations. In 2008 a staff member at the National Forum described the difficulty of defining and identifying existing programs to serve youth education access in the region. As outsiders, university partners identified this difficulty as a need and reached out to WHEN community organizations to discover additional university divisions developing higher education access programs in the neighborhood; none were found from the university, and few college access programs existed in the community at all. One study, sponsored by the Carpenter Foundation, showed that the neighborhood had no programs to support higher education access, and many WHEN partners saw this as validating their work and the ongoing partnership efforts. However, even with strong documentation of this issue, identifying college access as a community need was a challenge, because not all partners saw this as a priority. Data gathering is important, but it is not always sufficient to bring consensus among partners.

All partner contributions also had to be in line with WHEN's unique capacities. Community partners offered schooling, youth programming, and community relations. The National Forum partners offered research and administrative support, energy to build momentum, and higher education access expertise. Partners from larger organizations, including WCS and the university, negotiated their contribution with one foot in the partnership and one in their organization. They needed to cultivate institutional buy-in for any contributions that strayed from their central mission or capacities. Their involvement required the management of internal sets of expectations within WHEN and external expectations within their respective organizations. As they listened to the community partners, the other partners could mistake listening *to* community partners in order to coconstruct work as listening *for* the value for their organizations.

At times this tendency of institutional partners to filter community need in relation to their capacities served to narrow options when attempting to inclusively discover and describe needs. The National Forum's location in a School of Education meant that most students who worked with the partnership had an interest in education reform, particularly in improving higher education access. National Forum leadership expressed concern to colleagues about how universities can—knowingly or not—set agendas in partnerships. The challenge, for the National Forum leaders and others, is to figure out how to do this in a sustainable way that really serves community needs, not merely expresses some aspect of the university ego.

Additionally, early in the partnership, the National Forum was conscious of the need to manage community expectations through understanding institutional constraints. For example, in 2007, university students began a tutoring effort as volunteers because a community funding effort did not receive support, but the program ended when the lead university student graduated. Community expectations of this contribution were more than could be delivered, and reliance on this type of activity was not effective for the partnership. Careful listening for community need had to be balanced with institutional capability for sustained efforts. We learned that "[university partners should] constantly listen for the community's definition of need and priority, while maintaining a manageable effort from our end," stated a leading National Forum partner. For the National Forum, building sustainable efforts took precedence over direct action. Achieving understanding of community needs requires higher education partners' acknowledgement that too often they have been unable to sustain initiatives within communities due to lack of resources, institutional support, or transitions among faculty and staff. From the perspective of community leaders, this is a history which invites wariness and frustration.

Dynamic Community Need

The literature points to higher education institutions' slow decision processes (Smerek, Pasque, Mallory, & Holland, 2005) and responses to community (Maurrasse, 2002) as challenges in community partnerships. Within WHEN, movement and change were equally slow. In the case of the university and WHEN, the pace of decisions and action was a by-product of attempts to ensure inclusive coalition building and decision structures. Forum partners had additional reasons for not wanting to rush into activities. Many National Forum partners thought higher education change was necessary to meet community needs. But turning energy toward the university without explanation to Walnut Hills' partners was also seen as a distraction from meeting locally defined needs. The slow processes in WHEN were primarily attributed to the deliberative process, partnership growth, and staff turnover. Similarly, turnover occurred when students left the National Forum, causing dips in activities. The slowdowns were offset by growth that occurred as new community partners and university programs entered the effort. Dialogue and deliberation took time, but so did revisiting earlier conversations to bring new members up to speed. For example, Mark, the housing developer, expected a "slow building process" or an "open-ended type of discussion," and Ted, a leader at WCS, similarly called for "incremental steps" to build rapport and understand shared interests.

Concerns about the slow pace of coalition building were echoed by many WHEN partners, including those in higher education. Ronald, a master's student involved in the partnership, reminded the group of a Martin Luther King Jr. quote: "All progress is precarious, and the solution of one problem brings us face-to-face with another problem." The negotiation and renegotiation of relationships and outcomes to meet community need was evident in this work. In a related example, the WHBC pastor offered advice for partnering organizations, including higher education institutions:

> One of the main takeaways is listening to those who are in the community. Second of all, be willing to change and adapt however you're used to doing business to make sure that everybody's satisfied. And that's the same thing that I've told the community, as well.

Community and university partners envisioned change coming from the relationship. Neighborhood leaders expected WHEN partners to not only listen and "adapt," but also transform their typical organizational practices to align better with the needs within the neighborhood. From a neighborhood perspective, this was something Reverend Windsor claimed the community had learned and that "the community" was ready to change "to planning their strategy versus . . . just willy-nilly throwing something together." WHEN partners agreed about the pace at which change in the community would occur. No such shared agreement existed among the higher education partners. They did anticipate influencing the college environment (graduate student education, tenure-promotion policies, funding support, and curriculum) as an outgrowth of their work, though these outcomes were more vague and rarely shared with the WHEN community partners. Tom, a student in the National Forum, highlighted this need for change in higher education:

> I think if you don't change the culture of the university, you can't create a system whereby the community, the good of the community, is integrated into the good of the university. If they don't see each other as their welfare being tied to one another, then neither side is going to benefit from any of this.

Tom's vision framed higher education as interwoven into the fabric of the neighborhood *and* prioritizing the good of the community within the university. Interestingly, the university partners seldom discussed these institutional outcomes with neighborhood partners. From the perspective of community-based organizational partners such as the WHBC pastor, the community need was to come first in the partnership. In addition, it should be developed meaningfully through an inclusive and dynamic process. Partners worked together to create change slowly because it signaled transparency and mutual respect.

Second Contested Construct of Community: Reach to Residents

Partners in WHEN discussed community in terms of impact in two ways: impact on residents and impact on organizations. In this section, I explore how WHEN partners framed impact in terms of how their efforts should reach residents. Though these levels of impact overlapped at times, and I touch upon that here, the organizational impact is emphasized in the next section.

The National Forum leadership recognized that there were layers of community at different levels, including individual students and parents, families, community organizations, schools, and at multiple system levels. The recognition of this community complexity, though, rarely carried into the planning process as systematically as it was listed here. All parties involved in WHEN, however, defined *community* as residents or organizations, and sometimes the term referred to multiple levels simultaneously or even to the culture of the region.

WHEN partners often had the lofty vision that over time their collaboration would create measurable impact in the neighborhood as well as in the city. In one example, the 2011 WHC leader was asked how he would recognize successful action emerging from the WHEN partnership. He responded in a way that typified this grand vision:

> [When] I can see a tangible program working to be able to take children from wherever they are to success and their goals. When the community uniformly understands that this program is in this community the same way they know that there's a McDonald's [at an intersection in Detroit].

Although the partnership was able to support some students, WHEN did not reach residents outside of the WCS in its pilot year. It was, however, successful in establishing a local area college access network, partially funded by the state. But to date, the wide-reaching vision for WHEN has not been realized.

There are many reasons for this. Once the higher education access support was secured for WHEN, WCS played a more prominent role than the National Forum and the other organizations. WCS then measured resident impact for WHEN based on school outcomes. The higher education access support acquired by the WHEN partners was available primarily through the school partner, at least in the first years. Although the funding supported this model, the other partners learned that these offerings did not capture the vision of "community" originally carried by WHEN.

Other issues also intervened to decrease the impact for WHEN. Neighborhood-based partners expressed concern about partnering with organizations not anchored in the neighborhood. This area of concern included higher education institutions and other organizations that came into the partnership from outside the neighborhood. There were at times frank conversations about these relations. In one example early in the relationship, Reverend Windsor noted that universities and other outside organizations have strong "infrastructure" to write grants and acquire funds, but that the work supported through these funds sometimes neglects to create real change in the neighborhood. He called these partners "poverty pimps" due to their potential to benefit from the circumstances of poverty while making limited contributions to changing it. He stated,

> I hate to use this term because it sounds derogatory, but I think you'll get the point—one of the issues of trust revolved around *poverty pimps*, and

what I mean by that is those organizations that will come in, receive a great deal of money from foundations because they have the infrastructure to write the grant to do the work; however Reverend the work never hits the ground. You'll never see those resources leveraged in the community. (Windsor, personal communication, September 6, 2008)

External partners, including the National Forum, had to demonstrate an orientation toward helping residents and developing on-the-ground impact related to issues of resource sharing, commitment, and sustainability.

When higher education partners have offered direct outreach programming for youth, the contributions were not always aligned with the priorities of the community. For example, university students and Forum staff originally involved with WHEN from 2006 to 2008 tried to get "grassroots projects . . . up and running" (National Forum staff, internal communication) and offered college admission essay writing support and entrance exam preparation. Leadership at the National Forum indicated willingness to provide direct services in addition to making the research capacity of the National Forum available to WHEN. This prioritization was aligned with the expectations of Walnut Hills' partners that external partners would add value to the community.

This expectation for the university to do its part was a common theme for some community persons. One director of the WHC recognized the public mission of higher education and felt the university had an obligation to serve the region in a variety of ways: "People in this community are contributing to you" through taxes and other indirect ways, and as a result universities should provide "outreach" as a form of reciprocation (interview, September 17, 2008). Consistent with this sentiment, some Walnut Hills' leaders wanted university partners to offer leadership classes to develop resident's political advocacy skills to address the community goals. Funders, such as the Carpenter Foundation, shared this view that higher education should "help build capacity of community members" through leadership and group dynamics programming.

Higher education partners had expertise in issues related to college access, but, as noted earlier, higher education access programs were not the top priority among all partners within Walnut Hills. This focus was questioned as a strategic goal motivated by higher education's self-serving interest in increasing student enrollment (De La Rosa, Luna, & Tierney, 2006). The National Forum and other higher education partners had to overcome these suspicions. One approach to this was helping to evolve WHEN's mission to a broader set of goals aimed at defining and serving community needs related to improving educational opportunity, whether or not it benefited the involved institutions. At the same time, the National Forum and other education partners distanced themselves from the direct programming contributions (Hudson, 2013). When higher education partners again offered college preparatory programming, it was offered through the WCS partner and served only a small number of youth in the region. Thus, the focus on residents (students or others) and direct service did not serve as a primary frame for the community-institution partnerships with this project.

Third Contested Construct of Community: Community as Organizations

Community for many exclusively meant its residents, but it also meant organizations. In this section, I highlight how partners used the term *community* to refer to organizational relations.

The concept of community as organizational partners stifled a richer candid discussion and the potential for a partnership grounded more deeply in the needs of the neighborhoods' diverse residents. Complicating this scenario further, some community-based partners described their own organizational ends as being synonymous with community ends. For example, Walnut Housing Development leadership referred to *community* to describe both the organization's efforts and the WHC. The WHBC leadership also referred to work in the WHC, a membership coalition of 30 organizations, as indisputably serving the interests of the community.

Shared organizational goals were apparent in the partnership as well. A common goal of WHEN organizations was to draw the attention of funders to the neighborhood. Higher education partnership and the National Forum leadership brought new potential funders, and the community partnership offered legitimacy for the potential impact of partnership efforts from the National Forum's educational improvement programs in Walnut Hills. In one example, Forum leadership recruited students to help write grants for WHEN and maintained a role to support a fund-raising partnership. This dynamic entailed sharing resources with partnering organizations to raise and maintain funding. Early in the partnership, the National Forum leadership stated that the university and its students would "be available in whatever way we can to provide grant writing or technical support for your coalition interests" (National Forum staff, internal communication). However, the partnership was about action, and his primary aim in leveraging funds was to support the neighborhood in actions that would meet the needs of the community. If the partnership was successful in obtaining outside funding, the National Forum leadership saw that the financial disparity between the university and the neighborhood would have warranted that "the bulk of it should [go] to Walnut Hills as a community" (National Forum staff,

internal communication). But at the same time, he noted that he was also bat-
tling institutional constraints in that university students do not work for free,
and that it "does require resources" for students to carry out their internship
work (National Forum staff, internal communication).

As noted, research was another organizationally understood way that the
National Forum partners could serve WHEN or the network—gathering
data for grants administrators. In a 2007 grant application to the university,
however, the National Forum described its aims in partnership as "step[ping]
back from the work, shar[ing] it with a selected group of community partners and scholars, and chart[ing] the next phase of sponsored research and
community engagement efforts." This statement represents how the National
Forum saw the role of research in the community. It planned for research in
the region that would allow research partners to take time to synthesize the
existing findings, and then work with community partners and residents to
determine the next steps for research and programming in Walnut Hills. The
National Forum did not find financial support for this proposal. Searching
for funding support became a major role for the National Forum and part of
its role in service to the coalition of partners.

Early in the partnership, a WHC leader noted how the academic research
distanced higher education partners from authentic engagement with residents.

> [University] people have come in here and said, "We want to do a focus
> group." I tell you, that's the worst thing you can say now to people. . . .
> They will not come. They're tired. . . . They don't mind answering ques-
> tions, but what they do want is they want you to share your conclusions
> and the data with the community. I mean, if people are going to be part
> of a study, and if you are interviewing them the way you are me, you mail
> the information to them or give them a phone number or a self-addressed
> stamped envelope if they have any questions or they want to see—send
> them over the executive summary. (Lynn, interview, September 6, 2008)

Those who partnered with this or other universities in the past were skeptical.
We learned that our project and other higher education institutions involved
in engaged research have had to relationally compensate for the way communities have been treated in the past. This process of trust building took time.
As the preceding quote also illustrates, research was considered a university
aim, not something that could benefit the community. Higher education
partners have the power and privilege to choose whether or not to engage
in research and share subsequent findings with the community; the choice
not to share was considered problematic. The potential value of research was
recognized by community leaders, but it was valued in the partnership only

when it informed the community partners and when the community at large had access to it.

Organizational goals and funding support—those of the higher education partners and WHEN itself—often eclipsed the outcomes that were designed to serve residents. Because the National Forum is situated at Midwest University, it was sometimes easier to find support for research on education projects than to support other higher priority goals of the community. Though partners were able to collectively raise funds for some programs, at times the goal of finding network support contributed to shunting the network's direct service aims in favor of funding that redefined the vision for WHEN. Walnut Hills' community-based organizations that hoped to better serve youth through WHEN collaborations saw many successes. However, it is still debatable whether community reach was sufficient. Most of the approximately $200,000 raised for WHEN was allocated for research efforts and coalition building, and some of these funds were from partners who only supported research partnerships. The collaboration provided more than $20,000 for college scholarships and had several short-term programs for higher education access, but several coalition partners did not receive any resources or programming to enhance their capacity to serve youth.

Discussion

Scholars in higher education, such as Strand and colleagues (2003) and Maurrasse (2002), have cautioned about higher education's tendency to conflate the interests of representatives in community-based organizations with needs of the community at large. Dempsey (2009) takes this criticism a step further, arguing that the use of a broad concept of community homogenizes a region at the expense of those who are marginalized. This study reinforces these findings as it focuses on WHEN partner language related to community and its implications for developing equitable partnerships that serve the public good.

Community-based partners and higher education partners in WHEN often used the term *community* loosely, but this analysis suggests the need for a structured use of the term among partners in order to elucidate the complexity of networked partner interests. The construction of community in WHEN presents some challenges that can inform coalition partnership (a) at the relational level, to encourage a process in which partners approach one another with trust and mutual respect; (b) at the individual level, to consider the impacts of a collaborative reform effort on youth and residents through direct services and programming; and (c) at the organizational level, to build

TABLE 3.3

Community Constructs, Levels of Community, and Their Implications for Reciprocity

Contested Construct	Community Need as a Process	Reach to Residents	Community as Organizations
Community Level	Relational level	Individual level	Organizational level
Definition of *Community*	Process cultivates trust and mutual respect among partners	Coalition effort impacts on youth and residents through direct services and programming	Partners build and feel impact from organizational or coalition infrastructure to improve goal-meeting capacity
Implications for Reciprocity	Efforts should build a trusting, responsive relationship	Work results in impact for the lives of neighborhood residents and/or youth	Practices enhance the work of organizations within the coalition or the coalition's ability to serve the region
Essential Practices to Strengthen Multilevel Reciprocity	• Accessibility and responsiveness among partners • Transparent interactions • Structuring continuity for inevitable staff turnover • Inclusive decision-making processes	• Include youth and/or community residents formally in coalition • Designate organization partners to foster direct community impact • Formative and summative program assessment for youth-serving efforts with regular reporting	• Explicitly state each organization's expectations for their own and other organizational partnership contributions • Balance individual organizational outcomes for all partners with coalition outcomes • Designate responsible parties for specific coalition infrastructure-building practices (relationship management, fund-raising, assessment, etc.)

infrastructure to improve capacity among organizations and to meet goals of the network partnership. Each of these levels of community must be considered in order for the partnership to meet the needs of the diverse members of a network reciprocally. From these insights, I derive some implications and practices that can strengthen partnership (see Table 3.3). The analysis presented here provides some insight into how a multisector coalition can be built to strengthen impact for residents as well as community-based organizational partners. In the following sections, I offer practical insights, based on this research, into how an authentic mutual exchange may be accomplished through a multilayered understanding of reciprocity.

Community Need as Process and the Relational Level of Multisector Reciprocity

The stronger the relationships between institutional actors and community partners, the more likely community engagement efforts are to be valued by partners (Ferman & Hill, 2004; White, 2009). For partnerships to be considered authentic by those involved, need and benefit must be transparently communicated. However, defining *need* in a complex community effort is always incomplete, which makes attending to the coalition-building process even more important. Understanding how to work collaboratively in ways that uphold trust through an inclusive and dynamic process is essential, because the public good is contested and perhaps never settled. Additionally, understanding who benefits and how is essential for trust building and for all members to recognize the value of the partnerships. Authentically creating an inclusive, open, and transparent process makes achieving relational dimensions of reciprocity possible, which may be the best outcome that partners in a complex partnership can hope for.

Partners can make a process trustworthy by listening and adapting to feedback from other partners and being open to change. As a partnership becomes more inclusive, the ability to be flexible and listen to more and more perspectives comes into conflict with accomplishing partnership goals. Though partners understand network collaborations to be slow, messy, and partial, they need to balance progress with respect for the voices of those involved. Partners within a complex collaborative effort can make the stakeholder identification and need definition processes more transparent by formalizing them. Stakeholder identification should be an open and deliberate process. Those initially involved in brainstorming must have the ability to make contributions to solve challenges. Adding some structure to a planning process that partners agree to early in the partnership also helps to offset some suspicions that a partnership will leave some in the community behind or ignored.

Reach to Residents and the Individual Level of Multisector Reciprocity

WHEN's focus on educational opportunity meant that its efforts were expected to improve the lives of young people in Walnut Hills. Anything short of this would be considered a failure. The collaborative efforts helped to secure tutoring programs for youth, additional advising support for high school students, college visit programming for middle school students, and financial support for at least two students from the neighborhood. None of these direct service programs lasted, however, because of a lack of sustained funding. The coalition could have included youth and residents more formally into WHEN as it was being established in order to strengthen community impact while continually being mindful of the resident outreach. Additionally, we learned we should have designated community impact as a regular topic and charged specific groups with responsibility for examining more closely what it would require of each partner to obtain the impact we wanted.

The National Forum and the university, given the community mistrust of them as external partners, had to gain legitimacy as partners. To do this, the National Forum needed to participate, at least initially, in direct programming that served residents or make it clear that their work was mindful of these goals. People needed to see benefit. The higher education partners did not always find a place in this partnership to provide direct programming to serve youth in the community, but they supported the direct needs in other ways, such as by facilitating administrative functions and taking the lead in fund-raising efforts. Higher education partners can be a valued part of a network as long as the institutions keep the long-term goals at the heart of the partnership and play an active role in supporting that goal as part of the network system. The teaching, research, and service goals of the institutions can be accomplished, but the institutional agenda must be meshed appropriately with the community agenda.

Community as Organizations and the Organizational Level of Multisector Reciprocity

Organizational reciprocity occurs when partners are perceived to meet organizational needs in a networked partnership. The organizational level can mean infrastructural support that meets community needs, such as fund-raising, human resources, and research. This level of coalition reciprocity can do a great deal to improve trust and mutual benefits brought to the table by various partners. This type of sharing should be an important goal of multidimensional community partnerships as it facilitates a sense of equity and fairness that builds long-term relationships.

Further, in a networked partnership, higher education institutions can play important roles in supporting underresourced, nonprofit organizations by offering infrastructure support. Colleges and universities are particularly well suited for fund-raising and research activities. However, institutions need to contribute cautiously because these structural acts could be interpreted as self-serving and as part of historical parasitic and paternalistic behavior looking to capitalize from poverty.

In summary, this study promotes a richer conversation regarding neighborhood coalition efforts to improve educational opportunity. In networks, partners have complex expectations and need to disperse power equitably. This can be a challenging and complicated landscape. Without incorporating multiple levels of community to build a reciprocal partnership, these multisector partnerships risk eclipsing their fundamental goal—improving youth educational outcomes. As partners strengthen their work together and improve organizational capacities, they may lose sight of the individual level of community even as they improve capacities at the organizational and relational levels. In systemic, place-based partnerships, all collaborators, including higher education partners, should and will be held accountable by partners and residents at each of these three levels. This approach strengthens the potential for an equitable outcome for organizational partners *and* for residents in the community.

References

Braun, V., & Clarke, V. (2006). Using thematic analysis in psychology. *Qualitative Research in Psychology, 3*, 77–101.

Corbin, J., & Strauss, A. (2008). *Basics of qualitative research.* (3rd ed.). Thousand Oaks, CA: SAGE.

Corrigan, D. (2001). The changing role of schools and higher education institutions with respect to community-based interagency collaboration and interprofessional partnerships. *Peabody Journal of Education, 75*(3), 176–195.

De La Rosa, D., Luna, M., & Tierney, W. G. (2006). *Breaking through the barriers to college: Empowering low-income communities, schools, and families for college opportunity and student financial aid.* Center for Higher Education Policy Analysis, University of Southern California.

Dempsey, S. E. (2009). Critiquing community engagement. *Management Communication Quarterly, 24*(1), 359–390.

Ferman, B., & Hill, T. L. (2004). The challenges of agenda conflict in higher-education-community research partnerships: Views from the community side. *Journal of Urban Affairs, 26*(2), 241–257.

Grabill, J. T. (2001). *Community literacy programs and the politics of change.* Albany, NY: State University of New York Press.

Hudson, E. (2013). Promising commitments: Exploring the role of higher education to transform neighborhoods through one federal U.S. policy. *Journal of Higher Education Outreach and Engagement. 17*(3), 109–137.

Jones, S. R., Torres, V., & Arminio, J. (2013). *Negotiating the complexities of qualitative research in higher education: Fundamental elements and issues* (2nd ed.). New York, NY: Routledge.

Maurrasse, D. J. (2002). *Beyond the campus: How colleges and universities form partnerships with their communities.* New York, NY: Routledge.

Nicotera, N., Cutforth, N., Fretz, E., & Thompson, S. (2011). Dedication to community engagement: A higher education conundrum? *Journal of Community Engagement & Scholarship, 4*(1), 37–49.

Rubin, H. J., & Rubin, I. S. (2011). *Qualitative interviewing: The art of hearing data.* Thousand Oaks, CA: SAGE.

Smerek, R. E., Pasque, P. A., Mallory, B., & Holland, B. A. (2005). Introduction. Partnerships for engagement futures. In P. A. Pasque, R. E. Smerek, B. Dwyer, N. Bowman, & B. Mallory (Eds.), *Higher education collaboratives for community engagement and improvement* (pp. 7–9). Ann Arbor, MI: National Forum on Higher Education for the Public Good.

Strand, K., Marullo, S., Cutforth, N., Stoecker, R., & Donahue, P. (2003). *Community-based research and higher education: Principles and practices.* San Francisco, CA: Jossey-Bass.

Weerts, D. J., & Sandmann, L. R. (2008). Building a two-way street: Challenges and opportunities for community engagement at land-grant and urban research universities. *The Review of Higher Education, 32,* 73–106.

White, B. P. (2009). *Navigating the power dynamics between institutions and their communities.* Dayton, OH: Kettering Foundation.

4

COMMUNITY AGENCY AND COLLEGE-GOING CULTURE

The Use of Participatory Action Research

Esmeralda Hernandez-Hamed

"It takes a village to raise a child" is a commonly used adage, yet it remains unexamined by many education researchers. The claim suggests that communities possess preexisting networks that can mobilize to provide for the welfare and future opportunities of their children. University representatives cite this truism—often at a safe distance from the community they reference—and then seem surprised when the *village* fails them and, ultimately, itself. This chapter is a representative example of the actual application of this adage, meant to inspire communities and higher education scholars to work more effectively in concert with each other.

The challenge attributed to communities for the welfare of their youngest and most vulnerable members is most visible in the educational attainment in low-income communities. For example, in 2010 the immediate college enrollment rate of high school completers from low-income families was 52%, 30 percentage points lower than the rate of high school completers from high-income families (82%) (National Center for Education Statistics, 2012). In Detroit, Michigan, the setting of the study discussed in this chapter, 54.7% of the population's highest level of education is a high school diploma or less. Another 26.4% of the population has some postsecondary education but never received a degree (U.S. Census Bureau, 2013). Notably, these statistics show the persistent cycle of marginalization in communities that are most in need of the opportunities provided by higher and postsecondary education.

Policymakers, scholars, and the general public have focused on schools, universities, and supporting educational organizations as primary sources for the development of the college-going culture necessary to bolster postsecondary access and success of students (Corwin & Tierney, 2007; Knight-Diop, 2010; Ramsey, 2008). However, the community on the other side of the schoolhouse gate (i.e., parents, churches, neighbors) is still not a full partner in the broader conversation about educational aspirations and expectations.

The community, however, is the earliest arena where youth begin to form the conception of themselves as "college material" or not. In some communities, children receive constant messages and information resources from multiple community stakeholders that shape subsequent college-going expectations and behaviors, and this contributes to their social capital or their collective network of people, financial resources, and so on that propel them toward college (Bourdieu, 1985). The social capital in these communities contributes to what is often termed *college-going culture* at the community level, but many communities, particularly in low-income neighborhoods, do not have the same social capital related to college (Israel, Beaulieu, & Hartless, 2001); therefore, these communities do not exhibit the college-going culture necessary to begin to prepare students for postsecondary education earlier in their lives.

To develop college-going culture in a community suggests a process of *social change*. We know that social change is possible (Maton, 2008), but the process of building college-going culture at the community level continues to be a mystery, and the mechanisms that would aid the development of college-going culture remain unexplored. Given that higher education has been a catalyst for community social change in the past (Marullo & Edwards, 2000), there may be a role for universities to play in increasing college-going culture in communities. In this chapter, I explore one example of how institutions of higher education can enter communities as an equal partner and catalyst for social change. Specifically, I reflect on the benefits as well as the ongoing challenges of maintaining thoughtful and effective university research relationships between communities and higher education scholars. Furthermore, I explore the intended and unintended consequences of preparing for, and using, participatory action research in a 100-block area of Detroit for community members. I suggest the concept of community agency as a potentially important mechanism for building college-going culture and making sustainable social change.

University Methods for Social Change

When university researchers (URs) partner with communities for social change, they usually do so by applying traditional forms of university-community research partnerships (Bensimon, Polkinghorne, Bauman, & Vallejo, 2004). In other words, universities name issues, collect data, provide their interpretation, and disseminate the results to the appropriate academic journal or community partner. Recent literature indicates that this traditional relationship is problematic for many reasons (Pasque, Carducci, Kuntz, & Gildersleeve, 2012). For example, communities subjected to these types of research partnerships may experience research fatigue (Clark, 2008) or develop distrust of URs that may be dangerous (Milner, 2007; also see Chapter 5 in this volume). Moreover, when there is no foundation for a genuine relationship with that community, researchers may miss critical answers to their questions and may not elicit the sustainable social change they were expecting.

Given the National Forum on Higher Education for the Public Good's (National Forum's) belief that for community social change to be sustainable it must be rooted in active, authentic, and broadly endorsed community leadership, supported by widespread community input, the team began to think of alternative methods to engage with the community. This form of critical introspection has led us to ask the following questions: *What is the role of university partners and researchers in community social change? What practices can researchers use to gain a more nuanced understanding of educational issues in the community and be part of the solution to those issues?* The hope is that this chapter will provide some direction for answering these questions, inspire activist-scholars working in these areas, and serve as an impetus for further examination of these critical issues.

Reframing University-Community Partnerships Through Participatory Research

Innovative researchers are conceiving the relationships between the university and the community in new ways. Some scholars are focusing on local communities as primary spaces with their own concerns. Other scholars have noted different types of university-community research partnerships, such as those that involve a higher degree of community involvement and the researcher's role as contradistinctive to traditional conceptions. These shifts are apparent in a review of the common characteristics of university-community partnerships provided by Suarez-Balcazar and colleagues (2004) in which the authors note,

> "Within collaborative partnerships, communities are not merely seen as an extension of the laboratory experience. The traditional researcher's role of consultant or expert changes to collaborator and partner, and the research endeavor becomes a participatory process that is not necessarily under the control of the researcher." (p. 106)

Whereas research that gives agency to the researched (i.e., participants) is still not a predominant form of research in the universities, it is gaining popularity as a valid and desirable method of collecting data and driving positive social change. This method is participatory research.

Participatory research is a very broad term for methodology that encourages the "active participation of community members in the planning, implementation, or evaluation of research" (Taylor et al., 2002, p. 4). For this chapter, I use the terms *PAR* and *participatory research* interchangeably. Nevertheless, it is important to note that some literature posits two separate definitions for these terms.

Kurt Lewin introduced PAR formally in 1946. Unlike other forms of participatory research, it involved an added component of social action (Prilleltensky & Nelson, 2002). Participatory research methods had been in use long before the term had been established. Faculty working with farmers shortly after the Morrill Act is an example of early participatory research meant to bring research and practice closer together. In 1926, B. R. Buckingham used a form of PAR in schools for the similar purpose of understanding the issues that teachers and school administrators face, as well as influencing their practices to address those issues. Several approaches to participatory research have emerged across a number of disciplines. These approaches share several defining characteristics as outlined originally by the International Network on Participatory Research at a major conference in 1977 and reproduced by Selener (1997):

1. The problem originates in the community itself and is defined, analyzed, and solved by the community;
2. The ultimate goal of research is the radical transformation of social reality and improvement in the lives of the people involved. The primary beneficiaries of the research are the community members themselves;
3. Participatory research involves the full and active participation of the community in the entire research process;
4. Participatory research involves a whole range of powerless groups of people: the exploited, the poor, the oppressed, the marginal;
5. The process of participatory research can create a greater awareness in people of their own resources and can mobilize them for self-reliant development;
6. Participatory research is a more scientific method in that community participation in the research process facilitates a more accurate and authentic analysis of social reality; and
7. The researcher is a committed participant, facilitator, and learner in the research process, and this leads to militancy, rather than detachment. (pp. 10–16)

The research that utilized the PAR methodology thus far in higher education illuminated the ways universities may involve students, faculty, administrators, and staff in the research that may ultimately affect managerial and pedagogical practices within the institution (Bensimon, 2007; Bensimon et al., 2004; Eilola et al., 2011). Few have examined the use of PAR in communities from a higher education perspective.

Harkavy and Hartley (2012) argued that universities could forge genuine commitment to civic engagement when faculty and the institution embraced methodologies like PAR. Reflective of Harkavy and Hartley's argument, National Forum researchers utilized PAR methods to organize dialogues on access to postsecondary education in collaboration with a Detroit neighborhood. During the process, the team of URs and community researchers (CRs) recorded their experiences (primarily through journaling and interviews) to explore how the methods affected the data collected, the relationships between the community and university, and the individual outcomes of all researchers involved.

The Case of HOPE Village

In 2012, the National Forum was invited into a partnership with Focus HOPE—a civil rights organization engaged in action to overcome racism, poverty, and injustice in Detroit. The HOPE Village Initiative project was to take place in the 100-block area surrounding the Focus HOPE community organization. The HOPE Village Initiative was a concerted effort to develop safe, strong, and nurturing neighborhoods by launching six separate research projects targeted toward different areas of need in the community. The National Forum focused on educational access and success in these research projects with support from the Graham Institute—a provost unit at the University of Michigan focused on fostering sustainability through stakeholder-centric activities.

The research team consisted of graduate and undergraduate students at the National Forum under the leadership of John C. Burkhardt and Betty Overton. Initial conceptualization of the study included the use of dialogues to discuss the creation of a local college access network (LCAN). LCANs are community coalitions developed to strengthen the college-going culture and academic success of students in a determined community. The National Forum had experience establishing an LCAN in the nearby neighborhood of Brightmoor and thus felt strongly that HOPE Village would also benefit from a community coalition in their area. The partnership with Focus HOPE, therefore, began by taking on the traditional roles of universities and communities. The research team assumed the community had a deficit and offered their solution with the best of intentions.

The Alternative to LCAN: PAR

When consulting with a board of community representatives provided by Focus HOPE, it became clear that the communities' specific needs and concerns about access to higher education and career options were unknown. Furthermore, the community leaders were apprehensive about the creation of an LCAN in their community. The research team at the National Forum concluded that the best approach would be to consult community citizens more broadly about the state of access to higher education in their neighborhoods. This new approach was the impetus for the use of PAR to conduct community dialogues.

The community dialogues researchers had in mind were a particular type of conversation modeled after the Intergroup Dialogue theorized, modeled, and practiced at the Program of Intergroup Relations (IGR) at the University of Michigan (igr.umich.edu). Different from other forms of conversation, the dialogues in the HOPE Village community were intended to be conversations that move toward solving problems with a particular awareness of the sociohistorical legacies, stereotypes, and communities to which the participants belonged. They also discussed how these identities were reflected in societal institutions (Schoem, Hurtado, Sevig, Chesler, & Sumida, 2001). In this way, the team hoped to center the narratives of community members to expose the barriers to higher education in their community and identify the assets in that community that may have been ignored in other dominant conversations on the topic.

Importantly, the dialogues were meant to give community members voice on the issue. However, the only way the dialogues would go forward was *in partnership with* the community. The guidance of community members had given the URs invaluable insight up to that point. Thus, it was important to continue to have a community voice in their work and to bring that voice to the forefront of the research.

The research team was introduced to PAR as an alternative research method that would bring the important work closer to community members. Given the dearth of PAR in higher education studies of this kind, the National Forum approached the Kettering Foundation to ask for their support for an adjacent study to the HOPE Village Initiative, which would focus on how URs formed partnerships with CRs, and the subsequent outcomes of that partnership. With funding from the Kettering Foundation, the research team documented the PAR process through journaling and personal reflection at various points of the process. Furthermore, graduate students at the

National Forum who were not associated with the research team for this study conducted interviews with the URs and the CRs who would eventually join the team. These interviews were conducted during and following the research collaboration.

Recruitment

PAR required an additional amount of effort and preparation to recruit and train a new research team to lead this community project. There were already four students (graduate and undergraduate) under the leadership of John C. Burkhardt and Betty Overton who had been involved with the HOPE Village Initiative and would continue to be involved as URs. The research team sought to recruit members from the community to join these existing URs in February 2013. We placed few specifications on the qualifications for applying to avoid limiting the applicant pool and to recruit a diverse research group representative of the local community. Given the nature of the research and our proximity to the community, the URs recommended that interested community members have some knowledge of e-mail and basic word-processing software (i.e., Microsoft Word) but did not make that knowledge a requirement. In order to recruit community members who were interested in educational issues in their neighborhood, we asked applicants to write a few sentences expressing that interest. In all, there were two and a half weeks of open recruitment in which the researchers reached out to community organizations, programs, and schools that worked with community members to assist with the recruitment process. URs communicated the research opportunity to community members through community forums and flyers. They placed the flyers in areas where community members would be exposed to the information. URs also attended community events, such as "College Go Sunday," as a way to reach out to individuals attending higher education–related events who might be interested in positions as CRs.

The National Forum received and reviewed 15 applications during recruitment and interviewed applicants in person and over the phone. At the project's inception, researchers from the National Forum believed it would be ideal to have an equal number (four of each) of URs and CRs. However, the commitment and passion of many of the applicants made it very difficult for URs to choose just four members of the community. Ultimately, five CRs were hired, bringing the research team to a total of nine members.

Becoming a Team

As members of the university and, thus, not previously connected to the HOPE Village community, the URs made a commitment to build trust with CRs and to take on the difficult task of breaking down the assumptions

and hierarchical power dynamics prevalent in community-university relationships. The URs addressed assumptions and power dynamics with the
hope of producing a better research experience for all persons involved and
generating optimal conditions for successful dialogues.

One way the National Forum chose to address these issues was by paying the
CRs for their time. Although the number of paid hours that the National Forum
was able to confer was small, CRs earned the same amount per hour as the URs.
Another way in which the research team addressed traditional assumptions and
power dynamics was through intentional research training, which was the first
time all of the URs and CRs met. Park (2006) stated that when intentionally uti-
lizing PAR "ordinary people may not command requisite research skills or grasp
methodological issues involved, but it is one of the participatory researcher's
tasks to share the available options with the community, providing training if
necessary, so that the people can be partners in research" (p. 144).

Following PAR, the training incorporated several elements to get to
know everyone at the table, including icebreakers and personal identity activities. An external trainer gave the group an overview of the research process
and training on how to conduct dialogues. One CR discussed her experience
during the training:

> [From] the exercises that we did initially [in the training], I was able to see
> things a little differently. . . . For me that helped me deal with some things
> as it related to the team and to listen a little bit more intently and not really
> kind of looking down on somebody that may think differently than me
> or—not that I normally would do that—but it just helped me to be more
> conscious of it.

The consciousness of the team's differing backgrounds and varied experiences that she described was a quality that was desired of all team members.

One notable item that stood out to the URs was the fact that CRs were
already tremendous assets in the HOPE Village community. One CR was
the leader of a movement to board up abandoned homes that posed security issues in the local area. Despite being unemployed due to the city's economic downturn, another CR was a parent leader in the schools and was
very involved with organizing community events around educational issues
in schools and with other parents. An older community member repeatedly
brought to our attention the issue of access to higher education for seniors
and adults who want to return to school. Many community members were
already contributing in similar ways to the improvement of their neighborhoods. This active and daily community involvement was a crucial asset to
the research and the research team.

Challenges

There were some times that the team found it difficult to support the equal partnership between CRs and URs. Traditional research processes usually require some degree of flexibility, but the research team had to be even more aware of time and space as a result of working with CRs. Two areas where URs had to be adaptable were channels of communication and time and location of research team meetings. Some of the CRs had limited access to computers or the Internet at home. Therefore, e-mail was a challenge as a primary form of communication, which led to a subsequent discussion about how to improve communication (as well as a reflection on how this problem may create barriers for community development). During this discussion, the research team came to a consensus that phone calls and texts were best for immediate communication needs. In addition, we discussed options for accessing computers in other spaces (e.g., the Focus HOPE library).

Further, URs had to be flexible with the CRs' time schedules, as many of them had other jobs, children, or travel constraints that needed to be taken into account. The same was true of with university researchers, most of whom had their own student schedules and other commitments. To address these concerns, the team held meetings later in the day at a central location near the CRs' homes to accommodate their obligations. The URs did what they could to adjust to the CRs' needs, fully recognizing that it may be difficult for community members to participate in this research project. Stated another way, the URs wanted to assist in creating spaces within the community where all members of the research term could have access to and work in effectively.

Despite efforts to be flexible and accommodating, challenges still emerged. For example, in the final interviews both URs and CRs acknowledged the communication barrier. One CR noted this struggle in her final interview when she said that the implementation of a "lead CR" to facilitate the communication with the various CRs in Detroit was a good idea that was implemented too late. Although she lamented that the decision had not been implemented earlier, she also expressed that the research team embraced these learning opportunities, noting, "Those kinds of things we were building as we were going along, and so now going forward I think we see what really needs to be in place." This CR observed that decisions were evolving over the course of the project as challenges presented themselves. Being able to adapt to these challenges was critical to moving forward and learning from the experience.

The URs also experienced barriers to communication, which posed challenges and prompted discussions throughout the project. The physical distance between the HOPE Village and the University of Michigan (approximately a 40-minute drive) created travel barriers associated with time and weather. This significantly affected the amount of time it took to make decisions and slowed the collaborative progress. It also reduced the URs' presence within the community. Therefore, despite the best intentions to integrate URs into the community, some challenges were difficult to avoid. As one participant reflected,

> Communication could have improved a lot. It's really difficult for us here. I'm a student; I have to go to classes. Community researchers have children and jobs and other responsibilities in the community and don't always have access to computers, and so being so far away in Ann Arbor it was difficult to keep in close contact with the researchers. And so a project that technically could have taken maybe four months to complete is now into its seventh month, and that's kind of due to the sparse communication and having to deal with all these different schedules.

Problems may arise as distance increases between the university and community. One such problem is "windshield saturation," a phenomenon in which researchers are continually driving to or from the community, and community members feel unconnected to or even incapable of recognizing the URs. Both URs and CRs had scheduling, transportation, and communication needs to consider. These important issues should be discussed and accounted for early in the research process to minimize challenges and delays throughout the process. Ultimately these reflections contributed to how the National Forum thought about PAR and negotiated limitations.

The Dialogues

Despite the challenges, the research team managed to meet at least once a week to plan community dialogues—led by URs and CRs with participants from across the community. The research team created icebreakers, a research protocol, and, ultimately, a plan for leading the community dialogues. The dialogues focused on understanding what higher education meant to the community members present in the dialogues, their perceptions of what higher education meant in their community, the barriers and assets that were present for them personally, and what they perceived were more structural issues and resources.

The research team held three dialogues: One included only youth, another only adults, and the third both youth and adults. Each of the dialogues was facilitated by one UR and one CR. Both researchers met prior to their dialogue to discuss their facilitation style and how they would best work together. Not all researchers were able to lead a dialogue because too many researchers can be intimidating to community participants. Accordingly, some researchers conducted observations of the dialogues.

The dialogues highlighted major community frustrations with the school system, as well as economic and environmental factors that participants believed were negatively impacting youth in that community. Dialogue participants also focused on the positive impact that the community can have when all members are invested in the success of youth in that community. The full analysis of the dialogues can be found in the report to HOPE Village (National Forum, 2014). In addition to the direct answers provided by the dialogues, the conversation and the observation of the research team shed light on the possible importance of an unexpected concept—community agency.

An Analysis Through PAR: Community Agency

The analysis of the materials, dialogues, and interviews conducted with CRs reflected interesting paradoxes in the ways in which the community members participating in the dialogues and the CRs perceived themselves as contributors to the solution of the problem. These perceptions were evident in the various commonalities and differences in the dialogue between the participants and the CRs.

In terms of commonalities, the community participants all lived within or near the boundaries of the 100-block area designated for the study. Importantly, participants and CRs perceived that there were problems with access to higher education and success within these institutions for their children, many of which began even before high school. The residents and CRs perceived the reasons for a low college-going culture in similar ways. In addition, likely due to selection bias, participants in the dialogues were very involved in their communities. In some cases, the participants were just as involved as many of our CRs.

However, community participants and CRs differed in how they expressed their agency to bring about change in the college-going culture of their communities. In order for social change to take hold, community members must feel they have the agency to make change happen. Community agency, therefore, has the potential to be a powerful mechanism for social change.

As of yet, scholars have not offered a clear definition for *community agency*, nor has it been the focus of deeper study. Kretzmann and McKnight (1996) make important assumptions about the agency of communities when they are perceived as clients or members with assets. In other words, when community decisions are left to organizations that view community members as clients, residents no longer feel they have ownership over those decisions. Conversely, when residents are perceived as assets to community development and provided with the spaces to contribute to community change, they will do so.

Scholar Gilberto Arriaza (2004) began to explore community agency directly in the context of school reform (see also Mercado, 1993; Miron & Moely, 2006; Pérez, 2014). He noted the importance of concepts such as ownership and seizing democratic power to overcome the assumptions of those in power. Arriaza's argument is not very different from that of the National Forum. He states that "school reform initiatives—particularly those aiming at high schools—have greater chances at staying made when the community actively participates as an empowered change agent" (p. 10). Based on this research and the experiences in this project, the National Forum constructed its working definition of *community agency* as a community member's ability to feel ownership of and ability to exert democratic influence over issues that impact him or her.

Overall, evidence from the studies suggested that community members did not feel they had agency to enact change. For example, the following resident did not believe he could improve the college-going culture for his children, despite being very involved in the community.

> I thought that if I was involved as a parent that I could impact the education they would receive and the environment but I was unable to do that . . . .You know back when I believed in public education, then I thought that appearing onto PTAs [parent teacher association], staying on my kids at home would make them [successful], but there were many distractions. They're not stupid. They graduated, all of them, but the environment itself and the system that's in place didn't engage them.

This community member's sense of hopelessness may have originated from the lack of agency he had over the environment and system in which his children were developing. One might suggest that involvement in community spaces such as the PTA would increase the agency of community members involved in creating change in their communities. Yet, this particular community member did not feel agency to realize change for himself or his children as a result of his involvement with the PTA. When community members experience no sense of agency as a result of their involvement, there is the potential to develop a sense of hopelessness and disempowerment.

The CRs, in contrast, suggested a different, more hopeful experience having worked on the research team. CRs believed they could improve their college-going culture and had already taken some steps in the process of conducting the study. All community members believed that they had agency to shape their communities. The following is an example from the point of view of a CR:

> In talking to some of the young people I have been able to take information that I've had here, the hopelessness that some people express here, and have been able to share it with the young people in another group, and be able to talk to them from a different way, and have a greater impact on changing their thinking and encouraging them to go forward in their education. So it was like a training ground in a way.

Like this CR, many community researchers believed that they had gained valuable skills during the research process that would help them with the connections between research and practice as they work *with* community members. They also expressed using those skills to continue to make sustainable change in their own communities.

Increasing Community Agency Through PAR

One could argue that the involvement of CRs in the study is a form of community engagement similar to involvement in other community spaces like the PTA. However, there is some evidence that PAR provided a unique space to develop community agency and that the nature of PAR may have played a part in fostering and sustaining community agency. For example, the fifth key characteristic of PAR as outlined by Selener (1997) most closely aligns with the formation of community agency. Selener states, "The process of participatory research can create a greater awareness in people of their own resources and can mobilize them for self-reliant development" (p. 15).

How PAR facilitates these outcomes may depend on many issues. In the National Forum example, the effort made to genuinely include CRs in the research process may have had an impact on how they ultimately felt about their participation in the research process and whether they had the skills to create that change themselves.

In addition, the CRs highlighted several benefits that they received through their participation in the PAR process that may have contributed to an increase in their perceived community agency. The CRs expressed feeling that they added true value to the team. In the answers to journal questions posed at the end of each meeting, CRs expressed that they felt their experiences in the community had given them a great deal to contribute to the team. One CR described it in this way:

> Not only did I have an equal role, there were many times that I was asked certain things about the community where my opinion was really valued because I live four blocks from here, and I'm also a former Focus: HOPE employee, and I've been a volunteer for 14–15 years. So my feeling about the community and my recommendations about certain things, I feel, was highly valued.

It is possible that the feeling of having made a valuable contribution had a positive impact on the perception of community agency and that the PAR method provided a democratic space through which CRs could make decisions that would impact their community. Furthermore, knowing that their experiences are valuable gave them ownership over the process.

Community members also began to be identified by other residents as *researchers* who were working on the project. A UR recounted one of these moments to the interviewer:

> Some of the community researchers who would go around to different schools advertising for people to turn out to the community dialogues were more recognized. Every time they would walk down the street, some kid would be like, "Oh, hey, you went to our school and you talked about education."

Therefore, in addition to the internal perception of value, these feelings were being validated by other community members. This recognition by the broader community may solidify the feeling that what the CRs participated in was impacting other people, or that it had at least begun conversations that had not previously taken place. Again, this may have strengthened the CRs' perceptions of their agency in the community.

CRs increased their involvement in this project as well as projects beyond this one. One of the CRs joined the local SOUP group (detroitsoup.com). Detroit SOUP provides microgrants to projects around the community. Dinners are organized in which attendees (usually community residents) pay five dollars at the door for a plate of food and get to vote on one of four community proposals. These proposals are crafted by anyone with an idea and range from filling a pothole to starting a small local business. The proposal with the most votes is awarded all the money collected at entry to implement the community project.

After her work with the team, one of the CRs joined the SOUP committee responsible for reviewing community member proposals and deciding on which four proposals will be voted on by the rest of the community. Another CR is proposing a project to the SOUP to open a summer camp for students to keep them interested in learning while away from school. This further community involvement is a clear example of exercising agency and being involved in democratic processes within the community and taking ownership over community issues.

In their statements, URs and CRs expressed that they felt they were a valuable part of the research team and of the community, and went on to become involved in additional local efforts to inspire community change. These findings suggest that community agency may have an important role to play in community change and that future research and practice should explore the concept of community agency more directly.

Concluding Thoughts: Community Agency and College-Going Culture

As I have noted, building a college-going culture in communities remains largely unexplored, due to the lack of scholarship focused on this area. However, if we understand the development of college-going culture as a form of community empowerment and a move toward social change, we may gain clues as to how it might be formed and how community agency may serve as a mechanism in that formation. For example, the summer program for youth in the community that will be implemented by one of the CRs will be an additional asset toward building a college-going culture in that community. Other CRs now have the tools and knowledge to hold formal and informal conversations about college access with their neighbors. In this way, there is a ripple effect—community members participate in PAR and then continue the community efforts with other organizations. It is important that further studies in higher education address questions about community agency and the ways that universities can support its creation and transformation.

This chapter has served to explore methods of university-community research partnerships that differ from the many traditional methods that have formed out of an ambiguous history. Furthermore, it gives an overview of PAR as a form of engaged scholarship and university-community partnership that can have extensive benefits for community social change. This chapter has also presented the HOPE Village Initiative study, which used PAR methodology to conduct community dialogues about college-going culture in the HOPE Village community. Finally, this chapter made the case for a closer look at community agency as a mechanism for social change and at the use of PAR to increase community agency among residents.

The work that has been undertaken by the National Forum suggests there is sufficient evidence to merit future studies on community agency and the possible role community-university research partnerships may play in fostering community agency as a mechanism for social change. Given that there is still limited evidence in this study as to the nature of *community agency*, future studies could seek to understand this term with more intention, answering such questions as *What is community agency? What does it mean to community members? Which contexts facilitate or impede the creation of community agency?* and *Does community agency translate to social change outcomes?* We hope that the continuation of PAR with community-university partnerships may make concerted change in society.

These future studies will be important in furthering our understanding. However, it is equally important for interested scholars and administrators to become involved in communities and build relational contacts that will allow for genuine, respectful entry in ways that will allow for good data to be accessed. This is the persistent and continuous work of engagement. It begins before the design of the study, and it connects the academy to the community as part of the social fabric of our society.

References

Arriaza, G. (2004). Making changes that stay made: School reform and community involvement. *The High School Journal, 87*(4), 10–24.

Bensimon, E. M. (2007). The underestimated significance of practitioner knowledge in the scholarship on student success. *The Review of Higher Education, 30*(4), 441–469.

Bensimon, E. M., Polkinghorne, D., Bauman, G., & Vallejo, E. (2004). Doing research that makes a difference. *The Journal of Higher Education, 75*(1), 104–126.

Bourdieu, P. (1985). The forms of capital. In J. G. Richardson (Ed.), *Handbook of theory and research for the sociology of education* (pp. 241–258), New York, NY: Greenwood.

Buckingham, B. R. (1926). *Research for teachers.* New York, NY: Burdett.

Chahin, T., & Ortega, N. (2010). Hispanic Serving Institutions. In H. E. Fitzgerald, C. Burack, & S. D. Seifer, (Eds.), *Handbook of Engaged Scholarship: Contemporary landscapes, future directions, Vol. I: Organizational Change* (pp. 197–214). East Lansing: Michigan State University Press.

Clark, T. (2008). We're over-researched here! Exploring accounts of research fatigue within qualitative research engagements. *Sociology, 42*(5), 953–970.

Corwin, Z. B., & Tierney, W. G. (2007). *Getting there—and beyond: Building a culture of college-going in high schools.* Los Angeles, CA: Center for Higher Education Policy Analysis, University of Southern California. Retrieved from http://files .eric.ed.gov.proxy.lib.umich.edu/fulltext/ED498731.pdf

Eilola, C., Fishman, K., Greenburg, A., Moore, C. D., Schrijver, A., & Totino, J. (2011). Success with ACCESS: Use of community-based participatory research for implementation. *Journal of Postsecondary Education and Disability, 24*(1), 61–65.

Harkavy, I., & Hartley, M. (2012). Integrating a commitment to the public good into the institutional fabric: Further lessons from the field. *Journal of Higher Education Outreach and Engagement, 16*(4), 17–36.

Israel, G. D., Beaulieu, L. J., & Hartless, G. (2001). The influence of family and community social capital on educational achievement. *Rural Sociology, 66*(1), 43–68.

Kindon, S., Pain, R., & Kesby, M. (Eds.). (2007). *Participatory action research approaches and methods: Connecting people, participation and place.* New York, NY: Routledge.

Knight-Diop, M. G. (2010). Closing the gap: Enacting care and facilitating Black students' educational access in the creation of a high school college-going culture. *Journal of Education for Students Placed at Risk, 15*(1–2), 158–172.

Kretzmann, J., & McKnight, J. P. (1996). Assets-based community development. *National Civic Review, 85*(4), 23–29.

Marullo, S., & Edwards, B. (2000). From charity to justice: The potential of university-community collaboration for social change. *American Behavioral Scientist, 43*(5), 895–912.

Maton, K. I. (2008). Empowering community settings: Agents of individual development, community betterment, and positive social change. *American Journal of Community Psychology, 41*(1–2), 4–21.

Mercado, C. I. (1993). Caring as empowerment: School collaboration and community agency. *The Urban Review, 25*(1), 79–104.

Milner, H. R. (2007). Race, culture, and researcher positionality: Working through dangers seen, unseen, and unforeseen. *Educational Researcher, 36*(7), 388–400.

Miron, D., & Moely, B. E. (2006). Community agency voice and benefit in service-learning. *Michigan Journal of Community Service Learning, 12*(2), 27–37.

National Center for Education Statistics, U.S. Department of Education. (2012, May). *The condition of education 2012.* Retrieved from http://nces.ed.gov/pubs2012/2012045.pdf

National Forum on Higher Education for the Public Good. (2014). *The development of a community based coalition to promote career and college preparation in the HOPE Village neighborhoods of Detroit and Highland Park.* Retrieved from http://graham.umich.edu/media/files/HOPEVillageIA_Career-College.pdf

Park, P. (2006). Knowledge and participatory research. In P. Reason, & H. Bradbury-Huang (Eds.), *Handbook of action research: Concise paperback edition* (pp. 83–93). Thousand Oaks, CA: SAGE.

Pasque, P., Carducci, R., Kuntz, A. K., & Gildersleeve, R. E. (2012). *Qualitative inquiry for equity in higher education: Methodological innovations, implications, and interventions. ASHE Higher Education Report, 37*(6). San Francisco, CA: Jossey-Bass.

Pérez, M. S., (2014). Complicating 'victim' narratives: Childhood agency within violent circumstances. *Global Studies of Childhood, 4*(2), 126–134.

Prilleltensky, I., & Nelson, G. (2002) *Doing psychology critically: Making a difference in diverse settings.* Basingstroke, UK: Palgrave MacMillan.

Ramsey, J. (2008). *Creating a high school culture of college-going: The case of Washington State Achievers* (Issue Brief). Washington, DC: Institute for Higher Education Policy. Retrieved from http://files.eric.ed.gov.proxy.lib.umich.edu/fulltext/ED539703.pdf

Schoem, D., Hurtado, S., Sevig, T., Chesler, M., & Sumida, S. H. (2001). Intergroup dialogue: Democracy at work in theory and practice. In D. L. Schoem & S. Hurtado, (Eds.). *Intergroup dialogue: Deliberative democracy in school, college, community, and workplace* (pp. 1–21). East Lansing: University of Michigan Press.

Selener, D. (1997). *Participatory action research and social change.* The Cornell Participatory Action Research Network. Ithaca, NY: Cornell University.

Suarez-Balcazar, Y., Davis, M. I., Ferrari, J., Nyden, P., Olsen, B., Alvarez, J., & Toro, P. (2004). University-community partnerships: A framework and an exemplar. In L. A. Jason, C. B. Keys, Y. E. Suarez-Balcazar, R. R. Taylor, & M. I. Davis (Eds.), *Participatory community research: Theories and methods in action* (pp. 105–120). Washington, DC: American Psychological Association.

Taylor, R. R., Jason, L. A., Keys, C. B., Suarez-Balcazar, Y., Davis, M. I., Durlak, J. A., & Isenberg, D. H. (2002). Introduction: Capturing theory and methodology in participating research. In L. A. Jason, C. B. Keys, Y. E. Suarez-Balcazar, R. R. Taylor, & M. I.Davis (Eds.), *Participatory community research* (pp. 3–14). Washington, DC: American Psychological Association.

U.S. Census Bureau. (2013). *2009–2013 5-Year American Community Survey* [Data Table]. Retrieved from http://factfinder.census.gov/faces/tableservices/jsf/pages/productview.xhtml?pid=ACS_13_5YR_S1501&prodType=table

5

COLLABORATIVE APPROACHES TO COMMUNITY CHANGE

The Complexities of Power, Collaboration, and Social Change

Penny A. Pasque

Real [community-university] relationships mean, not that we come to do "show and tell" and "dog and pony shows" about "you want to give us some money"; it means sittin' down and saying, "these are what we're wrestling with, this is what we're failing against, this is what we're trying to do differently" . . . And, then we can begin to talk about what needs to be done together.

These words are from a community partner, Glenn,[1] as he passionately spoke to a national conference of approximately 150 university presidents, legislators, faculty, administrators, national association representatives, students, and community partners. The focus of this gathering was on community engagement and strengthening higher education for the public good. Glenn reflected on known relationships between community and university[2] partners as "shows" and stresses the importance of establishing strong, collaborative relationships with honest dialogue about barriers *before* discussing strategies for change. Glenn recognizaed a less effective approach to community-university partnerships and argued for a more complex framework for collaboration.

The issues mentioned in this quote serve as exemplars for the changes in perspective that are needed to foster effective community-university collaborative approaches for social change. More specifically, there are

A previous version of this chapter appeared in Pasque, P. A. (2010). "Collaborative approaches to community change." In H. E. Fitzgerald, C. Burack, & S. Siefer (Eds.), *Handbook of engaged scholarship: Contemporary landscapes, future directions: Vol. 2: Community-campus partnerships* (pp. 295–310). East Lansing: Michigan State University Press. Adapted with permission from Michigan State University Press.

elements of power, collaboration, and community change embedded in such relationships. In terms of power, Glenn described the unequal relationships between community and university partners where community partners are paraded out when needed or are used for objectification or show. Further, collaborative conversations include open discussions of the barriers communities and universities face, where people own mistakes and failures. Such authentic conversation is inclusive of the history of the organization and is reflective of different strategies for change that have already been attempted. Only then may collaborative strategies for community change be envisioned and enacted.

In this chapter, I consider the elements of power, collaboration, and social change in order to deeply explore the complexities of collaborative approaches between community and university partners for community change. This type of collaboration becomes critical during this time of crisis (e.g., environmental, educational, economic, health, housing), where these social issues are inextricably linked. A broad impact on local, national, and global communities is needed, and community-university collaborations have the potential to make deep community change that may impact people's daily lives.

First, I briefly share a research study on this topic that informs my perspective. Second, I offer reflections on power, collaboration, and social change as connected to community-university partnerships. In each of these sections, I draw from the words of Glenn (from the contextual research study) and use the actions of my own institution, the University of Oklahoma, as an example for further exploration of engagement and outreach for critical community change.

Contextual Research Study

A study on strengthening the relationships between higher education and society informs this current chapter, and I offer a cursory review of that research to provide context (see Pasque, 2007, 2010, 2012; Pasque & Neubauer, 2013). In this study, I explore higher education leaders' perspectives of higher education's relationships to society as found through (a) a macroanalysis of the current literature and (b) a microanalysis of face-to-face language during a national conference series. In this case, *leaders* includes community partners, university presidents, legislators, faculty, administrators, and graduate students. These individuals may not consider themselves to be leaders but have published or articulated their thoughts in various national contexts.

Through examination of the linguistic complexities of this national written and verbal discourse, I find something that is sadly commonplace and something quite original. The finding that is not new but is certainly unacceptable is that some women, people of color, graduate students, and community partners are silenced, or their perspectives are reframed or discounted in the national dialogue on engagement (see Chase, 2005; Gilligan, 1982, 1987, 1988; Green & Trent, 2005; Rowley, 2000; Smith, 2004; Stanley, 2006; Tannen, 1993, 1994). What is unique is that the emergent advocacy perspective about higher education's relationships with society is marginalized. In addition, these advocacy perspectives (presented by people with dominant and/or subordinate social identities; i.e., White male full professors, African American male community partners, Latina graduate students) that question the dominant perspectives are reframed or disregarded. In each case, the dilemmas presented by these advocates are not captured in recrafted models or in revised visions for change that hope to strengthen the relationships between higher education and society. Specifically, the dilemmas revealed by advocates are couched in broad, if not universal, agreement in final reporting mechanisms or are marginalized in the national literature.

It is important to elaborate on the content of the advocacy perspectives shared in the national (verbal and written) discourse, which have two similarities.[3] First, the authors state that there is mutual interdependence between the public and private good of higher education; the location where one ends and the other begins is blurred. Specifically, the private good argument is where educating the private individual through higher education will contribute to the public good through an increase in economic growth, thereby defining the *public good* as local, state, and national economic vitality. The public good argument is to educate students to participate in a diverse society, and this will contribute to the public good in terms of qualities such as increased civic engagement and appreciation of diversity.

Second, the authors each passionately describe a crisis in higher education where action from leaders is needed to shift the focus of the higher education from a capitalistic, market-driven emphasis to one that better serves the public good (Gildersleeve, Kuntz, Pasque, & Carducci, 2010; Giroux & Giroux, 2004; Kezar, 2005; Labaree, 1997; Parker, 2003; Pitkin & Shumer, 1982; Rhoades & Slaughter, 2004). Moreover, higher education's role in a democracy needs to acknowledge the public and private realms as well as privilege the interconnections between them. The authors view this interconnection as the crux of a crisis in the academy where change in leaders' perspectives about and behaviors regarding the academy is needed. Political capital and change to actualize a true and inclusive democracy is central.

Further, the authors believe it is particularly important for leaders within colleges and universities to initiate this change.

Most scholars with the *Advocacy* perspective identify people with an economic neoliberal view—who support the marketization of higher education—as a problem and believe there is a lack of leadership and governance within the academy. The authors fear that if there is not a change in how stakeholders perceive and act upon higher education's relationship with society, then higher education will be increasingly perceived as a private good, or a commodity. This will, in turn, reduce the collaborative connections between communities and universities that focus on social change. The authors often identify solutions as increased access to education, multicultural education, civic engagement for a diverse democracy, university engagement and outreach, and a change in leadership.

It is these *Advocacy* perspectives that are marginalized in the discourse and in national conversations (Pasque, 2010). In these instances, silencing is not necessarily connected to volubility (Tannen 1993); omitting comments from final reporting documents, rejecting critical approaches in national journals, and crafting committees where recommendations are filed (as opposed to considered and/or acted upon) are all methods of silencing perspectives. Marginalizing the perspectives from (a) community partners, people of color, graduate students, and women and (b) *Advocacy* perspectives limits our available strategies for community change.

Based on the findings from this study, and in the hopes of encouraging a shift in perspectives and action around higher education's relationships with society, I offer a tricuspid model of interconnected advocacy and educational change that requires (a) rethinking the role of power brokers, (b) centering marginalized perspectives, and (c) including voices of all people in society (Pasque, 2010). Principles of power, collaboration, and change are embedded in the tricuspid model. In addition, I argue that if a more thorough understanding of leaders' perspectives is not offered, then dominant perspectives shared in academic discourse genres may continue to perpetuate the current ideas of higher education's relationship with society—from an economic rationalization perspective—without consideration of alternative perspectives. The perpetuation of the current trajectory and the continued marginalization of *Advocacy* frames for educational change will be detrimental to working toward social justice and educational equity.

Additional models that specifically address community-university partnerships and reflect the exemplar are offered at the beginning of this chapter. Some of these models will be explored further in the following discussion of power, collaboration, and social change.

Complexities of Power

Social change efforts will not succeed if they do not deal directly with issues of power, difference, and diversity in the community-university relationship and within the communities in which they operate (see outreach and engagement discussions on diversity, including Association of American Colleges and Universities [AACU], 1995a, 1995b; Ibarra, 2006; O'Connor, 2004; Rowley, 2000). For example, Dewey (1916/1997) states,

> The notion that experience consists of a variety of segregated domains, or interests, each having its own interdependent value, material, and method, each checking every other, and each is kept properly bounded by the others, forming a kind of balance of powers in education. On the practical side, they were found to have their cause in the divisions of society into more or less rigidly marked off classes and groups—in other words, in obstruction to full and flexible social interaction and intercourse . . . resulting in various dualisms such as practical and intellectual activity, labor and leisure, individuality and association. (p. 323)

As Kezar and Rhoads (2001) reflect, "Dewey makes the compelling argument that distinctions emerged to serve the interests of power and privilege" (p. 161). These power dynamics of inequity need to be both acknowledged and addressed in community and university relationships for community change.

Inherent in power relationships and "rigidly marked off classes and groups" (Dewey, 1916/1997, p. 161) are target and agent social identities including race, class, gender, sexual orientation, age, religion, and other social identities. From the social identity approach, people with target identities are "members of social identity groups that are disenfranchised, exploited, and victimized in a variety of ways by the oppressor and the oppressor's system or institutions" (Hardiman & Jackson, 1997, p. 20). In contemporary U.S. society, this includes people of different abilities, people of color, non-Christians, working class/poor, gay/bisexual, and women/transgender people. Agents include "members of dominant social groups privileged by birth or acquisition, who knowingly or unknowingly exploit and reap unfair advantage over members of target groups" (Hardiman & Jackson, 1997, p. 20). In contemporary U.S. society, this includes people who are able-bodied, White, Christian, middle and upper-middle class, heterosexual men, and those who have assimilated to U.S. culture. Further, identities are fluid; they may change as people move through life, and the sociopolitical environment may also change over time. It is impossible to separate various personal social identities from people's social group memberships (Bell, 1997) as social identities are fundamentally connected to the cultures in which they are embedded (Bakhtin, 1981; Vygotsky, 1978).

Power (asymmetrical relationships) and *solidarity* (symmetrical relationships) are always operating between and among people (Tannen, 1994) from different social identities within community-university relationships. *Institutional power* comes from the operation of laws, policies, procedures, and historical and cultural paradigms. Foucault (1976) argues that whoever holds power regarding what counts as knowledge also has power over policies and systems. For example, power and solidarity may be found between community members and university students in Students for Access to Justice (SATJ). In March of 2004, the students in the University of Oklahoma College of Law started SATJ. The mission states that SATJ "promotes a culture of public service commitment by connecting students with meaningful pro bono volunteer opportunities" (SATJ, 2008, para. 2). Each spring, this program holds a fair where volunteer students and community members in need of legal information and support are brought together (with support from licensed attorneys). Students in the program have collaborated with organizations such as the American Civil Liberties Union, Legal Aid, Equal Opportunity Employment Commission, Oklahoma Indigent Defense System, Oklahoma Lawyers for Children, and Oklahoma Indian Legal Services.

As legal decisions and policies take place in a relevant historical, cultural and sociopolitical context, power around social identities, such as race, gender, class, religion, of the student and community partner may add to—or detract from—collaboration toward an integrative community-university partner relationship. In addition, the student has the institutional knowledge about the law and understands the complexities of legal policies and procedures. Similarly, the community partner has the expertise about the community agency and/or the people in the local community.

The Interdisciplinary Collaboration Model (ICM) is instructive in this situation (Amey & Brown, 2005). The ICM shows the transitions from Stage One collaboration, where relationships are top-down and individual, to Stage Three, where the relationships are "integrative, collaborative, team, [and] weblike" (p. 28). The "dog and pony shows" are more indicative of Stage One of the ICM, where there is a dominant discipline orientation and university partners serve as experts. The SATJ relationship has the opportunity to be transactional, such as is found in Stage One of the ICM (i.e., student gains legal experience, the organization gains knowledge and assistance), or transformational, as in Stage Three (i.e., all parties learn from each other and collaborate to make change from within or throughout the legal system). Further, attention to (a) rethinking the role of power brokers, (b) centering marginalized perspectives, and (c) including voices of all people in the relationship between community members and SATJ students may continue to deepen what is learned and what is gained from this relationship.

Moreover, *solidarity* is where people join together with other people who hold common social identities or roles. To continue with the SATJ example, a person in need of legal advice may connect with a person based on shared identity or experience. Discourse is often used as a way to signal solidarity. Comments such as "As another single mother, I also believe . . .," or "I'm also a Native American man and can relate to . . .," or "I, too, went to a rural high school and have faced . . ." are a way of showing solidarity and shared identity between the community member and the university student. Relationships of power and solidarity add further complexity to the community-university relationship as we work toward transformational community change.

It is also important to note that power and solidarity may be explored through the concept of *footing* (Goffman, 1981). "A change in footing implies a change in the alignment we take up to ourselves and the others present as expressed in the way we manage the production or reception of an utterance" (p. 128). For example, when a person says "I'm just a community organizer . . ." or shares an opinion and follows it up with "but, I'm only a student," the person changes his or her own footing in the conversation to a one-down position. The reverse changes a person's footing to a one-up position. This one-up happens, for example, when a person says, "As a full professor, I . . ." or "As a lawyer who works in Washington, DC, I know that . . . ." It is important to be cognizant of these verbal displays of footing, in addition to power and solidarity across social identities, in order to more completely understand the complexities of community-university relationships, as ignoring these issues may be detrimental to working collaboratively for community change and further entrench conceptualizations of power. This may, in turn, silence participants who could be less likely to share their perspectives when one-up footing is pervasive in the discourse.

Smith's (2004) concept of racial battle fatigue may be useful in uncovering more of the dynamics between community and university partners from target and agent identities as connected to issues of power and solidarity. Smith describes racial battle fatigue as "a response to the distressing mental/emotional conditions that result from facing racism daily (e.g., racial slights, recurrent indignities and irritations, unfair treatments, including contentious classrooms, and potential threats or dangers under tough to violent and even life-threatening conditions)" (p. 180). Further, Smith relates documented various psychological and physiological symptoms (tension headaches, backaches, trembling and jumpiness, chronic pain, upset stomach, extreme fatigue, constant anxiety and worrying, etc.) to the combat fatigue experienced by military personnel.[4] In addition, the anticipation of a racist event may add to the stressor. Smith further notes that "unfortunately for African American faculty . . . higher education was and continues to be much more racially exclusive, oppressive, and antagonistic than society at large" (p. 185). Community and university partners should be aware of such daily experiences of battle fatigue as related to social inequities around race, gender, class, and other social identities in order to eliminate the perpetuation of such fatigue when collaborating toward social change.

In addition to research about discussions across race in higher education, there is scholarship that addresses the relationship between community organizer and university partner (e.g., Glenn) and university faculty and staff. Bok (1982) mentions how community members' high hopes are often met with failures that "actually heightened local suspicions and frustrations rather than improving relations with the university" (p. 46). Rowley (2000) furthers this perspective and offers a major premise for considering the relationship between universities and Black urban communities. He states,

> The *habitus* of higher education inflicts symbolic violence on individual universities (by defining the traditional university mission and values), and universities in turn inflict symbolic violence on society by either contributing to urban social reproduction (restricted access to and limited distribution of dominant cultural capital) or refusing to help alleviate urban problems (placing little value on public service and civic responsibilities of universities). (p. 56)

Rowley's analysis also may help add insight into Glenn's community partner perspective quoted at the beginning of this chapter. Glenn may be attempting to make this symbolic violence visible and explicit through his narrative in this conference. In turn, his persistence in and dedication to expressing his advocacy perspective in the company of people who he perceives as having the "power" to make change may add to his own racial battle fatigue.

Hurtado (2007) emphasizes that "it is time to renew the promise of American higher education in advancing social progress, end America's discomfort with race and social difference, and deal directly with many of the issues of inequality in everyday life" (p. 186). If higher education leaders truly want to deal directly with issues of social and educational inequality in ways that will make change regarding race, class, and gender, then we must foster discussions about power and inequity, but in such a way that all voices and perspectives are included. Contrary to some people wanting to be "comfortable"[5] in these types of settings, I believe that discussing issues of power across race, class, and gender as connected to social inequity *is* going to be uncomfortable. And, further analysis of the language and enacted issues of power surrounding relationships between higher education and society constitutes one step toward collaboration for social justice and change.

Approaches for Collaboration

A complex framework for collaboration between communities and universities is critical when working toward broad and deep community change. For example, Bringle and Hatcher (2002) point out that community-university partnerships share similar complex dynamics to "interpersonal relationships" (p. 504). Based on this theoretical framework of relationships, they offer practical guidelines at an organizational level. From here, Fogel and Cook (2006) utilize this framework to address specific challenges in university-community partnership projects. They identify relationship formation, development, and maintenance as instrumental in addressing challenges. Glenn echoes the importance of collaborative relationships for community-university partnerships as he describes the importance of teams. Teams are strengthened through an intentional power analysis of who is involved. He asks,

> Who is your team? . . . The first question I will always ask people is, what is your power analysis? How many *trustees* are engaged in this conversation? How many of your top administrators are on your team, if you have a team at all? What about faculty, particularly tenured faculty, those that head departments, those who set the [rules], to make the decisions about who's going to be tenured or not? How many of those folk are part of this conversation? What about the support staff in your universities?

The importance of collaboration in teams across community-university partnerships cannot be stressed enough and has been discussed elsewhere (Bringle & Hatcher, 2002; Galura, Pasque, Schoem, & Howard, 2004; Thomas, 2004; Weerts & Sandmann, 2008; White, 2006). For such partnerships to truly exist in an integrative manner, a space is needed for multiple perspectives and voices—from all members of the team—in multiple venues including in the community, classrooms, end-of-the-year reports, dissemination of information, research, best practices articles, and policy changes. These efforts intentionally shift the focus from "dog and pony show" collaborations to true, equitable collaboration. Such a shift in climate would also require a shift in the social balance and institutional discourse (Miller &

Fox, 2004) so that people with advocacy perspectives, who directly address issues of power and privilege through a collaborative approach, are centered.

It is also important to consider whether the network of practices in higher education needs the current siloed structures that perpetuate inequity in order to exist. As Fairclough (2001) mentions, questions need to be asked about "whether those who benefit most from the way social life is now organized have an interest in the problem not being resolved" (p. 236). Jones, Torres, and Arminio (2006) echo this line of questioning when they ask higher education researchers to "address not only what is being said but also what is not, not only what was said and quoted but also what is being protected from public view and why" (p. 31). This raises the question of whether community and higher education leaders—we—benefit from the use of specific collaborations of outreach and engagement. For example, are concepts of community-university partnerships that reflect the "dog and pony show" model easier or more rewarding than advanced levels in the commitment to community engagement or interdisciplinary collaboration models? More specifically, how is social reproduction operationalized in this context? Is a market-driven, "private good" frame (where education is seen as increasing the local, state, and federal economies) more palatable and acceptable to policymakers and funders than a "social good" frame, which may in turn help support future funding possibilities? Moreover, is it easier to think of the private and public good as polarized and mutually exclusive in order to perpetuate dominant perspectives and practices?

On a related point, Bok (2003) contends that "the incentives of commercial competition do not always produce a beneficial outcome; they merely yield what the market wants" (p. 103). These days, our "market" is changing on a daily basis. State appropriations have decreased (Brandl & Holdsworth, 2003; Cage, 1991; Hansen, 2004), and faculty experience a tremendous amount of pressure to acquire additional external funds. For example, Slaughter and Leslie (1997) state,

> To maintain and expand resources faculty had to compete increasingly for external dollars that were tied to market-related research, which was referred to variously as applied, commercial, strategic, and targeted research, whether these moneys were in the form of research grants and contracts, service contracts, partnerships with industry and government, technology transfer, or the recruitment of more and higher fee-paying students. (p. 8)

Current faculty and administrators are experiencing pressure to alter agendas in order to guarantee financial support. In *Academic Capitalism and the New Economy,* Slaughter and Rhoades (2004) describe further the theory of academic capitalism and warn people in the field to be more cognizant of these influences. Such a push toward capitalism may reduce collaborations between communities and universities if they are not seen as profitable financially or academically. Numerous scholars have talked about the need for increased reward structures for faculty such as grants, tenure, and promotion that reflect the university's mission and commitment to engagement and outreach (AACU, 2002; Boyer, 1990; Buys & Bursnall, 2007; Checkoway, 2000, 2001, 2004; Colby, Ehrlich, Beaumont, & Stephens, 2003; Grunwald & Peterson, 2003; Holland, 1999; Jongbloed, Enders, & Salerno, 2008). Further, Weerts and Sandmann (2008) found that "promotion and tenure policies were the strongest barrier to faculty engagement with the community, especially at the land-grant universities" (p. 91) and is one example of where the public and private are interconnected. An infrastructure that provides rewards and creates an organizational structure that supports engagement and outreach efforts is vital.

The new Carnegie Community Engagement Elective Classification is arguably one process encouraging institutions to intentionally address issues of engagement through collaboration with community partners and is discussed in detail elsewhere in this book. The framework for institutions to document their engagement with communities was designed to

1. Respect the diversity of institutions and their approaches to community engagement;
2. Engage institutions in a process of inquiry, reflection, and self assessment; and
3. Honor institutions' achievements while promoting the ongoing development of their programs. (Driscoll, 2008, p. 39)

Although many have pushed for this type of accountability and recognition, others have discussed the questions that are included and absent in this new classification furthering the idea that the classification system may encourage isomorphic tendencies across campuses (Jaeger & Thornton, 2008).

The University of Oklahoma has actively been seeking this classification. As a member of the university's Community Engagement Committee, I had the privilege to gather with representatives from across the institution as they and we shared information about their community engagement and outreach efforts and struggled over the ways to represent such meaningful work in such small boxes on the application form. Representatives from across campus, including the medical school, education, business, student affairs, law, and women's and gender studies, articulated their established outreach and engagement programs and learned about the various efforts across campus. Although one aspect of this process was mechanical—the process of encouraging all faculty, staff, and student organizations to document their relationships with communities—there was another aspect that was quite collaborative. This process encouraged colleges and departments to talk across often-siloed areas of the institution about their efforts with communities. This dialogue has fostered further collaboration between departments and provided an institutionalized venue for recognizing these important efforts. Ongoing action committees that include students, community partners, faculty, and staff have been formed to further the process.

As the University of Oklahoma and other institutions across the country continue to reflect upon and strengthen collaborative approaches to community change, Fine's (1994) concept of "working the hyphen" across researcher-participant relationships is particularly salient for community-university collaboration. I have inserted these parallel terms where relevant in the following quote by Fine. She states,

> By *working the hyphen,* I mean to suggest that researchers [university faculty, staff, and students] probe how we are in relation with the contexts we study and with our informants [community members], understanding that we are all multiple in those relations. . . . Working the hyphen means creating occasions for researchers and informants [community and university partners] to discuss what is, and is not, "Happening between," within the negotiated relations of whose story is being told, why, to whom, [and] with what interpretation, and whose story is being shadowed, why, for whom, and with what consequence. (p. 72)

In a similar vein, community-university partners can learn to "work the hyphen" in their collaborations in order to uncover what is happening within and between the relationships in the current sociopolitical context. Working the hyphen deepens understandings of the complexities of the community story and consequences of action/inaction. Such awareness of positionality can foster stronger collaboration and set the foundation's partners to work in concert with each other toward social justice and change.

Strategies for Social Change

Higher education leaders have been called upon to change the current trajectory that perpetuates educational stratification (Giroux & Giroux, 2004; Rhoades & Slaughter, 2004). This change can be enhanced through strategic relationships between community-university partners as they work toward social change with deep and/or broad impact. Instructive in these efforts for change are Harro's cycle of socialization (2000a) and cycle of liberation (2000b).

Harro (2000a) describes the cycle of socialization process as "*pervasive* (coming from all sides and sources), *consistent* (patterned and predictable), *circular* (self-supporting), *self-perpetuating* (intra-dependent) and often *invisible* (unconscious and unmanned)" (p. 15). More specifically, we are born into a preexisting world and socialized with rules, norms, and expectations. These perspectives are reinforced through institutional and cultural messages that result in dissonance, silence, collusion, ignorance, violence, and internalized patterns of power. The cycle of socialization offers two options: Do nothing and perpetuate the status quo, or make change by raising consciousness, interrupting patterns, educating oneself and others, and taking action.

Harro (2000b) also offers a cycle of liberation regarding individual, collaborative, community, and culture change. Change, in this instance, requires a "struggle against discrimination based on race, class, gender, sexual identity, ableism, and age—those barriers that keep large portions of the population from having access to economic and social justice, from being able to participate fully in the decisions affecting our lives, from having a full share of both the rights and responsibilities of living in a free society" (p. 450). Such change interrupts dominant paradigms of oppression through the use of transformational and collaborative relationships. This cycle begins on the intrapersonal level, where social inequities create cognitive dissonance when people cannot rectify in their own minds what they see happening versus what they think should be happening to address critical social issues. From here, a person gets "ready" by empowering himself or herself to dismantle collusion, privilege, and internalized oppression. At this point, the person reaches out toward others, seeks experiences, names injustices, and uses tools for change. Next is the interpersonal phase in which people build community. In this work with others, we seek people "like us" for support and people "different from us" for building coalitions and questioning assumptions in structures and systems (p. 464). Coalescing is an important stage where people engage in organizing, action planning, fund-raising, educating, renaming, learning about being an ally, and moving into action. Creating such systemic change critically transforms institutions and creates a new culture through influencing policy, structures, leadership, and a shared sense of power. This work is maintained as additional systemic changes are initiated.

I argue that such collaborative efforts must also utilize idiosyncratic methods for critical social change, as a single approach for breaking the cycle of oppression is not enough to combat years of ingrained socialization.

Al Gore's approach toward addressing global warming exemplifies such a multifaceted strategy. In myriad speeches and in his movie, *An Inconvenient Truth,* Gore (2006) discusses the layered complexities of global warming and then offers numerous strategies to simultaneously address this problem with a worldwide approach. In a similar vein, multiple methods for community-university collaborations for social change need to offer differentiated and critical change on multiple levels simultaneously. This idiosyncratic approach toward change reflects the so-called new science perspective. Wheatley (1999) explains,

> In organizations, which is the more important influence on behavior—the system or the individual? The quantum world answered the question for me with a resounding "Both." There are no either/ors. There is no need to decide between two things, pretending they are separate. What is critical is the relationship created between two or more elements. (pp. 35–36)

Love and Estanek (2004) expand on the new science perspective and discuss its relevance for student affairs in higher education. The authors argue for a "both/and" perspective where the Newtonian science and the new science of chaos and unpredictability are combined in dialectical thinking. Their conceptual framework for the future of organizational behavior in student affairs also includes transcending paradigms, recognizing connectedness, and embracing paradox.

Community-university partnerships have the potential to engage in such liberation. The University of Oklahoma's K20 Center for Educational and Community Renewal (2008) offers the following example:

> We envision interactive learning communities where citizens identify, analyze, and help solve problems in their local and global communities. Through cutting-edge research and development, local and international networking, school-university-industry partnerships, and interdisciplinary degree programs, we envision empowered citizens working for the creation of a global society rid of poverty, crime, racism, and other forms of inequality. (para. 1)

This interdisciplinary research and development center creates action-oriented partnerships among schools, universities, industries, and community and governmental agencies. For example, their four-phase model for school and community renewal has engaged 794 (45%) of schools in 520 (96%) of districts in Oklahoma, and 1,400 K–12 superintendents and principals have participated in this sustained professional development opportunity designed to support learning communities and the integration of digital game-based learning. Among other things, this project has developed digital game-based learning programs to strengthen math and science scores for children in a way that engages young people and increases educational outcomes (Wilson, Whisenhunt, & Eseryel, 2008). This project includes 10 community and industry partners and is funded with grants from 6 foundations or funding sources, including the National Science Foundation and the Bill and Melinda Gates Foundation.

The levels of commitment to community engagement is a useful model when considering the complexities of the relationships between communities and universities in this context (Holland, 1997/2006). The model explores various elements of the university (e.g., mission statement, tenure and promotion, curriculum, and fund-raising) across four levels of relevance for said institution. For example, when considering the element "leadership" in level one: low relevance, an institution does not mention engagement as a priority; in level four: full integration, there is a broad leadership commitment to a sustained engagement agenda with ongoing funding support and community input. The various levels and descriptors are particularly useful for universities interested in assessment efforts and may serve as the impetus for deeper collaborative approaches for community change. The K20 Center reflects Holland's (1997/2006): full integration for a number of reasons, including its utilization of multiple leadership collaborations in order to interrupt the cycle of educational inequity and make change for young children, and their futures.

Leaders who situate themselves to make this type of systemic change have been described as boundary-crossers (Thomas, 2004). *Boundary-crossers* are defined as listeners who connect multiple contrasting views and ideas. They focus on long-term goals, relationships, and follow a dialogic and inclusive process. Boundary-crossers are at ease with numerous people, are comfortable in informal or structured conversations, and continually refine perspectives. I extend this definition to include that boundary-crossers acknowledge the various historical and contemporary boundaries that propagate power relationships (Foucault, 1976) and sustain cyclical oppression. Further, they operate with an awareness of Bourdieu's (1986) notion of social capital, which connects sources of capital (economic, cultural, and social) in order to create an aggregate of resources linked to a network of relationships. Bourdieu considers such capital to be grounded in theories of symbolic power and social reproduction where social capital is a tool of reproduction for the privileged. In addition, boundary-crossers in community-university partnerships will work to break the cycle of socialization and operate with a cycle of liberation strategy for community change.

Concluding Thoughts

The "dog and pony shows" of community-university partnerships need to be a thing of the past if we are to work together to interrupt the cycle of socialization and inequity and make critical social change. We need to increase our awareness of the complexities of power, build an infrastructure for strong collaborative teams, and work to make strategic community change that has direct impact on the lives of people in our local, national, and global communities. Such strategies have the potential to make change in communities around critical social issues such as education, health care, housing, the economy, and the environment.

In this chapter, I explored notions of power, collaboration, and change in the hopes of offering different ways in which we may "work the hyphen" of community–university partnerships to address inequities in society and collaborate on working toward social justice and change. This chapter builds upon—and should be viewed as interconnected with—the other chapters in this handbook so that we may break siloed efforts and work toward collaborative approaches toward community change.

Notes

1. A pseudonym.
2. The term *university* is meant to be inclusive of all higher and postsecondary institutions.
3. An analysis of the process of the discussions and a more detailed analysis of the content may be found elsewhere (Pasque, 2007, 2010).
4. Smith does mention that he is not equating the daily experiences of people in the military with daily experiences of faculty of color, but he is suggesting a useful metaphor.
5. A quote from a participant (Pasque, 2007, 2010).

References

Amey, M. J., & Brown, D. F. (2005). Interdisciplinary collaboration and academic work: A case study of a university-community partnership. *New Directions for Teaching and Learning, 102*, 23–35.

Association of American Colleges and Universities. (1995a). *American pluralism and the college curriculum: Higher education in a diverse democracy.* Washington, DC: Author.

Association of American Colleges and Universities. (1995b). *The drama of diversity and democracy: Higher education and American commitments.* Washington, DC: Author.

Association of American Colleges and Universities. (2002). *Greater expectations: A new vision for learning as a nation goes to college.* Washington, DC: Author

Bakhtin, M. M. (1981). *The dialogic imagination.* Austin: University of Texas Press.

Bell, L. A. (1997). Theoretical foundations for social justice education. In M. Adams, L. B. Bell, & P. Griffin (Eds.), *Teaching for diversity and social justice* (pp. 1–4). New York, NY: Routledge.

Bok, D. (1982). *Beyond the ivory tower: Social responsibilities of the modern university.* Cambridge, MA: Harvard University Press.

Bok, D. (2003). *Universities in the marketplace: The commercialization of higher education.* Princeton, NJ: Princeton University Press.

Bourdieu, P. (1986). The forms of capital. In J. Richardson (Ed.), *Handbook of theory and research for the sociology of education* (pp. 241–258). Westport, CT: Greenwood Press.

Boyer, E. (1990). *Scholarship reconsidered: Priorities of the professoriate.* Princeton, NJ: Carnegie Foundation for the Advancement of Teaching.

Brandl, J., & Holdsworth, J. M. (2003). On measuring what universities do: A reprise. In D. R. Lewis & J. Hearn (Eds.), *The public research university: Serving the public good in new times.* New York, NY: University Press of America.

Bringle, R. G., & Hatcher, J. A. (2002). Campus-community partnerships: The terms of engagement. *Journal of Social Issues, 58,* 503–516.

Buys, N., & Bursnall, S. (2007). Establishing university-community partnerships: Processes and benefits. *Journal of Higher Education Policy and Management, 29*(1), 73–86.

Cage, M. C. (1991, June 26). Thirty states cut higher education budgets by an average of 3.9% in fiscal 90–91. *The Chronicle of Higher Education,* pp. A1–2.

Chase, S. E. (2005). Narrative inquiry: Multiple lenses, approaches, voices. In N. Denzin & Y. Lincoln (Eds.), *The Sage handbook of qualitative research* (3rd ed., pp. 651–679). Thousand Oaks, CA: SAGE.

Checkoway, B. (2000). Public service: Our new mission. *Academe, 86*(4), 24–28.

Checkoway, B. (2001). Renewing the civic mission of the American research university. *The Journal of Higher Education, 72*(2), 125–147.

Checkoway, B. (2004). Dilemmas of civic renewal. In M. Langseth & W. M. Plater (Eds.), *Public work and the academy: An academic administrator's guide to civic engagement and service-learning.* Bolton, MA: Anker.

Colby, A., Ehrlich, T., Beaumont, E., & Stephens, J. (2003). *Educating citizens: Preparing America's undergraduates for lives of moral and civic responsibility.* San Francisco, CA: Jossey-Bass.

Dewey, J. (1916/1997). *Democracy and education.* New York, NY: Simon & Schuster.

Driscoll, A. (2008). Carnegie's community engagement classification: Intentions and insights. *Change, 40*(1), 38–41.

Fairclough, N. (2001). The discourse of new labour: Critical discourse analysis. In M. Wetherell, S. Taylor, & S. J. Yates (Eds.), *Discourse as data: A guide for analysis.* Thousand Oaks, CA: SAGE.

Fine, M. (1994). Working the hyphens: Reinventing self and other in qualitative research. In N. K. Denzin & Y. S. Lincoln (Eds.), *Handbook of qualitative research* (pp. 70–82). Thousand Oaks, CA: SAGE.

Fogel, S. J., & Cook, J. R. (2006). Considerations on the scholarship of engagement as an area of specialization for faculty. *Journal of Social Work Education, 42*(3), 595–606.

Foucault, M. (1976). *The archaeology of knowledge.* New York, NY: Harper & Row.

Galura, J. A., Pasque, P. A., Schoem, D., & Howard, J. (Eds.). (2004). *Engaging the whole of service-learning, diversity, and learning communities.* Ann Arbor, MI: OCSL Press.

Gildersleeve, E. R.., Kuntz, A., Pasque, P. A., & Carducci, R. (2010). The role of critical inquiry in (re)constructing the public agenda for higher education: Confronting the conservative modernization of the academy. *The Review of Higher Education, 34*(1), 85–121.

Gilligan, C. (1982). *In a different voice: Psychological theory and women's development.* Cambridge, MA: Harvard University Press.

Gilligan, C. (1987). Moral orientation and moral development. In E. F. Kittay & D. T. Meyers (Eds.), *Woman and moral theory* (pp. 19–33). Totowa, NJ: Rowman & Littlefield.

Gilligan, C. (1988). Two moral orientations: Gender differences and similarities. *Merrill-Palmer Quarterly, 34*(3), 223–237.

Giroux, H. A., & Giroux, S. S. (2004). *Take back higher education: Race, youth, and the crisis of democracy in the post-civil rights era.* New York, NY: Palgrave Macmillan.

Goffman, E. (1981). *Forms of talk.* Philadelphia: University of Pennsylvania Press.

Green, D. O., & Trent, W. (2005). The public good and a racially diverse democracy. In A. J. Kezar, A. C. Chambers, & J. Burkhardt (Eds.), *Higher education for the public good: Emerging voices from a national movement.* San Francisco, CA: Jossey-Bass.

Gruggenheim, D. (Director). (2006). An inconvenient truth: A global warning [DVD Documentary], Hollywood, CA: Paramount.

Grunwald, H., & Peterson, M. (2003). Factors that promote faculty involvement in and satisfaction with institutional and classroom student assessment. *Research in Higher Education, 44*(2).

Hansen, H. (2004, March 15). *Granholm, Cherry announce commission on higher education and economic growth.* Retrieved from www.michigan.gov/printer-Friendly/0,1687,7–168—88248—,00.html

Hardiman, R., & Jackson, B. (1997). Conceptual foundations for social justice courses. In M. Adams, L. A. Bell, & P. Griffin (Eds.), *Teaching for diversity and social justice.* New York, NY: Routledge.

Harro, B. (2000a). The cycle of socialization. In M. Adams, W. J. Bluenfield, R. Castañeda, H. W. Hackman, M. L. Peters, & Z. Zúñiga (Eds.), *Readings for diversity and social justice* (pp. 15–20). New York, NY: Routledge.

Harro, B. (2000b). The cycle of liberation. In M. Adams, W. J. Bluenfield, R. Castañeda, H. W. Hackman, M. L. Peters, & Z. Zúñiga (Eds.), *Readings for diversity and social justice* (pp. 463–469). New York, NY: Routledge.

Holland, B. (1999). Factors and strategies that influence faculty involvement in public service. *Journal of Public Service & Outreach, 4*(1), 37–43.

Holland, B. (1997/2006). Levels of commitment to community engagement. *Michigan Journal of Community Service Learning, 4,* 30–41.

Hurtado, S. (2007). Linking diversity with the educational and civic missions of higher education. *The Review of Higher Education, 30*(2), 185–196.

Ibarra, R. (2006). Context diversity: Reframing higher education in the 21st century. In B. Holland & J. Meeropol (Eds.), *A more perfect vision: The future of campus engagement.* Providence, RI: Campus Compact. Retrieved from http://www.compact.org/20th/papers

Jaeger, A., & Thornton, C. (November). *Perspectives on the state and future of engagement in higher education: A critical and committed view.* Paper presented at the Association for the Study of Higher Education, Jacksonville, Fl.

Jones, S. R., Torres, V., & Arminio, J. (2006). *Negotiating the complexities of qualitative research in higher education: Fundamental elements and issues.* New York, NY: Routledge.

Jongbloed, B., Enders, J., & Salerno, C. (2008). Higher education and its communities: Interconnections, interdependencies and a research agenda. *Higher Education, 56,* 303–324.

K20 Center for Educational and Community Renewal. (2008). *Vision and purpose at K20 center.* Retrieved from http://k20network.ou.edu/about/vision

Kezar, A. J. (2005). Challenges for higher education in serving the public good. In A. J. Kezar, A. C. Chambers, & J. Burkhardt (Eds.), *Higher education for the public good: Emerging voices from a national movement.* San Francisco, CA: Jossey-Bass.

Kezar, A., & Rhoads, R. A. (2001). The dynamic tensions of service learning in higher education. *The Journal of Higher Education, 72*(2), 148–171.

Labaree, D. F. (1997). *How to succeed in school without really learning.* New Haven, CT: Yale University Press.

Love, P. G., & Estanek, S. M. (2004). *Rethinking student affairs practice.* San Francisco, CA: Jossey-Bass.

Miller, G., & Fox, K. J. (2004). Building bridges: The possibility of analytic dialogue between ethnography, conversation analysis and Foucault. In D. Silverman (Ed.), *Qualitative research: Theory, method and practice* (2nd ed.). Thousand Oaks, CA: SAGE.

O'Connor, J. (2004). Success and challenges of community-based teaching, learning and research: A national perspective. In J. Galura, P. A. Pasque, D. Schoem, & J. Howard (Eds.), *Engaging the whole of service-learning, diversity, and learning communities* (pp. 14–19). Ann Arbor, MI: OCSL Press.

Parker, W. (2003). *Teaching democracy: Unity and diversity in public life.* New York, NY: Teacher's College Press.

Pasque, P. A. (2007). Seeing the educational inequities around us: Visions toward strengthening the relationship between higher education and society. In E. P. St. John (Ed.), *Readings on equal education* (Vol. 22). New York, NY: AMS Press.

Pasque, P. A. (2010). *American higher education, leadership, and policy: Critical issues & the public good.* New York, NY: Palgrave Macmillan.

Pasque, P. A. (2012). *Deliberative turns in national policy gatherings: A reflective memo.* Dayton, OH: Kettering Foundation.

Pasque, P. A., & Neubauer, H. (2013). Beyond discourse toward emancipatory action: Lessons from an undergraduate. *About Campus, 18*(2), 10–19.

Pitkin, H. F., & Shumer, S. M. (1982). On participation. *Democracy, 2,* 43–54.

Rhoades, G., & Slaughter, S. (2004). Academic capitalism in the new economy: Challenges and choices. *American Academic, 1*(1), 37–59.

Rowley, L. L. (2000). The relationship between universities and black urban communities: The class of two cultures. *Urban Review, 32*(1), 45–62.

Slaughter, S., & Leslie, L. (1997). *Academic capitalism: Politics, policies and the entrepreneurial university.* Baltimore, MD: Johns Hopkins University Press.

Slaughter, S., & Rhoades, G. (2004). *Academic capitalism and the new economy: Markets, state and higher education.* Baltimore, MD: Johns Hopkins University Press.

Smith, W. A. (2004). Black faculty coping with racial battle fatigue: The campus racial climate in a post-civil rights era. In D. Cleveland (Ed.), *A long way to go: Conversations about race by African American faculty and graduate students* (Vol. 14, pp. 171–190). New York, NY: Peter Lang.

Stanley, C. A. (2006). Coloring the academic landscape: Faculty of color breaking the silence in predominantly white colleges and universities. *American Educational Research Journal, 43*(4), 701–736.

Students for Access to Justice (SATJ). (2008) *Mission statement.* Retrieved from http://adams.law.ou.edu/satj/

Tannen, D. (1993). The relativity of linguistic strategies. In D. Tannen (Ed.), *Gender and conversational interaction.* New York, NY: Oxford University Press.

Tannen, D. (1994). *Talking from 9 to 5: Women and men in the workplace: Language, sex and power.* New York, NY: Avon.

Thomas, N. (2004). Boundary-crossers and innovative leadership in higher education. In J. Galura, P. A. Pasque, D. Schoem, & J. Howard (Eds.), *Engaging the whole of service-learning, diversity, and learning communities* (pp. 26–30). Ann Arbor, MI: OCSL Press.

Vygotsky, L. S. (1978). *Mind in society: The development of higher psychological processes.* Cambridge, MA: Harvard University Press.

Weerts, D. J., & Sandmann, L. R. (2008). Building a two-way street: Challenges and opportunities for community engagement at research universities. *The Review of Higher Education, 32*(1), 73–106.

Wheatley, M. J. (1999). *Leadership and the new science: Discovering order in a chaotic world* (2nd ed.). San Francisco, CA: Berrett-Koehler.

White, B. P. (2006). Sharing power to achieve true collaboration: The community role in embedding engagement. In B. Holland & J. Meeropol (Eds.), *A more perfect vision: The future of campus engagement.* Providence, RI: Campus Compact. Retrieved from http://www.compact.org/20th/papers

Wilson, S., Whisenhunt, T. G., & Eseryel, D. (2008). *An instructional design and development model for effective game-based learning environments.* Paper presented at the annual meeting of the Association for Educational Communications and Technology Conference, Orlando, FL.

REFLECTIVE NARRATIVE

Finding Voice in *Communidad*

Estefanía López

I am walking alongside a massive crowd, an immense sea of protesters.

¡Se ve! ¡Se siente! ¡El pueblo estapresente!

This narrative is not solely about my experiences, my struggles, or my successes; all these things are interwoven into the broader fabric of my *communidad*. My story mirrors many of the experiences, struggles, and successes that feed into the passion and resilience of my community. That passion is a force to be reckoned with.

On March 25, 2006, thousands of people took to the streets to protest proposed federal legislation that would further criminalize undocumented immigrants, discipline those who attempted to help them, and move toward greater militarization of the border. Donning white clothing as a sign of peace, more than 500,000 Angelinos demonstrated their opposition to anti-immigrant laws in one of the biggest demonstrations in recent U.S. history. There, at 15 years old, I first found a voice in unison with my *communidad*.

People of all beautiful shades of brown boldly took to the streets, making their presence known. The sounds of our voices echoed through downtown Los Angeles. Every so often, we passed protesters blasting lively music, prompting many to dance to the lovely beats of our native countries. Mothers nestled their babies, while older children made a game of running among the intricate maze of people. People waved flags from their home countries, representative of a diversity of backgrounds found in our community.

At a distance, a man's voice began to grow hoarse. Partly engulfed by the crowd, he strained into the microphone until his voice gave out and other fresh voices led the chants. I was overcome with joy in the *communidad*. We chanted. We danced. We laughed. That day we stepped out of the shadow of our criminalized existence and walked under the hot sun, in unison, to demonstrate the capacity, power, and impact of our voices.

Breaking Spirits

Seventeen years ago, I arrived at San Ysidro, California, and embraced my parents for the first time in the United States. Their hugs and beaming smiles indicated more than happiness—a passionate pursuit for a better life filled their enthusiastic spirits. At a very young age, I learned to embrace that pursuit. It became manifest in a commitment to my academic journey.

That journey to a college education was a dream, but an elusive one. Despite the obstacles I encountered, I became one of those students now identified as "DREAMers," undocumented students seeking a college education. Navigating college without federal financial assistance and little familial support presented a challenge. The hardest critic was my mother, now a single parent, who could not fathom why I put myself through such hardships to obtain what she felt was an unachievable dream. Time and time again, she berated me for the physical strain I forced on my body, the emotional anguish to which I subjected my mind, and the incomprehensible stubbornness I carried in my spirit by undergoing such a difficult journey. I could not understand why she expressed such adamant opposition to my academic advancement. Had she let go? Acquiesced? Abandoned the zealous pursuit for better opportunities that she risked her life to pursue for her family? I struggled to comprehend the force that had taken hold of her previously indomitable spirit.

Arriving home from work one evening, my mother presented me with an article her employer had shared. The article listed reasons why professional training programs were superior to a postsecondary education in achieving economic advancement. As the daughter of a housecleaner, I was not encouraged to pursue higher education but rather to remain in the positions designated for people of "my" socioeconomic status and cultural background. Fortunately for me, the aspiration for a better life had become irreversibly engrained in my being. My mother may have given up, but I refused to yield to low expectations.

In the pursuit of a better life, I learned to aspire to certain standards of academic achievement and success in hopes of achieving the coveted American dream. Throughout my educational journey, I was careful to pursue the normative demands of institutional structures and social interactions in desperate hopes that my undocumented status would not ultimately conflict with my objective to obtain the first bachelor's and graduate degrees in my family. In other words, I worked to be accepted. I was not always successful. At points, I even adopted some of the characteristics of the idyllic "DREAMer," actively promulgated in news outlets and political platforms—smart, hardworking, humble and appreciative, patriotic—converted into sound bites and offered as attributes of "good" undocumented people. "It is not their fault that they came here; their parents brought them over without their consent. . . . They are exceptional students. . . . They can contribute taxpayer dollars to the economy." To adopt the language of "fault" and preclude myself from that fault meant I needed to accept the assertions that my parents had committed an offense in attempting to provide me with a better life; that DREAMers were exceptional students, and I must denigrate hardworking students who did not achieve "exceptional" academic accomplishments; that undocumented people should contribute tax dollars to the economy, and, if they didn't, they did not deserve basic human rights.

Despite my earnest efforts to assimilate into American culture and attain high academic achievements, my struggle was insignificant to people like my mother's employer, whose views of my future remained chained to low expectations. Precisely *because* of my earnest efforts to pursue higher education, my struggle was dismissed by otherwise well-meaning people who believe only "deserving" undocumented immigrants were entitled to human rights. I was not the valedictorian of my class—I was a student who worked hard to help provide for her family and who struggled with several of her classes. Through different contexts but in similar ways, advocates and opponents placed constraints on my educational achievements.

Finding Voice

But I did make it to college. There I developed greater consciousness about the systemic roots of the issues and began to acquire the language to articulate these struggles. Through this journey, rather than developing the ability to integrate and conform, I developed the ability to navigate through a multitude of institutional forces that insisted I did not belong.

I came to understand that my mother had not acquiesced in the face of adversity, but that her spirit had been *broken* by prevailing inequalities embedded in the social structure that continuously obstructed her pursuit for greater opportunities. The time came when I no longer wished to integrate into a society that restricted and rejected me.

Within Community

I had help in coming to these new insights. As an aspiring scholar and educator, I investigated the factors that contribute to the academic success of underprivileged and marginalized youth. I was deeply influenced by my involvement with a number of projects that were built in thoughtfully engaged research in my work. In my work at the National Forum on Higher Education for the Public Good, I collaborated with doctoral, master's, and undergraduate students to develop research studies that addressed educational access, diversity, community engagement, and the role of higher education in facilitating public good. I began to acquire the theories and concepts that confirmed and extended my views, and I learned new language to express my struggles and my successes.

Within the National Forum's Immigration Team, I led coordinating efforts for the University Leaders for Educational Access and Diversity (uLEAD) project to provide research, resources, and support for postsecondary leaders and practitioners seeking to expand access and benefits for undocumented students. This connected me directly to resources and research that could help my community and my decisions. It also provided me with a group of colleagues who shared my concerns and my educational journey and constituted a support network.

Throughout my educational career I know I will continue to address issues of access, equity, retention, and support within higher education for people like me and those in other marginalized communities. My desire to assist other students who are on journeys similar to mine has become stronger. I plan to be a socially conscious educator, activist, and scholar who uses engaged research so that I never forget to work with my community on these issues.

REFLECTIVE NARRATIVE

Making Herstory: Inside and Outside the Walls of Academia

Lena M. Khader

Decades before my Taiwanese mother and Palestinian father met in the United States, their mothers shared a similar fate; neither *Ama* Run Chi nor *Sitti Tamam* Abu Kamleh would earn a college degree. In fact, my *Sitti* never stepped foot into an elementary school and was a newlywed at the age of 12, and my *Ama* merely had a sixth-grade education. Yet my grandmothers both ensured that each of their children received an education past elementary school. When my father almost stayed in Jordan to help provide for his family, my *Sitti* urged him to travel to the United States—amid disapproval from other family members—to receive a college degree and provide better lives for his future children. My ancestors continue to be guiding lights in my journey within the ivory tower, and their perseverance and resiliency remind me that an education will be my path to true wealth.

Receiving a college education, however, has not been an easy task. As immigrants in a foreign land, my parents did not understand the varying inequalities in the U.S. education system. Thus, I attended a local high school where my peers and I were bombarded with negative media press; the media dubbed our school the "dropout factory" due to our high dropout rate and low standardized test scores. U.S. Grant High School, located in south Oklahoma City (OKC), boasted an average 17.7 ACT score and a 40.9% dropout rate (Education Oversight Board, 2009).

During my senior year, several things occurred: I and other students received low ACT scores, Advanced Placement (AP) courses were omitted from the high school curriculum even though they were promised, capable students were given only minimal college and career counseling, and the "turnaround model"—mandated by the federal government—was to be implemented at my high school. Due to persistently low national Adequate Yearly Progress reports, the turnaround model would result in either a "turnaround," "restart," "school closure," or "transformation" at U.S. Grant High School (Kutash, Nico, Gorin, Rahmatullah, & Tallant, 2010). Because teaching and learning that support strong ACT scores, AP courses, college and career counseling, and Adequate Yearly Progress reports should be afforded to every young person, I was angry with our school officials, the federal government, and the media. How could individuals (who had rarely, if ever, stepped foot into our high school) make decisions about students' futures or discuss pertinent issues regarding our school without consulting students?

Upon graduation, I was lucky enough to receive a fully funded Clara Luper Scholarship to attend a local, private institution, Oklahoma City University (OCU). My experiences at OCU were twofold: On the one hand, my experiences were stained with tears, I had difficulty comprehending material, and I had an inferiority complex that almost dashed my dreams of graduating from college. On the other hand, my experiences also provided me with important opportunities outside of my predominantly White institution that radically politicized my entire being.

For example, as a 2011 Organization of Chinese Americans intern placed at the National Education Association in Washington, DC, I was exposed to the words I had felt for so long, yet never had the opportunity to express throughout my educational experiences. Through weekly "*Sama Sama*" (Tagalog for "together, together") workshops with 28 other Asian Pacific Islander American (APIA) interns, I was exposed to concepts, issues, and academic terminology that engaged me in conversations around White privilege, my parent's immigration stories, women of color (WOC) feminist perspectives, the model minority myth, the struggles of undocumented families, and other issues pertinent to traditionally marginalized groups. That summer, I realized I was not taught to be a politically active and socially conscious person throughout my educational career. I was not taught to critically analyze the world or to read books written by radical queer WOC, the working class, or other marginalized people. I was not taught to question the usage of standardized tests to gauge my intellectual capabilities, the lack of curriculum regarding the atrocities people of color faced in the United States, and the lack of education about the contributions and advancements made by people of color. Instead, I was taught to be a complacent student who *believed*, rather than a sentient student who *questioned*. After that fateful summer, I had the critical consciousness to understand the systemic and institutionalized racism I endured as a Taiwanese-Palestinian woman raised in south OKC.

After graduating from OCU, I received a $500 grant from Young People For, a progressive organization that actively works with 100 to 150 activists across the nation to create a Social Justice Blueprint during a year-long fellowship (Young People For, 2015). Based on my high school experience of feeling silenced by school administrators and academia, I had a dream for my Blueprint: to create a youth empowerment organization in south OKC that provided high school WOC with a created safe space to discuss and learn about WOC feminism, ethnic studies, and their own rich "herstories" as a form of social, self, and political empowerment. Yet, my dream felt difficult to attain due to the lagging community organizing resources and organizations in south OKC, as well as my own frustrations finding allies who were willing and able to support my endeavors. However, after teaching an Introduction to APIA Studies and Women's Studies course for my alma mater, Upward Bound, one student raised his hand and asked, "Where do we go from here? Can we continue meeting?" Thus, my Upward Bound students and I collectively founded Making Herstory—we responded to the need of a WOC-organized, youth-led, community-based organization promoting positive, sustainable, and revolutionary curriculum.

After two years of hosting weekly Making Herstory facilitations at Southern Oaks Library in south OKC, I have watched Making Herstory members speak at local protests; create a social media campaign; and raise $250 in honor of Luis Rodriguez, a victim of police brutality. I, along with other admirable WOCs, have raised over $2,000 in donations and grant funding and have successfully facilitated over 50 workshops around WOC feminism, ethnic studies, and our members' personal narratives. The Making Herstory staff and members have been featured in local newspapers, magazines, and national social media blogs.

Due to members' earnest requests, during our second year we began hosting beginner and intermediate workshops. The beginner's space focused on accessible, interactive workshops as a primer to social justice issues, and the intermediate workshops focused on advanced curriculum around academic theory through an intersectionality lens (Collins, 2000; Crenshaw, 1991; Davis, Brunn, & Olive, 2015). These accomplishments and public praise have been essential to my own confidence in the continuation of, and member's pride in, Making Herstory.

But the most meaningful Making Herstory experiences are during intimate moments with members—when they have shared their stories of being undocumented, of embracing their sexuality as queer youth, of surviving domestic and sexual abuse, or describing how Making Herstory is "home." The most meaningful experiences have been the "lightbulb" moments—when members created a political cartoon about the detrimental nature of standardized tests, when members questioned Eurocentric beauty standards and patriarchy, when members expressed anger because the Tulsa Race Riots were not discussed in their schools' textbooks, and when members began sharing their own vision of future Making Herstory curriculum. Or, when members began slowly shifting their narratives into one of empowerment, and started questioning themselves; society; and, most important, Making Herstory staff members. We openly encourage Making Herstory members to cultivate critical thinking abilities in the hope that they will be willing and able to and confident about questioning authority figures.

As a graduate assistant of Penny Pasque, I have had the privilege of reading and editing this volume. This opportunity helped me understand the ways in which "engaged research and practice" can be effectively approached in the contemporary higher education arena. I now realize the immense value academic research could have in my community—ensuring the academic credibility and support of endeavors similar to Making Herstory. Through reading the research and stories in this volume, I see the ways in which engaged research and practice can work in tandem to ensure broad societal change.

I have witnessed the immense power that curriculum around WOC feminism, ethnic studies, and storytelling can have on low-income and/or immigrant students from impoverished communities. As a future school counselor, I plan to merge my passion for social justice, critical consciousness, and education through a personal school counseling framework. I will continue working with high school students and community members to uplift our silenced and marginalized communities.

My *Ama, Sitti,* and ancestors guided me toward a path of education as true wealth, and I hope to continue their legacy in ensuring high school students—whether through engaged research, practice, or both—become radically politicized through spaces such as Making Herstory. Social justice efforts such as these exemplify true wealth, which permeates beyond financial resources to include wealth in living a socially just and critically conscious life. As such, each day I strive to embody the wishes of my Taiwanese and Palestinian ancestors.

References

Collins, P. H. (2000). *Black feminist thought: Knowledge, consciousness, and the politics of empowerment* (2nd ed.). New York, NY: Routledge.

Crenshaw, K. (1991). Mapping the margins: Intersectionality, identity politics, and violence against women of color. *Stanford Law Review, 43*(6), 1241–1299.

Davis, D. J., Brunn, R. J., & Olive, J. L. (Eds.). (2015). *Intersectionality and research in education: A guidebook for higher education and student affairs professionals.* Sterling, VA: Stylus.

Education Oversight Board. (2009). *2009 school report card.* Oklahoma City, OK: Oklahoma City Public Schools.

Kutash, J., Nico, E., Gorin, E., Rahmatullah, S., & Tallant, K. (2010). *The school turnaround field guide.* Boston, MA: FSG Social Impact Advisors.

Young People For. (2015). *Blueprints.* Retrieved from http://youngpeoplefor.org/the-fellowship/blueprints/

REFLECTIVE NARRATIVE

The Education of a *Fontanero*

Jessica L. Cañas

I n a small town in the Cloud Forest Mountains of the Central American country of Honduras, I find myself far from the lecture halls, laboratories, and classrooms of the ivory tower of academia. I swing on a white and blue hammock, as the theories and best practices I have been taught swirl around in my head. With all the education of an Ivy League institution and the best intentions in my heart, I traveled to this community to work on sustainable agricultural initiatives with the descendents of the first agriculturalists of the Americas. I think of my own community back home on the northwest side of Chicago and wonder: Who is working with them to create a more sustainable community? My thoughts are interrupted by the murmur of children coming through the open shutters of my small, whitewashed adobe house.

One of them arrives at my doorstep and says, "*Se fue el agua y no tenemos. ¿Nos regala?*" "The water is gone and we do not have any. Would you share some with us?" The water in town comes from the forest's microwatershed through a system of underground PVC tubing that travels down from the mountain to the homes. If a pipe breaks or is clogged, *el fontanero* (the plumber) is quickly called to repair it. He is the sole caretaker of the water system and the only one in town with the knowledge and skills to repair it. I began to wonder: If the *fontanero* was not available to repair a broken pipe or if he came across a problem too complicated to solve on his own, what would he do, what would we do? There was a saying in town, "*Nadie nace fontanero*" or "No one is born a *fontanero*," meaning no one is born with all the knowledge and skills necessary; you learn them. This made me realize the risk we run as a society when we do not share equal educational opportunity with all people. We deprive communities of their own *fontaneros*, of individuals who carry the knowledge, skill, creativity, talent, and passion necessary to sustain the well-being and flourishing of their own communities.

Months later I am back in my hometown of Chicago, sitting around a large red wooden table, in a maroon-colored conference room lined with maps of Chicago's neighborhoods and pictures of people from around the world. I am working in the Department of Environment, Culture, and Conservation at the Field Museum, and we are discussing how to foster a love for nature and an awareness of environmental issues in the community where we work. But none of us are originally from the community, which is under-resourced and consists primarily of *minoritized*[1] people. I am the only minoritized person at the planning table. I wonder why that is so. Surely some of them are interested in what's happening to their environment. And how did I get here? How did I make it to this table to have a voice in this discussion?

I look at the participants sitting around the table in hopes of pinpointing the one thing we all share in common. After one look around, it comes to me: We all have college degrees in the sciences. At that exact moment I knew what I had to do in order to diversify that planning table and provide seats for the voices of the communities that are too often left out, the minorities not at the table. First, I had to find out why there were so few minoritized people with science degrees. Second, I had to identify what changes and efforts had to be made to increase that number. Most villages, especially a village like Chicago, need many *fontaneros*. Third, I had to reserve a seat for them at the table and learn how to add more seats.

I knew that if minoritized people do not have more than a token seat, then environmental conservation efforts in their communities will never be sustained, and efforts touted to serve their needs will end up advancing the good of others (e.g., landfills in poor communities). Stated another way, an effort cannot be sustained without the representation and participation of all stakeholders, especially of the minoritized whose marginal positions limit their histories, stories, cultural wealth, and interests from entering the dominant discourse and influencing power. In a circuitous way, this goal—to bring the voices of minoritized people to the environmental conservation planning table by means of education—became my driving motivation and led me to the field of higher education.

This take on education has been the driving force behind my sisters' and my passion to bring to our minoritized people the educational opportunities we benefited from. The environmental conservation movement cannot remain defined by the voice of the dominant few. The knowledge and experiences needed to care for the water system that is the assemblage of our natural resources, ecosystems, and communities must be shared and must derive from diverse *fontaneros* across our communities in order for our collective efforts to be sustainable.

Through my time at the National Forum on Higher Education for the Public Good (National Forum), I have started to explore further the reasons why I had a seat at the table while other minoritized people did not. In formal and informal ways, this has become my research quest. The National Forum has been a place for me to engage in dialogues with my peers on this topic and other issues related to widening access to higher education, especially in the sciences, for those who have been marginalized and to include their stories, histories, and cultural knowledge in postsecondary education institutions. It's been a place for me to learn to help other students to be better prepared to welcome and seek knowledge from these communities in areas related to the environment.

As the National Forum works with communities that are building capacity, through shared research and information sharing, I get to see how my use of engaged research might be a way to add seats but also to build new tables where more people can join in the conversation about a sustainable environment. I join in that work, understanding that good research is a means to empowerment. The results of research and the appropriate use of it develop skills, voice, and place. Through my graduate study, as I continue to seek my own voice and seat at the table, part of my role is to not only be a *fontanero* but also work toward the empowerment and preparation of future *fontaneros*. As an environmental educator, a conservationist, and only newly an educator, I have often questioned my engagement in the National Forum and the field of higher education. Was this the right route to take to pursue my goal? What does higher education and this work at the National Forum have to do with my passion for sustainable environmental conservation? It took me some time, but I now know: It has everything to do with it. Colleges and universities that create learning environments and engage those around them; who welcome the histories, stories, cultural wealth, and language of *diverse* people; and that conduct research with them and on their behalf are part of a capacity-building infrastructure for not only these communities but also the nation. This is the public good.

Note

1. The use of the term *minoritized* instead of minority speaks to the notion that the overrepresentation of one racial group and its dominant cultural norms renders other racial groups minorities, thus resulting in the social construction of underrepresentation and subordination. Minoritized groups are only minorities in certain situations and institutional environments (Harper, 2011).

Reference

Harper, S. R. (2011). Foreword. In S. Museus & U. Jayakumar (Eds.), *Creating campus cultures: Fostering success among racially diverse students* (pp. ix–xi). New York, NY: Routledge.

Part Three

ENGAGING THE INSTITUTIONAL LEVEL

6

CHALLENGES TO DIVERSITY
Engaged Administrative Leadership for Transformation in Contested Domains

Cassie L. Barnhardt

*H*ow *do colleges and universities engage with society? How might colleges and universities pursue social problems to ignite social transformation around fundamental matters of inclusion?*

Increasingly, the rhetoric associated with university engagement calls upon higher education leaders and their institutions to deliberately connect with pressing social issues in the hope of activating sweeping or transformative changes that bring widespread benefits to society. This is typically viewed as the enactment of higher education's public good purpose. The logic holds that universities' raw materials of knowledge, expertise, and innovative discoveries and their abilities to bring people together from diverse fields and/ or to produce skilled people in high-need domains can serve to stimulate the sorts of changes necessary to overcome long-standing collective problems. There is a hope, and at times a belief, that higher education can engender social progress on enduring social problems like disregard for human rights, inequality in all its forms, poverty, global warming, disease, and more.

At first glance, it is reasonable to suggest that the public's best interest is served by higher education addressing and optimally solving any of the aforementioned social problems. For instance, respecting human rights evokes broad consensus, thus rendering any disregard for human rights as a serious matter worthy of institutional intervention (Sankowski, 1996). Under the general umbrella of protecting and improving human rights, a campus may turn its attention to engaging in activities directed toward addressing, for example, systematic (mis)treatment of immigrants and/or racial groups (among other potential social problems). This particular framing of human rights holds the potential to swiftly push the boundaries of a one-dimensional conceptualization of what constitutes "human rights" in a general way. Specifically, the (mis)treatment of immigrants and racial groups as a human rights social problem conjures up a complicated landscape of multiple meanings that are topically diffuse, contentious, and politicized. These complicated meanings surface much public dissensus from an array of stakeholders within and external to the university. As a result, competing questions arise over how to conceptualize the problem, the explanations and causes for the current state of affairs, and the suitability of any proposed solutions or actions that the university pursues.

Perhaps most relevant to university public engagement, disagreement manifests over whether higher education is serving the public's interests by engaging with this specific focus on human rights, because the criteria for what counts as a public interest are also contested. Given the pluralistic context of U.S. society stemming from diverse values, preferences, beliefs, economic circumstances, religion, race, or ethnicity, there is tremendous variation in what is deemed beneficial to the public (Calhoun, 1998; Chaves, 1998; Mainsbridge, 1998; Prewitt, 2006). This raises questions such as the following: Does a particular engagement topic serve those individuals or agencies who hold the power to decide what is in the public's proverbial interest? Does the topic serve those who do not hold power, thus rendering it worthy of the university's attention?

Mainsbridge (1998) opines that there is little value in establishing a precise shared meaning for what is meant by the *public good*, but to instead acknowledge that the term invites a "contest over what is public and good" (p. 17). Moreover, a public good rationale used to justify university engagement with a particular social issue will stand on disputed ground. Given the complicated dynamics associated with focusing on matters that lack social consensus, it is easier for universities to pursue engagement activities (and the accompanying issues) that are devoid of politics or controversy, rather than risk potentially attracting public scrutiny or trying to convince an array of parties that the work is justifiable. If universities shy away from contentious topics or look only to topics where many people (or powerful people) agree, then their public interactions and engagement activities might engender more noncontroversial or benevolent support, while simultaneously preventing universities from working on issues where their resources and unique organizational capacities hold great promise for creating social change.

The unintended result of universities focusing on social causes that engender vast public support may be the cost of public support for universities in the long term. It is the thorniest of social issues, where university engagement is perhaps the most necessary to generate transformative solutions, meanings, or relationships that cultivate social change. Transformation is learning and discovery (Clark, 1993; Freire, 1997; Mezirow, 1997); this is what universities do, with respect to students, communities, and society. Transformation is what emerges after overcoming a state of perpetual dispute and contestation, morphing into an altogether different reality that evokes new meanings, strategies, and tools for action, power distributions, and collective ambitions for what the community holds in mutual high regard. As such, universities' public engagement with the most-disputed social issues better positions them to realize their potential as servants of the public's welfare and long-term advancement of human progress. Universities can do what they are most capable of, such as teaching, discovering, transforming, and innovating, when they immerse themselves where these tools are most needed.

In 2012, the locus of attention at the National Forum on Higher Education for the Public Good (National Forum) turned toward examining potential pathways and processes that would encourage higher education institutions (and their leaders) to actively engage with social issues that evoke a particularly high level of dissensus in the public domain. In order to pursue this path, staff at the National Forum looked at conceptions of (a) how universities perform public engagement activities, and (b) idealized examples of long-lasting and dramatic social changes that had an association with universities' sustained engagement. Together, these paths merged to inform the initiatives of a multicampus project, entitled Leadership for Higher Education's Role in Promoting Diversity and Social Transformation: Extending Pathways of Inclusion in the U.S., which was funded by the Carnegie Corporation of New York, with matching funds from each of the partnering institutions. The focus of this project was on the work of campus administrators in specific roles and was designed to harness the capabilities of the university and a community—as a strategic community of administrative practice. This chapter provides a foundational argument for what led to the creation of this project and the accompanying strategies and approaches that flowed from these conceptualizations. The hope is that this chapter will provide a useful model for other partnerships working toward social change.

Conceptions of Universities' Public Engagement

Broadly speaking, publicly engaged campuses serve the community and provide models of action for common problems, or tools, to support the basic and emerging needs within civic life (National Task Force on Civic Learning and Democratic Engagement, 2012; U.S. Department of Education, 2012). The manner in which colleges have engaged in the task of supporting the nation's collective needs has adapted according to fluctuations in the broader American narrative.

Historically, U.S. higher education institutions engaged with public needs by preparing community leaders (who, at the time, were elite, White men) who could provide moral and virtuous leadership and support the structure and function of running civil society and local government (Rudolph, 1990). As the Morrill Acts of the late nineteenth century unfolded, the proliferation of colleges and universities supported states' agricultural and mechanical needs, thus fostering economic development and promoting the general welfare of the populace and the overall vitality of communities (Chambers, 2005; Gunn & Lucaites, 2010; Roper & Hirth, 2005). Throughout much of the twentieth century, higher education institutions' approaches to public engagement emphasized dissemination and application of knowledge (Roper & Hirth, 2005; Weerts & Sandmann, 2008), culminating in a model of outreach that focused on cultivating economic growth or institutional profits (O'Mara, 2012; Slaughter & Rhoades, 2011). These conceptions of engagement have been construed as bidirectional in nature, where the relationships involve contributions from each partner and yield reciprocal value for both entities (e.g., university, industry, social service agency, school) (Roper & Hirth, 2005; Weerts & Sandmann, 2008). A challenge with a bidirectional view of university engagement is that it promotes a transactional or dyadic view of the university's relationship to its community partners that may be prohibitive for seeing other collective benefits. When engagement work is viewed as largely reciprocal it may not compel the university to closely identify its engagement as being connected to a larger purpose or responsibility to society (Brickson, 2005). Brickson (2005) asserts that in order for organizations to pursue actions that consistently align with the broader welfare of society, they must possess an organizational identity that binds the organization's fate to the fate of its collaborators; without such a framing, organizations will restrict their focus to the direct benefits that flow to them from working with community partners or the negotiated obligations they are required to fulfill.

Another way to understand university engagement is to consider it from the perspective of contemplating how universities' sustained patterns of activities function in society. Stevens, Armstrong, and Arum (2008) argue that higher education operates as a temple, a sieve, an incubator, or a hub in terms of how its actions affect broader society. In their example, the temple alludes to higher education as a secular mecca for knowledge creation, resource development, and innovation for addressing common problems; the sieve idea acknowledges the role that higher education plays in stratifying societies; the incubator connotes the process and experience of education and how this affects students (or those who partake in education); and the hub metaphor describes the connective function that universities have as institutions to intersect with other sorts of social institutions—the labor market, the nonprofit sector, religious institutions, government bodies, nongovernmental organizations, and so on. Of these four portrayals, the hub metaphor is decisively structural. It denotes the ways in which higher education acts as a kind of agent linking the professions, the labor market, the state, the cultural institutions, the economy, the social institution of the family, and the nonprofit sector, a conceptualization quite consistent with perspectives on university engagement. Conceptualizing the university as a hub of engagement provides an agentic view of the university as an organization (King, Felin, & Whetten, 2010; Scott & Davis, 2007) with the capacity to connect solutions to problems, people to resources, knowledge to communities, and so on. Essentially, hubs of connection are produced when sustained patterns of organizational activities and administrative actions are pursued to respond to discrete and emergent needs in the external environment. The challenge for universities is, then, knowing what particular organizational arrangements and practices are most conducive for creating and sustaining productive hubs of engagement activity.

The dyadic and reciprocal perspectives regarding the instrumental value of university engagement as well as the structural perspective of the university engaging as a hub of connective tissue between different sectors of society provide a generalized framework of what university engagement is, but these conceptions do not provide a road map for administrators in terms of what must be done to implement or perform engagement work. To address this topic, a more nuanced body of literature provides insights.

How Does a University Approach Engagement?

Over time, research and writing about university public engagement have captured a range of organizational models and activities. Particular forms of university public engagement have drawn the sustained attention of researchers. These descriptions include university-based commercial and economic activities, engaged pedagogies or research efforts that evoke faculty community involvement, service-learning pedagogies and/or curricula that cultivate civic awareness and knowledge among students, and university engagement with stakeholder groups (e.g., alumni, foundations, or private corporate donors) that foster institutional advancement objectives (Doberneck, Glass, & Schweitzer, 2010; Wanat, 2006). The work in these areas has correspondingly resulted in detailed descriptions of administrative practices and work procedures that emphasize the ways in which universities perform engagement.

One form of university public engagement that has received much attention, as well as a scholarly critique, is the engagement that contributes to, cultivates, and fosters capitalistic or economic and revenue-generating ventures (Slaughter & Leslie, 1997; Slaughter & Rhoades, 2004). The research in this area has provided insights into how university leaders and administrators conduct technology-transfer processes and provide incentives and procedural pathways for faculty to move their research into commercially viable ventures that are beneficial for both the university and industry (Rhoades & Slaughter, 1991). Similarly, research on university engagement with alumni has specified administrative practices that are useful for building and sustaining relationships that facilitate institutional advancement aims such as fund-raising, volunteerism, or public/vocal support (Gallo, 2013; Gasman & Bowman, 2013; Weerts & Ronca, 2008). Research into both of these domains has helped develop a community of practice (Wenger & Snyder, 2000) of administrative professionals working in these areas (university economic engagement, alumni engagement). That is, campus administrators responsible for administering economic or alumni engagement have shared, particular professional knowledge and expertise to inform how and what they actually do in the course of their work routines and administrative practices (Wenger & Snyder, 2000).

Another variant of university engagement falls under what is generally termed the *scholarship of engagement*. This form of university public engagement is closely associated with Ernest Boyer's (1990) framing of the modern academy in his seminal piece *Scholarship Reconsidered*. Boyer argued for higher education to more robustly pursue its research, teaching, and service missions in ways that deliberately align with the community. *Scholarship of engagement* is an umbrella concept for many forms of university-based community initiatives, all of which feed into the larger guiding ideals of organizational practices that cultivate engaging with society's needs (Cox, 2006; Sandmann, 2008).

Since Boyer's declaration, research investigating the *scholarship of engagement* has functioned to emphasize what faculty are doing (or should be doing) in their teaching, research, and service capacities to act in engaged ways (Sandmann, 2008). The research in this domain has also provided an abundance of information about community service and/or service-learning initiatives and programs, as well as the effect of such programs on cultivating prosocial civic attitudes among students (Astin, Sax, & Avalos, 1999; Bringle & Steinberg, 2010; Eyler, Giles, Stenson, & Gray, 2001; Jones & Abes, 2004; Sax, 2004). Of these two foci (faculty forms of engagement versus service/volunteerism) in the broad area of the scholarship of engagement, community service and service-learning are typically termed *civic engagement*. However, when the term *civic engagement* is used to describe a university's activities, it tends to describe aspects of program administration or educational outcomes related to the act of individuals performing a service or volunteering in the community (e.g., students being civically engaged), rather than evaluating or describing the university's organizational capacity to exhibit agency as a civic actor as related to fundamental social problems.[1]

Even with its broad definition, studies on the *scholarship of engagement* have produced insights into how campus leaders and administrators can encourage these efforts, with the findings framed as strategies for institutionalizing university engagement (Furco, 2010; Lounsbury & Pollack, 2001). For example, Butin and Seider's (2012) volume provides details about how campuses can organize the curriculum to better prepare students for civic involvement during and after college. Also, Campus Compact (a pioneer in campus-community engagement) routinely synthesizes findings from research that provide direction for university administrators responsible for implementing engagement efforts on how to best implement service and volunteer programs on their campuses (see Zlotkowski, et al., 2004).[2] Campus Compact also promotes institutional policies and practices that incentivize faculty members' pursuits of engaged research.[3] In journals across an array of disciplines (especially in journals from professional fields such as education, social work, the health professions, and engineering), case examples and analyses of campus initiatives that foster engaged research among faculty are ever growing (see Bringle, Games, Foos, Osgood, & Osborne, 2000; Nokes, et al., 2013; Sorenson & Lawson, 2011). These have helped to provide templates of action for campus leaders and administrators who seek to encourage parallel types of engagement on their campuses.

In 2006, the Carnegie Foundation for the Advancement of Teaching initiated its Carnegie Community Engagement classification to complement its generalized classification system of postsecondary institutions. This Community Engagement classification defines *engagement* as the

> collaboration between institutions of higher education and their larger communities (local, regional/state, national, global) for the mutually

beneficial exchange of knowledge and resources in a context of partnership and reciprocity. The purpose of community engagement is the partnership of college and university knowledge and resources with those of the public and private sectors to enrich scholarship, research, and creative activity; enhance curriculum, teaching and learning; prepare educated, engaged citizens; strengthen democratic values and civic responsibility; address critical societal issues; and contribute to the public good. (New England Resource Center for Higher Education [NERCHE], n.d.)

In many ways the community engagement classification has helped to actively bundle universities' array of engagement pursuits together to encourage campuses to take stock of their overall engagement portfolios across multiple arenas. Correspondingly, Carnegie's definition of *community engagement* has emerged as the prevailing vision of university engagement (Smith, Else, & Crookes, 2014). As of 2016, 361 campuses have obtained the classification (NERCHE, n.d.).

The community engagement classification application and review process requires that campuses assess the structural and procedural aspects of their engagement activities, where campuses document resourcing patterns, staffing commitments, policies, programmatic efforts, data gathering, and evidence of outcomes or impact. These elements are indeed critical factors in an organization's overall institutionalization (Selznick, 1996) of engagement. However, the classification process is somewhat lacking in terms of taking stock of any substantive shifts or transformations in collective sentiments or psychic motivations that discretely tie the university's engagement activities to social problems or focused social change ambitions. Instead, the classification process requires documenting formal organizational artifacts, such as mission statements, marketing materials, and organizational goals, as material resources for assessing the degree of commitment to the ideals of engagement. Such formal artifacts do not necessarily reflect distinctive organizational patterns of action or aims to shift cultural meanings; rather, such artifacts have been observed to reflect existing normative views and meanings that ensure legitimacy among similarly situated organizational peers (Taylor & Morphew, 2010).

Essentially, aspirations and a vision for what university engagement can accomplish in various forms has prompted organizations to modify their existing philosophies, structures, and practices to pursue these aims. These efforts have been discussed, studied, assessed, and analyzed. Collectively these processes have the formalization and professionalization of administrative roles associated with university engagement activities (Wanat, 2006). At present, there exists a cadre of university administrators who are responsible for stewarding different facets of universities' ambitions for engagement, with each aspect of engagement (commercial advancement, scholarship of engagement, civic engagement) associated with a niche professional identity that includes criteria for what engagement is and how to perform it (Engagement Scholarship Consortium, n.d.).

This cultivation of a cadre of people "doing" engagement work, and thus learning about and reflecting on how to do it better, is crucial for organizational capacity building of the sort that allows universities to become more responsive to community needs or discover common challenges present in the work (Academy of Community Engagement Scholarship, 2014). To date, the commercial and the service and service-learning aspects of university engagement have become legitimate endeavors and are prominent aspects of how universities contribute to the public good. Other forms of university engagement, including alumni engagement, engaged research, and curricular approaches to engagement have, over time, developed into a community of practice that provides a basis for doing this work.

Critiques of the State of Engagement

Despite the successes and expansion of university public engagement in many respects, there is a concern that what contemporary university engagement has evolved into reflects a different reality than the aspirational vision of what university engagement was imagined to be—something that would evoke social transformation around society's most pressing and intractable challenges (Boyte, 2005; Butin, 2012; Hollander, 2012). The last 30 years have included the infusion of public and private financial resources to incentivize and formalize university engagement efforts (Butin, 2012; Furco, 2010), largely based on the hope and potential of what university engagement might bring to broader society.

Specifically, Hollander (2012) asserts that by and large both universities' public engagement activities and the scholarship about it has been categorically apolitical, reflecting a shortage of attention to dimensions of power and political processes, and without reference to an overarching theory to guide systemic change. She suggests that some of this may be intentional on the part of university leaders out of fear that university engagement that connects to political issues or processes may jeopardize funding or other forms of public support that institutions receive. These conditions make it of little wonder that university engagement efforts have yet to connect to their communities in ways that are fully suitable for addressing truly complicated public problems—the sort of matters that cannot be divorced from politics, contention, or the disruption of power or allocation of cultural value in society.

Now, rather than dissecting what is known about what engagement is or should be, where have there been inspirational moments of transformative university engagement? And, what do these stories and examples convey about universities engaging or intervening in critical social issues?

Models of Inspiration

Despite potential disincentives for higher education institutions to pursue engagement associated with remedying or making a dent in the thorniest of social problems, there have been moments when campuses have been central features in such circumstances. Correspondingly, society has seen poignant changes flow out of higher education institutions' engagement.

Following the Civil War, few venues in society offered any substantive hope for implementing structural changes that would directly expand the opportunities for the social inclusion of Blacks. Higher education was one of a few exceptions. At that time, under the veil of widespread public sentiment (and policy) in the South, which insisted upon segregationist education, individual colleges and universities had limitations on how they could expand educational access to Blacks (Anderson, 1980; Rogers, 2012). Even within this restrictive cultural context, the educational structure was altered to allow poor, southern Blacks to access a system of compulsory education (Flexner, 1952). These changes were facilitated with support from the Peabody Fund, a private foundation, which helped to fund a normal school in Tennessee that trained teachers to teach Black students (Flexner, 1952). This initial act helped set in motion a series of events that enabled subsequent expansion and increased access for Blacks to education. Specifically, also with foundation support, Fisk, Hampton Agricultural and Industrial College, and Atlanta University were among the early adopters to provide scholarship support (at a level that was comparable to what White students were receiving at the time) to train students for entering teaching positions in the south (West, 1966). From this example, it seemed evident that the kernels of widespread and long-standing change started with only a handful of campuses, and foundation resources were an important catalyst in these processes.

The civil rights era also stands out as a time when higher education was intimately involved with social change. Campus disruptions emerged across the nation for a sustained period of time Involving the civil rights struggle, questions over free speech, and the Vietnam War (Astin, Astin, Bayer, & Bisconti, 1975; Foster & Long, 1970; Higher Education Executive Associates, 1970; Light & Spiegel, 1977; Nichols, 1970; Scranton, 1970). Campus activism contributed to fueling a broader shift in public sentiment that ultimately assisted with opening doors for greater inclusion of Blacks and women in society. Even so, this campus activism was largely something that was *happening to* higher education, rather than universities purposefully seeking out the social issues that inspired the campus protests. In fact, it was in this era (1966, to be precise) that *The Chronicle of Higher Education* began publishing. The impetus for its publication was, in part, to satisfy university leaders' needs for news and perspectives about the substantive issues surrounding the campus protests and details of what occurred so they could determine a way to respond (Carnegie Corporation of New York, 2006).

What university leaders were making sense of was a robust pattern of protest activity; the U.S. Senate Committee of Government Operations documented 471 protest-type incidents occurring on 211 U.S. campuses between the fall of 1967 and the spring of 1969 that produced 6,158 arrests (Harris, 1969). Ultimately there was great variation in the ways administrators chose to engage or respond to the campus protests and activism, and the attention that the *Chronicle* brought to these events operated as a productive tool for campus leaders to make sense of what was happening. The unintentional engagement that many campuses had with student protests and grassroots activism during this era created a lasting cultural imprint on society, forever tying together college, students, disruption, and social change ambitions (Zald, 1996). From this example, it is apparent that the media and communication flows were an important tool in providing campus administrators a framework for calculating their own localized response to the activism. Also, the media was active in cultivating a collective psychological link from what was happening on campus to what was happening more broadly in society.

Further, during the civil rights era and throughout the early 1970s a handful of campuses became intentionally engaged with substantive social problems through the development of knowledge in critical areas related to those social issues. Specifically, working in partnership with the Ford Foundation, Black studies (Rojas, 2003, 2007) and women's studies (McCarthy, 1985; Proietto, 1999) programs and/or research centers were established at some of the most elite universities. Between 1969 and 1971 Ford allotted grants to 20 universities for work related to Black studies (Rojas, 2003), and between 1972 and 1975 Ford made grants to 16 universities to aid them in advancing women's studies programs and research (McCarthy, 1985; Proietto, 1999).

In addition to supporting the work on campuses, the Ford Foundation provided resources to develop a network connecting knowledge and resources by funneling support to fund the organizing of professional associations and academic journals (Roelofs, 2003; Rojas, 2003). The campuses that were earlier adopters of dramatic curricular changes gave rise to a larger wave of other campuses that would follow them in the ensuing decades (Roelofs, 2003; Rojas, 2003). Roelofs (2003) and Rojas (2003) both argued that the efforts of the first few campuses helped legitimate these domains of study, and correspondingly worked to advance the position of Blacks and women in society. From these examples, it seems that the most diverse and inclusive campuses were among the leaders in taking on issues of social identity by transforming their core processes to be more inclusive. This set the stage for changes to unfold at other institutions. Essential pieces that supported the universities' engagement with social challenges, and the accompanying organizational changes, were the infusion of external foundation funding and the momentum secured through creating and sustaining a professional network.

The post-Civil War era and the civil rights era examples provide instances of where higher education made important inroads on pressing social problems. Seemingly, higher education's ability to engage in a truly transformative fashion with contested social issues has been, in part, a function of (a) a handful of universities acting as leaders for the rest of the field, (b) partnerships with private foundations, and (c) a process to efficiently share insights and information about what was happening with other similarly situated campuses and the public (either in the news or in a professional/academic network). The lessons from these tangible examples of higher education–mediated social change, coupled with what the work on the philosophies, structures, and administrative processes associated with what university public engagement has produced, provide the backdrop for how the National Forum pursued its project with the Carnegie Foundation of New York and its campus partners.

Leadership for Social Transformation

The activities pursued in the Carnegie grant were designed to invoke a transformative approach to university engagement focused on contested matters of public concern. The project was intentionally crafted to address long-standing debates about who is worthy of social inclusion and what should happen as the central features of the organizing framework. With this focus, the inherent political and power dynamics embedded in these debates would be unavoidable. What we generated was a multifaceted project involving four focus campuses with uniquely different approaches to contemplating university engagement. Even within the different approaches, the activities were designed to evoke a degree of synergy by building on the scholarship of engagement, the idealized models of transformation that have occurred in higher education, and the amplifying support of a foundation's financial and cultural resources.

The Issue

The contested social issue selected for the Carnegie project was immigration, with the specific project focus on how universities contribute to the inclusion of undocumented immigrant college students in higher education and society. Undocumented immigration was an optimal selection of a contentious topic because it holds parallels to the structure of the problems present in the idealized models of social transformation that we explored. That is, at present, undocumented immigrants are categorically excluded from political and civil inclusion in the United States (Glenn, 2011), just as Blacks and women have been at different times in U.S. history. Therefore, the paths for their social integration are few, leaving higher education as one of the only viable venues for undocumented immigrant youth to pursue.

In fact, the federal action related to immigration in recent years has functioned to further affirm higher education's role in providing legitimate pathways for undocumented immigrants to pursue a brighter future in the United States. Both the 2012 Deferred Action for Childhood Arrivals (DACA) criteria (Napolitano, 2012) and President Obama's November 2014 executive action (The White House, Office of the Press Secretary, 2014) included reprieves or preferences for undocumented individuals enrolled in higher education (with the 2014 action emphasizing facilitating visas for those pursuing degrees in science, technology, engineering, and math fields in particular).

Moreover, if campuses are sufficiently motivated to take action, the nature of the problem itself presents an opportunity to encourage or facilitate the social integration and mobility of undocumented immigrant students. Ultimately, universities' choices to act (and in what manner) on this topic hold the potential to shape the way the nation constructs its narrative and justification for inclusion or exclusion of immigrants, and how it comes to understand education's role in fulfilling its potential to be a conduit of transformation.[4]

It is also worth highlighting that in addition to undocumented immigration being a structurally compelling and contentious context for considering university engagement, the topic of immigration inspires much social conflict and public dissensus, thus furthering the need for a transformation of meaning to generate a measure of resolve beyond the existing cultural stalemate that exists in society. Public opinion data continue to reveal that 7 out of 10 people feel that there should be a legal way for undocumented immigrants to remain in the United States (Pew Research Center, 2013, 2015). These same data also demonstrate that the public disagrees over how that should be accomplished as a matter of public policy (Pew Research Center, 2013, 2015). Following President Obama's November 2014 executive action on immigration, public opinion data revealed that the country was divided almost in half (50% disapprove to 46% approve) about whether the administration's approach was suitable (Pew Research Center, 2015).

Perspectives on the executive action fall along partisan lines, although not completely so, with differences of opinion also emerging according to one's ethnic and/or racial identity (Pew Research Center, 2015). Further, it seems that the formal policy solutions are either out of reach or only short-term adjustments, whereas higher education will maintain its responsibility to admit and enroll students for the broad purpose of training people to become active contributors to a global society, including beyond the boundaries of a particular nation-state.

Exploring University Public Engagement Where Social Conflict Exists

The project activities were facilitated by researchers, educators, and administrators from four campuses: the University of Michigan (as the leading/organizing campus), the University of Iowa, the University of Texas–Austin, and Columbia University. Over the course of a two-year period, each site was responsible for applying its expertise in understanding and activating pathways of inclusion for undocumented immigrants in society. From a university engagement perspective, this meant that the project activities were focused on the role of the campus and its leaders in shifting meaning, tying it to action, and leading others in higher education to do the same.

Similar to the research that focused on the work of campus administrators responsible for overseeing engagement activities, the Carnegie project focused on the administrative work of university professionals who were likely to be connected to public matters of contention. By shifting the focus from organizing for engagement outcomes (e.g., economic engagement, service, institutional advancement) to organizing for responses to conflicts related to external interactions, we were able to more actively infuse the political and power dynamics into the nature of the administrative processes. Specifically, it required that the Carnegie project focus on the work of administrators in three particular roles: general/legal counsel, chief diversity officers (CDOs), and senior campus communications/external relations officers. Each of these administrators has a unique role in guiding the university through how it will respond to contested matters of diversity and social inclusion.

In brief, staff from the general counsel's office provide legal opinions to guide the institution's adherence to or interpretation of relevant laws; CDOs are asked to be the standard bearers for the institution's moral and value commitments via education, assessment, and outreach to staff, faculty, and students; and campus strategic communication professionals are charged with voicing the institution's position on diversity and inclusion to a number of constituencies, such as prospective students and parents, alumni, elected officials, and the press. The professionals who inhabit these roles are expected to anticipate and interpret contentious matters of diversity and inclusion with an eye for the reciprocal effects that the institution can or will encounter. In making these assessments, they are subsequently responsible for formulating a position and then disseminating it to campus leadership, the internal community, or external audiences, respectively; they perform contentious engagement work.

For each of the project sites, the emphasis was designed to actively cultivate a professional community (much like the administrative communities of practice described in the engagement literature), one oriented toward transformation and social change to provide greater inclusion for undocumented students on their campuses. The strategies for creating such a community were accomplished through (a) sharing stories and examples of specific instances of inclusive organizational actions relating to undocumented students, (b) building relationships among individuals in parallel administrative roles so they could rely on one another or act together when faced with similar challenges, and (c) formalizing a coterie of campus administrators willing to publicly communicate about the moral and social responsibilities of the problems of society's (mis)treatment of undocumented immigrant youth. The project infused elements of knowledge dissemination, professional community building, and research as the central tasks of the project. Each site led a distinctive set of activities focused on the processes of transformation.

Columbia University's Center for Institutional and Social Change (www .changecenter.org) has a track record of generating scholarship that reveals the ways in which lawyers can approach their work with an eye toward social transformation. As a result, the project activities at Columbia were focused on the role of general/legal counsel campus administrators. The discrete goal for this work was to build a team of legal professionals who have access to information, influence, and shared commitments to advocate for inclusive university policies and practices. The University of Texas–Austin brought its extensive experience to the broader field of higher education in two administrative areas—strategic communications and chief diversity functions. The University of Texas–Austin project site hosted meetings for a slate of campus administrators from across the country who were responsible for overseeing diversity efforts and strategic communications in order to cultivate greater cooperation and narratives around inclusion for undocumented immigrant college students. The goals for the work situated at the University of Texas–Austin were the following: Increase the visibility and strategic orientation of CDOs and assist them in leveraging influence for framing complex issues of campus diversity and enhance the capacity of strategic communications officers to assess and articulate complex issues of diversity beginning with the challenge of access for undocumented immigrant college students. The University of Iowa focused its efforts on studying the professional tactics and competencies of campus administrators when they are confronted by contentious issues. This work covered facets of each of the key focus areas in the project, including research on the relative impact of university administrators' public advocacy around issues of diversity and morality, predictive modeling of campuses inclined to be involved in legal advocacy relating to diversity, and the work routines of CDOs.

The National Forum at the University of Michigan weaved the threads of multiple sites together to produce a national network of campus administrators focused on navigating the political contestation internal and external to their universities, while specifically providing pathways for the inclusion of undocumented immigrant college students. Their efforts were directed toward creating intentional synergies across activities. Moreover, the overarching objective for the work conducted by the National Forum was to maximize the inherent potential of higher education institutions to assert strategic leadership around contentious national issues related to diversity and inclusion, and to provide a sustainable process and repository that could be recycled for other campuses as they chose to subsequently become more active in their support for undocumented students, or when responding to issues of contested matters of diversity.

Early Insights

Some of the emergent research findings from the project are revealing the extent to which the strategic communications, legal positioning, and diversity work are connected to university engagement on contentious issues. For example, the University of Iowa site explored patterns in senior campus leaders' (here, university president, provost, dean, or associate dean) public advocacy in order to take stock of how strategic communications officers might need to refine their organizational strategies to engage with controversial social issues (Barnhardt, Liu, Parker, Sheets, & Valdes, 2014). Analyses of a national survey of approximately 23,000 students and 9,000 campus professionals (staff, academic administrators, and student affairs administrators) demonstrated that there are strong positive effects associated with senior leaders publicly advocating for moral and ethical issues, being active and involved citizens, or valuing diverse perspectives.

Specifically, each of these forms of senior leaders' advocacy was associated with far greater agreement among campus community members who actively promoted domestic and international social, political, and economic issues. Despite the potential utility of senior leaders' advocacy in encouraging a campus commitment to broader social issues, the frequency of senior leaders' advocacy was not necessarily robust. More than 60% of senior leaders viewed themselves as frequent public advocates of diversity, but just 33.4% of students and approximately 45% of faculty and staff viewed senior leaders as frequent public advocates. Seemingly the senior leaders' public advocacy was neither heard nor seen by the internal campus community.

Further, though there was more agreement between senior leaders and the rest of campus relating to the frequency with which senior campus leaders publicly advocated for moral or ethical issues, the patterns in the data were not altogether different from the findings related to diversity advocacy. Less than 30% of students and professionals believed that senior campus leaders advocated around moral/ethical topics. Together, these findings allude to the apolitical nature of public communications by the positional leaders on campus and suggest that strategic communications officers have some work to do in situating their campus leaders' messaging to more actively engage with issues that require a degree of position taking on the moral/ethical dimensions of social issues, the worthiness of allotting respect to diverse people and ideas, or the worthiness of taking action on pervasive social problems.

Other data from the project helped to evaluate which types of campuses have demonstrated a willingness to engage in legal advocacy around issues of diversity. The *Abigail Fisher v. University of Texas–Austin* Supreme Court of the United States (SCOTUS) case of 2013 was used as a context to explore an instance where campuses could willfully opt in to advocate a position by submitting a legal brief to the Supreme Court for its consideration before rendering a decision (Barnhardt et al., in press). These analyses demonstrated that, in total, 321 campuses had some sort of affiliation to a legal brief that was submitted to SCOTUS. Even so, more than half of these submissions were authored by campus stakeholder groups such as faculty, students, alumni, or a research center, as opposed to the formal embodiment of the campus (the administrative figurehead such as the president/chancellor, or the campus listed by its formal name or its board of governors) acting as a signatory on the brief. Campuses that advocated for the legal use of race in selective college admissions (315 of the 321 campuses affiliated with a brief) were also those with superior records of enrolling and graduating students of color (by 15 or more percentage points) when compared to all other nonprofit institutions that granted associate degrees or higher qualifications. These findings highlight the semblance of a connection between a campus's value commitments to educating diverse students and their being willing to take a particular legal position on matters of social inclusion.

Still another finding generated from this project involved evaluating the work routines of CDOs or their administrative equivalent labeled with a different moniker and how campuses responded to undocumented immigrant college students. We analyzed data from 23 CDO-type administrators (Barnhardt, Phillips, Young, & Sheets, 2016). These data revealed that campuses that include undocumented students among those eligible for in-state tuition pricing are also far more inclined to document and disseminate their campus diversity goals publicly. Also, campuses that allow undocumented students to be eligible for campus-based forms of financial aid were observed to routinely engage in the practice of data monitoring to evaluate the demographic compositions of students who enroll and which students persist. Furthermore, we observed that campuses that make concerted efforts to include undocumented students by charging them in-state tuition, allowing them to be eligible for campus-based financial aid, and enshrining a policy (as opposed to merely a practice) that undocumented students are categorically eligible for campus-based financial aid are also those campuses that by and large have a CDO that routinely communicates the campus's diversity objectives with on- and off-campus audiences.

Concluding Thoughts

When campuses face an uncertain situation (e.g., determining whether and how to respond to undocumented immigrant college students) the stakes are high in terms of evaluating the possible threats to organizational resources, reputation, or identity. In fact, O'Kane, Mangematin, Geoghehan, and Fitzgerald (2015) assert that administrators who manage university engagement activities, let alone engagement activities focused on a contentious issue, can feel immobilized by having to satisfy the pragmatic expectations of their administrative positions, while stabilizing or even increasing the university's reputation, resources, or ranking, and ensuring that their work addresses inherent moral, ethical, and civic questions.

Often, the organizational decisions that flow from having to wrestle with contentious issues are built on a compendium of advice from strategic actors (e.g., general counsel, diversity officers, and strategic communications officers). These people are the de facto administrators who hold responsibility for public engagement with political and contested issues. The advice and guidance from the administrators in these key positions is a function of their personal professional competence, their knowledge of the substantive contentious matter (undocumented immigrant students' challenges), their awareness of effective models of practice to address the issue, and their assessment of the organization's ability to act in an efficacious manner that aligns its practices with its institutional identity (socially responsible commitments).

Stulberg and Chen's (2013) research is providing new evidence that, in fact, university administrative leaders' moral interpretations of social justice are a central component of a university's choice to take inclusive action for underrepresented students. Their historical data suggest that campuses have purposefully modified their organizational practices because administrators believed "their institutions should participate in this kind of social change" (p. 40). Our work in this project is most certainly compatible with their work, suggesting the administrators must possess moral and ethical perspective to connect what they do through their campuses as holding discrete ties to fundamental principles of human dignity.

The activities, meetings, and research that made up the Carnegie and National Forum project were intentionally created to cultivate a community of practice among administrators most likely to come into contact with contentious social issues. The process was designed to unfold over time but also to embolden campuses to act on their stated commitments to inclusive and equitable education. Ultimately, history will judge whether the project activities described here will be worthy of the term *transformative*. The hope is that by more directly activating processes of how universities understand, interpret, and characterize the challenge of educational access and opportunity for undocumented students, universities will be more adept at creating sustainable pathways of inclusion for undocumented immigrant youth and be able to apply a set of similar administrative strategies to other difficult contexts. Infusing meaning with particular organizational actions is an emergent and generative process, but it does not need to be done passively—rather it can be done in active ways that allow higher education to lead the conversations and ask critical questions that society must face together.

Notes

1. Doberneck, Glass, and Schweitzer's (2010) typology provides an expansive analysis of the wide-ranging array of terms and phrases that denote different discrete forms of university public engagement.

2. See Campus Compact's resources for campus engagement at www.compact .org/initiatives/engaged-campus-initiative

3. Campus Compact's tool-kit on universities supporting engaged research can be found at www.compact.org/initiatives/trucen/trucen-toolkit

4. A full exploration of the history and policy context of undocumented immigrant students in education and postsecondary education is beyond the scope of this chapter. However, some excellent references for further context include Olivas, M. (2012). Dreams deferred: Deferred action, prosecutorial discretion, and the vexing case(s) of DREAM Act students. *Williams & Mary Bill of Rights Journal, 21*(2), 463–547; Olivas, M. (2009). Undocumented college students, taxation, and financial aid: A technical note. *Review of Higher Education, 32*(3), 407–416.

References

Academy of Community Engagement Scholarship. (2014). *Academy of community engagement scholarship concept paper.* Retrieved from http://engagementscholarship.org/upload/aces/FinalRevisedConceptPaper2014withFounders.pdf

Anderson, J. D. (1980). Philanthropic control over Black higher education. In R. F. Arnove (Ed.), *Philanthropy and cultural imperialism: Foundations at home and abroad* (pp. 147–177). Bloomington: Indiana University Press.

Astin, A. W., Astin, H. S., Bayer, A. E., & Bisconti, A. S. (1975). *The power of protest.* San Francisco, CA: Jossey-Bass.

Astin, A. W., Sax, L. J., & Avalos, J. (1999). Long-term effects of volunteerism during the undergraduate years. *The Review of Higher Education, 22*(2), 187–202. doi: 10.1353/rhe.1999.0002

Barnhardt, C., Liu, J., Parker, E., Sheets, J. E., & Valdes, P. (2014). *What happens when campus administrators speak out? University leaders' public advocacy. Report for the National Forum on Higher Education for the Public Good.* Ann Arbor: University of Michigan.

Barnhardt, C., Young, R. L., Sheets, J. E., Phillips, C. W., Parker III, E. T., & Reyes, K. A. (in press). Campus strategic action in the *Fisher* case: Organizational stakeholder advocacy across the field of higher education. *Research in Higher Education.*

Barnhardt, C. L., Phillips, C. W., Young, R. L., & Sheets, J. E. (2016). The administration of diversity and equity on campuses and its relationships to serving undocumented immigrant students. *Journal of Diversity in Higher Education.* doi .org/10.1037/a0040025

Boyer, E. L. (1990). *Scholarship reconsidered: Priorities of the professoriate.* Princeton, NJ: Carnegie Foundation for the Advancement of Teaching.

Boyte, H. C. (2005). *Everyday politics: Reconnecting citizens and public life.* Philadelphia: University of Pennsylvania Press.

Brickson, S. L. (2005). Organizational identity orientation: Forging a link between organizational identity and organizations' relations with stakeholders. *Administrative Science Quarterly, 50*(4), 576–609.

Bringle, R. G., Games, R., Foos, C. L., Osgood, R., & Osborne, R. (2000). Faculty fellows program: Enhancing integrated professional development through community service. *American Behavioral Scientist, 43*(5), 882–894.

Bringle, R. G., & Steinberg, K. (2010). Educating for informed community involvement. *American Journal of Community Psychology, 46,* 428–441.

Butin, D. W. (2012). When engagement is not enough: Building the next generation of the engaged campus. In D. W. Butin & S. Seider (Eds.), *The engaged campus: Certificates, minors, and majors as the new community engagement* (pp. 1–14). New York, NY: Palgrave Macmillan.

Butin, D. W., & Seider, S. (2012). *The engaged campus: Certificates, minors and majors as the new community engagement.* New York, NY: Palgrave Macmillan.

Calhoun, C. (1998). The public good as a social and cultural product. In W. W. Powell & E. S. Clemens (Eds.), *Private action and the public good* (pp. 20–35). New Haven, CT: Yale University Press.

Carnegie Corporation of New York. (2006). Chronicling higher education for nearly forty years. *Carnegie Results,* 1–12.

Chambers, T. C. (2005). The special role of higher education in society: As a public good for the public good. In J. C. Burkhardt, A. Kezar, & T. C. Chambers (Eds.), *Higher education for the public good: Emerging voices from a national movement* (pp. 3–22). San Francisco, CA: Jossey-Bass.

Chaves, M. (1998). The religious ethic and the spirit of nonprofit entreprenuership. In W. W. Powell & E. S. Clemens (Eds.), *Private action and the public good* (pp. 47–65). New Haven, CT: Yale University Press.

Clark, M. C. (1993). Transformational learning. In S. B. Merriam (Ed.), *An update on adult learning theory* (p. 57). San Francisco, CA: Jossey-Bass.

Cox, D. N. (2006). The how and why of the scholarship of engagement. In S. L. Percy, N. L. Zimpher, & M. J. Brukardt (Eds.), *Creating a new kind of university: Institutionalizing community-university engagement* (pp. 122–135). Boston, MA: Anker.

Doberneck, D. M., Glass, C. R., & Schweitzer, J. (2010). From rhetoric to reality: A typology of publicly engaged scholarship. *Journal of Higher Education Outreach and Engagement, 14*(4), 5–35.

Engagement Scholarship Consortium. (n.d.). *Home.* Retrieved from http://engagementscholarship.org/

Eyler, J. S., Giles, D. E., Stenson, C. M., & Gray, C. J. (2001). *At a glance: What we know about the effects of service-learning on college students, faculty, institutions, and communities, 1993–2000* (3rd ed.). Nashville, TN: Vanderbilt University Press.

Fisher, A., et.al. v State of Texas, et.al. (12013). (Case no. 11-345) United States Court of Appeals.

Flexner, A. (1952). *Funds and foundations.* New York, NY: Harper.

Foster, J., & Long, D. (1970). *Protest! Student activism in America.* New York, NY: William Morrow.

Freire, P. (1997). *Pedagogy of the oppressed.* New York, NY: Continuum.

Furco, A. (2010). The engaged campus: Toward a comprehensive approach to public engagement. *British Journal of Sociology of Education, 58*(4), 375–390.

Gallo, M. L. (2013). Higher education over a lifespan: A gown to grave assessment of a lifelong relationship between universities and their graduates. *Studies in Higher Education, 38*(8), 1150–1161.

Gasman, M., & Bowman, N. (2013). *Engaging diverse college alumni: The essential guide to fundraising.* New York, NY: Routledge.

Glenn, E. N. (2011). Constructing citizenship: Exclusion, subordination, and resistance. *American Sociological Review, 76*(1), 1–24.

Gunn, J., & Lucaites, J. L. (2010). The contest of faculties: On discerning the politics of social engagement in the academy. *Quarterly Journal of Speech, 96*(4), 404–412.

Harris, D. (1969). Staff study of campus riots and disorders, October 1967–May 1969. In United States Senate Permanent Subcommittee on Investigations of the Committee on Government Operations (Ed.) Washington, DC: U.S. Government Printing Office.

Higher Education Executive Associates. (1970). *Final staff report to the Michigan senate committee to investigate campus disorders and student unrest.* Lansing, MI: Higher Education Executive Associates.

Hollander, E. L. (2012). De Toqueville rediscovered: Community-based civic engagement. In D. W. Butin & S. Seider (Eds.), *The engaged campus: Certificates, minors, and majors as the new community engagement* (pp. 187–194). New York, NY: Palgrave Macmillan.

Jones, S., & Abes, E. (2004). Enduring influences of service learning on college students' identity development. *Journal of College Student Development, 45*(2), 149–166.

King, B. G., Felin, T., & Whetten, D. A. (2010). Finding the organization in organizational theory: A meta-theory of the organization as a social actor. *Organization Science, 21*(1), 290–305. doi:10.1287/orsc.1090.0443

Light D., Jr., & Spiegel, J. (1977). *The dynamics of university protest.* Chicago, IL: Nelson-Hall.

Lounsbury, M., & Pollack, S. (2001). Institutionalizing civic engagement: Shifting logics and the cultural repackaging of service-learning in U.S. higher education. *Organization, 8*(2), 319–339.

Mainsbridge, J. (1998). On the contested nature of the public good. In W. W. Powell & E. S. Clemens (Eds.), *Private action and the public good* (pp. 3–19). New Haven, CT: Yale University Press.

McCarthy, K. (1985). The short and simple annals of the poor: Foundation funding for the humanities, 1900–1983. *Proceedings of the American Philosophical Society, 129*(1), 3–8.

Mezirow, J. (1997). Transformative learning: Theory to practice. In P. Cranton (Ed.), *Transformative learning in action: Insights from practice* (Vol. 74, pp. 5–12). San Francisco, CA: Jossey-Bass.

Napolitano, J. (2012, June 15). *Exercising prosecutorial discretion with respect to individuals who came to the United States as children* [Memorandum]. Washington, DC: U.S. Department of Homeland Security.

National Task Force on Civic Learning and Democratic Engagement. (2012). *A crucible moment: College learning and democracy's future.* Washington, DC: Association of American Colleges and Universities.

New England Resource Center for Higher Education. (n.d.). *Community engagement classification.* Retrieved from http://nerche.org/index.php?option=com_con tent&view=article&id=341&Itemid=92#CE%20def

Nichols, D. C. (1970). *Perspectives on campus tension: Papers prepared for the special committee on campus tensions.* Washington, DC: American Council on Education.

Nokes, K. M., Nelson, D. A., McDonald, M. A., Hacker, K., Gosse, J., Sanford, B., & Opel, S. (2013). Faculty perceptions of how community-engaged research is valued in tenure, promotion, and retention decisions. *Clinical and Translation Science, 6*(4), 259–266.

O'Kane, C., Mangematin, V., Geoghehan, W., & Fitzgerald, C. (2015). University technology transfer offices: The search for identity to build legitimacy. *Research Policy, 44*(2), 421–437. doi:10.1016/j.respol.2014.08.003

O'Mara, M. P. (2012). Beyond town and gown: University economic engagement and the legacy of the urban crisis. *Journal of Technology Transfer, 37*(2), 234–250.

Pew Research Center. (2013, March 28). Most say illegal immigrants should be allowed to stay, but citizenship is more divisive. *U.S. Politics & Policy.* Retrieved from http://www.people-press.org/2013/03/28/most-say-illegal-immigrants-should-be-allowed-to-stay-but-citizenship-is-more-divisive/

Pew Research Center. (2015, January 15). Unauthorized immigrants: Who they are and what the public thinks. *Publications.* Retrieved from http://www.pewresearch .org/key-data-points/immigration/

Prewitt, K. (2006). American foundations: What justifies their unique privileges and powers. In K. Prewitt, M. Dogan, S. Heydemann, & S. Toepler (Eds.), *The legitimacy of philanthropic foundations: United States and European perspectives.* New York, NY: Russell Sage Foundation.

Proietto, R. (1999). The Ford Foundation and women's studies. In E. C. Lagemann (Ed.), *Philanthropic foundations: New scholarship, new possibilities* (pp. 271–284). Indianapolis: Indiana University Press.

Rhoades, G., & Slaughter, E. L. (1991). Professors, administrators, and patents: The negotiation of technology transfer. *Sociology of Education, 64*(2), 65–77.

Roelofs, J. (2003). *Foundations and public policy: The mask of pluralism.* Albany: State University of New York Press.

Rogers, I. H. (2012). *The Black campus movement: Black students and the racial reconstitution of higher education, 1965–1972.* New York, NY: Palgrave MacMillan.

Rojas, F. (2003). *Organizational decision-making and the emergence of academic disciplines* (Doctoral dissertation). The University of Chicago, Chicago.

Rojas, F. (2007). *From Black power to Black studies: How a radical social movement became an academic discipline.* Baltimore, MD: Johns Hopkins University Press.

Roper, C. D., & Hirth, M. A. (2005). A history of change in the third mission of higher education: The evolution of one-way service to interactive engagement. *Journal of Higher Education Outreach and Engagement, 10*(3), 3–21.

Rudolph, F. (1990). *The American college and university: A history.* Athens: University of Georgia Press.

Sandmann, L. (2008). Conceptualization of the scholarship of engagement in higher education: A strategic review, 1996–2006. *Journal of Higher Education Outreach and Engagement, 12*(1), 91–104.

Sankowski, E. (1996). Racism, human rights, and universities. *Social Theory and Practice, 22*(2), 225–249.

Sax, L. J. (2004). Citizenship development and the American college student. In J. C. Dalton, T. R. Russell, & S. Kline (Eds.), Special issue: Assessing character outcomes in college (*New Directions for Institutional Research No. 122,* pp. 65–80). San Francisco, CA: Jossey-Bass.

Scott, W. R., & Davis, G. F. (2007). *Organizations and organizing: Rational, natural, and open systems perspectives.* Upper Saddle River, NJ: Pearson Education.

Scranton, W. W. (1970). *The report of the president's commission on campus unrest.* Washington, DC: U.S. Government Printing Office.

Selznick, P. (1996). Institutionalism "old" and "new." *Administrative Science Quarterly, 41*(2), 270–277.

Slaughter, S., & Leslie, L. L. (1997). *Academic capitalism: Politics, policies, and the entrepreneurial university.* Baltimore, MD: Johns Hopkins University Press.

Slaughter, S., & Rhoades, G. (2004). *Academic capitalism and the new economy: Markets, state, and higher education.* Baltimore, MD: Johns Hopkins University Press.

Slaughter, S., & Rhoades, G. (2011). Markets in higher education. In P. G. Altbach, P. J. Gumport, & R. O. Berdahl (Eds.), *American higher education in the twenty-first century: Social, political, and economic challenges* (3rd ed., pp. 433–464). Baltimore, MD: Johns Hopkins University Press.

Smith, K. M., Else, F., & Crookes, P. A. (2014). Engagement and academic promotion: A review of the literature. *Higher Education Research & Development, 33*(4), 836–847. doi:10.1080/07294360.2013.863849

Sorenson, J., & Lawson, L. (2011). Evolution in partnership: Lessons from the East St. Louis action research project. *Action Research, 10*(2), 150–169.

Stevens, M. L., Armstrong, E. A., & Arum, R. (2008). Sieve, incubator, temple, hub: Empirical and theoretical advances in the sociology of higher education. *Annual Review of Sociology, 34*, 127–151.

Stulberg, L. M., & Chen, A. S. (2013). The origins of race-conscious affirmative action in undergraduate admissions: A comparative analysis of institutional change in higher education. *Sociology of Education, 81*(1), 36–52.

Taylor, B. J., & Morphew, C. C. (2010). An analysis of baccalaureate college missions statements. *Research in Higher Education, 51*(5), 483–503.

U.S. Department of Education. (2012). *Advancing civic learning and engagement in democracy: A road map and call to action.* Washington, DC: Author.

Wanat, J. (2006). Weaving engagement into the fabric of campus administration. In S. L. Percy, N. L. Zimpher, & M. J. Biukardt (Eds.), *Creating a new kind of university: Institutionalizing community-university engagement* (pp. 211–222). Boston, MA: Anker.

Weerts, D. J., & Ronca, J. M. (2008). Characteristics of alumni donors who volunteer at their alma mater. *Research in Higher Education, 49*(3), 274–292. doi: 10.1007/s11162-007-9077-0

Weerts, D. J., & Sandmann, L. (2008). Building a two-way street: Challenges and opportunities for community engagement at research universities. *Review of Higher Education, 32*(1), 73–106.

Wenger, E. C., & Snyder, W. M. (2000). Communities of practice: The organizational frontier. *Harvard Business Review, 78*(1), 139–145.

West, E. A. (1966). The Peabody education fund and Negro education, 1867–1880. *History of Education Quarterly, 6*(2), 3–21.

White House, Office of the Press Secretary. (2014). Fact Sheet: Immigration accountability executive action [Press release]. Retrieved from http://www.whitehouse.gov/the-press-office/2014/11/20/fact-sheet-immigration-accountability-executive-action

Zald, M. N. (1996). Culture, ideology, and strategic framing. In D. McAdam, J. D. McCarthy, & M. N. Zald (Eds.), *Comparative perspectives on social movements: Political opportunities, mobilizing structures, and cultural framings* (pp. 261–274). Cambridge, UK: Cambridge University Press.

Zlotkowski, E., Duffy, D. K., Franco, R., Gelman, S. B., Norvell, K. H., Meeropol, J., & Jones, S. (2004). *The community's college: Indicators of engagement at two-year institutions.* Providence, RI: Campus Compact.

7

ACCESS POINTS TO THE AMERICAN DREAM
Immigrant Students in Community Colleges
Kyle Southern, Teresita Wisell, and Jill Casner-Lotto

Nearly half of undergraduate students in the United States are enrolled in the nation's community colleges (Century Foundation, 2013). Among the community college population, an estimated one in four students comes from an immigrant background (Horn & Nevill, 2006). The immigrant student population is far from monolithic, representing a variety of ethnicities and cultures and including individuals with limited English proficiency and low levels of prior education in their native countries. This population also includes large numbers of highly skilled immigrants with advanced degrees and credentials earned outside the United States.

In this chapter, we discuss the vital and ongoing role of community colleges as facilitators of empowerment and advancement for students in American higher education and the workforce. In particular, we focus on immigrant students who study at community colleges, including students who lack documentation of their residency in the United States. Often referred to as "democracy's colleges," community colleges are inclusive institutions that provide the most accessible and affordable path to postsecondary education and workforce training for all who desire to learn, regardless of wealth, heritage, or previous academic experience (Boggs, 2010). Today, immigrants and their children are among those students who depend on community colleges as entry points to higher education.

We also present the work of a national consortium of community colleges as an example of engaged scholarship from which professional educators in the two-year sector can draw insights on how these institutions may support the educational success of immigrant students. Trustees, presidents, chief academic officers, deans, faculty, student affairs administrators, and other representatives of consortium member institutions act to address the hurdles many undocumented immigrant students encounter in their pursuits of postsecondary credentials. Partnerships across institutional offices and with local businesses and nonprofit organizations are essential. As educators work to lower barriers and facilitate partnerships that benefit students' educational efforts, their work reflects a commitment to the democratic ideas of the community college sector and the public good mission of postsecondary education. By sharing practices and experiences across institutions in different settings across the country, community colleges serving immigrant populations, including the undocumented, also reflect the kind of engaged scholarship required to best meet students' needs.

The Community College Consortium for Immigrant Education (CCCIE) is a national network of institutions that share a commitment to serving this student population. Established in 2008, with major support from the J.M. Kaplan Fund and other private funders and hosted by Westchester Community College, in Valhalla, New York, CCCIE works to strengthen and expand college programs that increase educational and workforce opportunities for immigrant students. CCCIE's work is guided by a blue-ribbon panel that includes national associations, including the American Association of Community Colleges (AACC), and research institutions such as the Migration Policy Institute, an independent nonprofit organization that provides analysis, development, and evaluation of migration and refugee policies at local, national, and international levels.

The nearly 30 members of the panel bring CCCIE a variety of perspectives, but they are united by a common mission: "to raise awareness of the important role community colleges play in delivering educational opportunities to immigrants and to promote and expand the range and quality of programs and services for immigrant students among community colleges around the country" (CCCIE, 2014, para. 2). After discussing the development of this network, its key initiatives, and the practices shared by member institutions, we propose areas for further research to provide insight and tools community college leaders need to best serve immigrant students and, in so doing, to meet the public good mission intrinsic to this sector of American higher education.

We hope the engaged scholarship practiced by CCCIE and its member institutions may inform community college professionals and illuminate potential practices that can benefit immigrant students nationwide. Scholars may also identify questions for empirical investigation that can inform further engagement with immigrant student communities in ways that enhance their educational experiences in the two-year sector.

Pursuing a Mission of Immigrant Student Support

Prior to the creation of CCCIE, no national voice or concerted initiative spoke to the role community colleges play in immigrant education or shared expertise and innovative strategies promoting that work. To fill this void, the consortium has adopted three primary goals and activities:

1. raising visibility and providing leadership through website resources, articles, and conference planning and presentations
2. encouraging innovation through action-based research, technical assistance, and sharing promising practices that encourage replication of model programs
3. impacting policy changes and strengthening the field through cross-sector strategic partnerships (CCCIE, 2014)

To carry out these activities, CCCIE has mobilized the resources of its blue-ribbon panel. The panel includes member colleges from across the country—urban, suburban, and rural—from a dozen different states. Members come from areas as diverse as suburban Kansas City, Kansas; Miami-Dade County, Florida; south Texas; and Queens, New York. They share a commitment to CCCIE's goals and overall mission. Serving immigrant students is an important part of each institution's identity and mission.

The panel includes prominent associations and institutions bringing expertise in policy research and advocacy. The AACC represents 1,200 institutions (AACC, 2014). AACC partners with CCCIE on issues of increased access and success for immigrant and undocumented students.

Each year approximately 65,000 undocumented students graduate from high schools in the United States, only to face uneven prospects for postsecondary education due to legal, financial, and other barriers tied to their immigration status. Despite an increased trend of state-level laws and policies offering in-state tuition and access to financial aid for undocumented students, the majority of states have not adopted tuition equity measures to help students continue their education. Addressing the needs of a student population this large, in a country with approximately 11.2 million undocumented residents (Passel & Cohn, 2011), requires concerted effort by a group with CCCIE's national reach.

Immigrant Education as a National Imperative

As CCCIE member colleges and other community colleges continue to provide accessible educational options for immigrant and undocumented students, they do so under the constraints of limited resources. According to a recent Century Foundation (2013) report, community colleges serve nearly half of this country's undergraduate students of color, who disproportionately come to college from lower socioeconomic backgrounds relative to the overall undergraduate population. As indicated in the report, "If our nation does not assist community colleges in better serving their students, it will be less economically competitive and poorer. The American Dream will remain out of reach for millions of our fellow citizens" (p. 11).

Undocumented students are not citizens, but removing the undocumented population from the United States would be impractical from a logistical standpoint, indefensible from a moral one, and not in the nation's economic interests. Undocumented immigrants represent nearly one-third of all immigrants residing in the United States and nearly 4% of the overall population (Passel & Cohn, 2011). Approximately 8 million undocumented immigrants participate in the workforce, comprising 10% of the total workforce in Nevada, 9.7% in California, and 9% in Texas. The fact that 71.4% of undocumented residents participate in the workforce—compared with 63% of the overall American population—indicates the disproportionate share who are of working age and motivated by work to risk life without documentation (Mui & Jayakumar, 2013; Passel & Cohn, 2011). Undocumented residents paid an estimated $10.6 billion in state and local taxes in 2010 (Institute on Taxation and Economic Policy, 2013). According to the Migration Policy Institute, unauthorized workers have contributed at least an estimated $50 billion in Social Security taxes (Papademetriou, 2013).

Many of the tax dollars of undocumented immigrants finance public schools, which many of their children attend. In a 5-to-4 majority 1982 ruling, the Supreme Court affirmed the right of all school-aged children to receive a K–12 education at the public expense, regardless of their immigration status. The court found a Texas district's attempt to charge tuition for undocumented students unconstitutional on Fourteenth Amendment equal protection grounds. Writing for the majority in the case, *Plyler v. Doe*, Justice William Brennan noted, "Paradoxically, by depriving the children of any disfavored group of an education, we foreclose the means by which that group might raise the level of esteem in which it is held by the majority" (*Plyler v. Doe*, 1982, III A). Restricting access to education would, in Brennan's estimation, render a "permanent caste of undocumented resident aliens, encouraged by some to remain here as a source of cheap labor, but nevertheless denied the benefits that our society makes available to citizens and lawful residents" (*Plyler v. Doe*, 1982, III A). Community colleges represent a first line of defense against the perpetuation of a permanent caste of undocumented, undereducated residents.

Increasing Access for Undocumented Students

States and higher education systems have attempted to address the educational needs of undocumented students, but the variety of approaches they have taken reflects the failure of the federal government to take comprehensive action to reform the country's broken immigration system. First introduced in Congress by Senators Richard Durbin (D-IL) and Orrin Hatch (R-UT) in 2001, the Development, Relief, and Education for Alien Minors (DREAM) Act would provide a path to citizenship for undocumented youth who pursue higher education or serve in the military. Congress has considered various versions of the DREAM Act numerous times since 2001 but has failed to pass any version. Although the House of Representatives passed the DREAM Act near the close of the congressional session in 2010, the Senate failed to overcome the necessary threshold to bring the bill up for a vote.

In the years since that failure, members of Congress have discussed and proposed a variety of measures to reform America's immigration system. In 2013, a bipartisan "Gang of Eight" senators introduced a comprehensive overhaul plan (SB 744). According to the Immigration Policy Center (2013), the bill "makes changes to the family and employment-based visa categories for immigrants, provides critical due-process protections, increases the availability of nonimmigrant workers to supplement all sectors of the workforce, and provides legal status to 11 million undocumented immigrants within the United States" (para. 3). After several rounds of amendments, senators passed it by a vote of 68 to 32. To date, the House has yet to take up a comparable approach to immigration reform.

As a temporary measure to encourage undocumented residents to register, the Obama administration in June 2012 announced the Deferred Action for Childhood Arrivals (DACA) program. An initiative of the Department of Homeland Security, DACA allows undocumented residents who were younger than 31 years old as of August 15, 2012, to defer deportation on a two-year, renewable basis and to apply for temporary work permits. DACA recipients must meet several requirements, including enrollment in or completion of an educational program or being active in or having received an honorary discharge from a branch of the armed forces. "DACAmented" students can be considered lawfully present for the purposes of receiving educational benefits, although such a determination can still take place at the state or institutional level (Immigration Equality, n.d.).

States across the country have interpreted DACA differently regarding availability of services and benefits for these students. Immigration, therefore, represents a dynamic national policy issue. As of this writing, 18 states have adopted tuition equity laws, enabling undocumented students to obtain in-state residency tuition benefits (National Conference of State Legislators, 2014). At least four others—California, New Mexico, Texas, and Washington—have also opened public financial aid programs to this student population, and Minnesota and Illinois have extended privately funded financial aid to undocumented college students. Other states have adopted policies with more restrictive stances toward undocumented students, either expressly disqualifying undocumented students from in-state tuition rates or banning their enrollment in public institutions altogether. A third group of states leaves approaches to undocumented students largely up to institutional decision makers.

Table 7.1 lists states according to their status of higher education policies—inclusive, restrictive, and unstipulated—toward undocumented students. The growing trend of increasing tuition equity for undocumented students will likely lead to increasing rates of students pursuing postsecondary education, heightening the need for institutions serving the needs of this student population to share practices.

The DACA program represents a temporary approach to providing lawful presence for young undocumented people. Upon President Obama's announcement of DACA in 2012, Joseph Hankin, then president of New York's Westchester Community College (WCC), noted in an op-ed article published by *Community College Daily* that the new initiative offers opportunities for improving the educational and career prospects of undocumented students and represents opportunities for community colleges as well. Hankin wrote, "Colleges can play a major role educating their current and prospective students about deferred action and getting them connected to the organizations and resources, including legal expertise, that can help" (Hankin, 2012, para. 7). CCCIE seeks to provide professional resources across an institutional network to enable community colleges to better meet the needs of undocumented students.

Opportunities and Challenges Serving Immigrant Students

In serving a high proportion of immigrant students, community colleges can empower people with the skills and knowledge they need to succeed and contribute to our country's society, public life, and economy. Many such

TABLE 7.1

Undocumented Student Inclusive, Restrictive, and Unstipulated States by Postsecondary Educational Access and Affordability

Inclusive States	Restrictive States	Unstipulated States
California	Alabama*	Alaska
Colorado	Arizona^	Arkansas
Connecticut	Georgia^	Delaware
Florida	Indiana^	Idaho
Hawaii[1]	New Hampshire[¡]	Iowa
Illinois	North Carolina[#]	Louisiana
Kansas	South Carolina*	Maine
Kentucky		Mississippi
Maryland		Missouri
Massachusetts		Montana
Michigan[2]		Nevada
Minnesota		North Dakota
Nebraska		Pennsylvania
New Jersey		South Dakota
New Mexico		Tennessee
New York		Vermont
Ohio[3]		West Virginia
Oklahoma		Wisconsin
Oregon		Wyoming
Rhode Island[4]		
Texas		
Utah		
Virginia[5]		
Washington		

1 University of Hawaii
2 University of Michigan, Wayne State University, and Western Michigan University
3 Ohio Board of Regents Policy only applies to students qualifying for DACA.
4 Rhode Island Board of Governors Policy
5 Virginia DACAmented students qualify for in-state tuition at public institutions.
* Ban enrollment of undocumented students in public institutions.
^ Ban in-state tuition for undocumented students.
[¡] Students must sign affidavits (HB 1383) attesting they are U.S. citizens to qualify for in-state tuition rates.
[#] Undocumented students may attend community colleges but must pay out-of-state tuition rates.

Source. National Immigration Law Center, 2014.

students—given their low-income backgrounds, limited English proficiency, lack of familiarity with community college systems, and undocumented or mixed-status immigration households—are ill prepared for college, and CCCIE member institutions and community colleges must address myriad personal, educational, financial, and employment needs of immigrant students.

The implementation of DACA and the increased national focus on comprehensive immigration reform allow for discussion about the role of educators in the linguistic, civic, and economic integration of new Americans in the workforce. Recognizing the restraints presented by limited resources, community colleges serving high proportions of immigrant students have a variety of opportunities, such as the following:

- Community colleges can provide a range of high-quality services supporting educational attainment and career enhancement for this fast-growing segment of the U.S. population, including certificates and two-year degrees, transfer to four-year colleges, career training and employer-recognized credentials, English as a Second Language (ESL) instruction, civics education, and citizenship preparation. These services are best delivered through partnerships with community organizations, employers, adult education systems, K–12 schools, four-year colleges, and workforce investment boards.
- Prominent political, business, nonprofit, and philanthropic leaders are working on a national degree/certification completion agenda that complements and strengthens community college initiatives.
- Immigrant students bring a diversity of cultures and perspectives and can be effective mentors and role models for peers. Colleges can support these experiences on campus and in the community. They can also work with immigrant youth-led networks such as United We Dream to facilitate immigrant students' completion of postsecondary programs.
- Institutional leaders can collaborate with immigrant youth movements and other immigrant rights groups in advocating for in-state residency tuition and other educational benefits for undocumented students.

Institutional leaders play an essential role in identifying resources to serve immigrant students and ensuring that students can access available resources. They can also advocate for policies and practices designed to promote the educational and personal success of immigrant students, including undocumented students.

Community colleges have limited resources and complex challenges. These challenges affect daily institutional practice, and efforts to overcome them require creative energy and sustained commitment by institutional leaders. They include rapidly changing demographic trends, especially growth of the Latino/Hispanic population. More than 40 million immigrants live in the United States—more than 17 million of them are natives of Mexico, Central America, and South America. Among the undocumented population, approximately 1 million people are younger than 18, and an additional 4.5 million have at least one parent lacking documentation (Pew Hispanic Center, 2011). Politics concerning immigration and access to public benefits are controversial, particularly in a time of increased focus on cost containment and performance measures. The changing economy also means community colleges must adapt to prepare students for the jobs of the future.

Community colleges are well positioned to serve a diverse immigrant population. However, the services required by immigrant students often go beyond the usual academic and financial assistance. As a result of strict budget constraints, colleges may lack adequate resources to meet these needs in a time of increased demand for immigrant education. Immigrants and their children are expected to account for almost all of the nation's future labor force growth. By 2030, nearly one out of five workers will be an immigrant (Gelatt, Batalova, & Lowell, 2006). By 2050, first- and second-generation immigrants are predicted to make up a record 37% of the U.S. population (Pew Research Center, 2013). Much sooner than that, by 2018, almost two-thirds of all jobs will require at least some postsecondary education (Carnevale, Smith, & Strohl, 2010). Yet in 2011, half of the 40 million immigrants aged five years and older had limited English proficiency, and one-third of the 34 million immigrants aged 25 years and older lacked a high school diploma (Britz & Batalova, 2013). Immigrant college students are at higher risk of dropping out of college than their native-born peers (Erisman & Looney, 2007; Teranishi, Suarez-Oroco, & Suarez-Oroco, 2011). Their college completion rates remain distressingly low compared to the general population (Lumina Foundation, 2013).

The education and training immigrant college students receive must equip them to make fuller contributions to the economy and to society. By making strategic decisions when allocating resources, community colleges can establish support structures to facilitate the educational and personal success of these students.

Strategic Resource Development

Institutions are starting to designate full-time staffing or to create resource centers to serve their immigrant student population. In Lexington, Kentucky, Bluegrass Community and Technical College (BCTC) has established a holistic support model for Hispanic students that also provides support for undocumented students. Further, the college's Office of Latino Outreach and Services provides immigrant students with help in financial aid, enrollment, and academic support. Activities coordinated by that office include the following:

- Help with the college application process
- Help with FAFSA application and personalized scholarship searches/coaching
- Personalized academic advising and coaching
- Career counseling
- Educational access and immigration policy information and referrals to social services, legal services and leadership programs. (BCTC, 2014, para. 2)

Other institutions have adopted support models to fit the needs of the students they serve. In its report *Dreaming Big: What Community Colleges Can Do to Help Undocumented Immigrant Youth Achieve Their Potential* (Casner-Lotto, 2012), CCCIE offers community colleges recommendations in five critical areas: increasing college access, making college affordable, supporting college readiness and success, offering alternatives for adult learners, and improving college retention. The practices that Miami Dade College (MDC), South Texas College (STC), and WCC use to support their undocumented students are described in the following sections.

Miami Dade College

Over 174,000 students attend MDC, and approximately 35,000 are immigrants. The college estimates that nearly 500 of those students are undocumented. When President Obama first announced DACA, MDC launched a campaign to educate its student body, faculty, and staff about that federal initiative. The college collaborates with student organizations such as Students Working for Equal Rights, immigrant advocacy groups, and trusted immigration attorneys to conduct DACA information sessions for students and their families. Along with these partners, MDC also provides assistance to eligible students in applying for deferred action and work permits.

MDC's collaboration with its local K–12 school district ensures that administrators, counselors, teachers, and students are aware that the college welcomes undocumented students and is committed to helping them succeed. In June 2014, Republican Governor Rick Scott signed legislation enabling undocumented students who have attended at least three years of high school in the state to qualify for in-state tuition rates at public postsecondary institutions. At MDC, the out-of-state tuition rate for 12 credits per term is more than three times the in-state rate of $1,346. MDC has complied with the state laws and regulations regarding Florida residency for tuition purposes and has also granted reduced tuition rates to DACA-approved students on a case-by-case basis.

In addition, MDC was one of 12 colleges selected to participate in the first round of awards under the The Dream.US initiative, a new $25 million private scholarship fund that provides financial assistance to undocumented students unable to access Pell Grants or other financial aid. MDC met the program's rigorous selection criteria: a focus on college completion and a demonstrated record of serving low-income students by helping them to graduate with career-ready degrees and find employment; providing academic and social support services to underresourced students; designating a student adviser to help undocumented students develop and manage education plans; and offering associate or bachelor's career-ready degrees for less than $12,500 and $25,000, respectively, for tuition and fees (TheDream. US, 2014).

South Texas College

Located in the Rio Grande Valley along the Mexican border, STC also participates in the TheDream.US initiative. The college has equipped its counseling staff with tools and resources needed to address the immigration status of students, including referrals to legal services and assistance in finding financial aid and scholarship resources, as well as guidance in navigating educational and career pathways. The Office of Admissions and Records provides training workshops for outreach and admissions counselors, and the college has increased the number of counselors equipped to assist undocumented students.

Dual enrollment programs are particularly important for undocumented high school students as both college preparation and cost-saving measures. These courses enable students to begin college-credit courses for free or at discounted prices while still in high school. STC's Achieve Early College High School Initiative introduces eligible high school students to the rigors of a college curriculum and encourages college completion. The program is open and free to all students, irrespective of immigration status. Hidalgo Early College High School serves as a statewide model in preparing students for college or career and technology education. The program grants preference to applicants who are from low-income families, are the first member of their family to attend college, or are English language learners (Nodine, 2010).

Another initiative at STC, the Broadband Technology Opportunity program, bridges the digital divide by increasing computer literacy among low-income and out-of-school adults, including a growing population of adults from immigrant and language minority communities. STC is one of 63 organizations in 6 national sites participating in the online Learner Web Partnership. The program, funded by the U.S. Department of Commerce, operates through the Continuing Education Department and is open to all immigrants, regardless of their status. The Learner Web system is a blended model, combining online learning with face-to-face support by trained tutors and computer assistants (Learner Web, 2010). Although ESL instruction is not the primary objective, participants acquire English language skills through the program. The program also has attracted people to the college who otherwise might not have ventured onto the campus, and they are enrolling in ESL or GED programs (Learner Web, 2010).

Westchester Community College

Despite its location in a county popularly known for its affluence, WCC serves a broadly diverse population. With one in four Westchester residents born outside the United States, the college's Gateway Center provides targeted programs for immigrant and international students, as well as U.S.-born students. Gateway houses a welcome center that helps new students navigate the campus; the English Language Institute, which serves about 5,000 ESL students annually; business and modern language programs; a professional development center that provides workforce training (including ESL courses) to local companies and their employees; and centers for financial literacy and entrepreneurial studies that offer targeted curricula for English language learners.

Studies have indicated that undocumented students can serve as powerful role models and mentors for other students by sharing their personal stories, showing how they overcame barriers, and emphasizing the importance of staying in school (Pérez, Cortés, Ramos, & Coronado, 2010). The *Mi Hermana Mayor* (My Older Sister) mentoring and community service program is a partnership among El Centro Hispano, WCC, Manhattanville College, and the White Plains school district in Westchester County. The program pairs Latina middle school students with Latina bilingual and bicultural "sisters," or mentors in college, who provide academic tutoring and serve as successful role models for the younger girls, encouraging them to continue with their own education.

Many of the mentors and mentees are undocumented students, and pairing older, academically successful students with younger students makes a significant difference. The program improves mentees' grades, their attitudes toward school and their future education, and their work habits by providing intensive tutoring, one-on-one mentoring, academic support, and weekly motivational sessions with successful professionals. Mentors also benefit as they learn the value of helping others succeed, gain tutoring skills, and earn stipends for their community service.

Directions for Future Research

The practices described in the previous sections of this chapter represent only a sample of the many efforts community college leaders have undertaken to address the educational needs of immigrant students, particularly those from the undocumented and DACAmented populations. They also reflect the commitment of community colleges to serve as access points to this country's system of postsecondary education and economic opportunity. Engaged scholarship facilitates an ongoing conversation among practitioners and scholars of higher education, and helping undocumented students achieve postsecondary success requires sharing effective strategies. Empirical study of these practices can help leaders implement their own strategies for addressing these needs of this underserved community. Engaged scholarship can thereby help empower undocumented immigrant students to overcome barriers to educational opportunities beyond high school.

Beyond case studies such as those from MDC, STC, and WCC more comprehensive research—both quantitative and qualitative—is needed to better understand the experiences and outcomes of a diverse immigrant student population and the critical role community colleges can play in improving their educational and workforce opportunities. Such research could also deepen understanding of the state and federal policies that can affect students' academic and career pathways. Both longitudinal studies that track the transitions of students across educational and workforce systems and best practice research efforts are needed to better inform practitioners and policymakers in their quest to improve immigrant students' college and career readiness. Three areas for further research may deepen the connection between research and practice: enhanced data collection, redesigned remedial education, and cross-sector partnerships.

Enhanced Data Collection

One area for further investigation is to examine how data can be used to better understand the needs and strengths of various immigrant subgroup populations in order to track student progress and outcomes, properly allocate resources, and set policy priorities.

Questions to explore might include: *What types of data collection systems could track the progress of English language learners from the noncredit ESL to the credit ESL and academic departments at community colleges? How can the data be best used to support or drive practices and policies at the institutional, programmatic, state, and federal levels, including educational reforms to increase college degree and certificate completion rates? What types of data are needed, and at what points can they be collected?* For example, community college information systems do not generally ask about immigrant students' prior educational experiences or credentials earned in their native countries—valuable data for addressing the needs of foreign-educated, highly skilled immigrants.

Redesigned Remedial Education

Research and practice over the past few years have begun to transform the way faculty, colleges, and state systems deliver remedial education, based on conclusive evidence "that remedial education as commonly designed and implemented—that is, sequences of several semester-long courses that students must complete before gaining access to college-level gateway courses— does not work" (Charles A. Dana Center, 2012, p. 1). Many ESL students are assigned to remedial or developmental education programs, usually spending several years there before ever reaching college-level work or, all too often, dropping out.

Innovations in the field can benefit all underprepared and underresourced students, such as accelerated and contextualized pathways that integrate basic skills instruction with academic programs or with job skills training (e.g., I-BEST models, bridge programs, stackable credentials, vocational ESL, and dual enrollments). However, more attention is needed to understand the ESL immigrant student experience, outcomes in these initiatives, and the targeted interventions that may be required to meet student needs. Among the issues to be explored are developing more comprehensive assessment measures that use diverse approaches to measure proficiency, addressing cultural differences, and capturing the full picture of immigrant students' unique needs and strengths (Casner-Lotto, 2011).

Cross-Sector Partnerships

Community colleges alone cannot adequately provide the comprehensive menu of services that immigrant students require to succeed in college. Colleges are increasingly developing partnerships with a variety of key stakeholders, including K–12 schools, four-year colleges, adult education systems, community-based organizations, employers, and workforce investment boards. These cross-sector partnerships increase immigrant students' opportunities for further education, training, and job placement.

Further research is needed to better understand the key elements contributing to partnerships that promote smooth student transitions. Finally, we recommend further work on how to leverage public and private funding streams as a way to sustain partnerships, incentivize employers as partners in developing ESL and job skills training at work, and successfully replicate and scale partnerships.

Conclusion

Leaders across government, industry, and philanthropy have recognized the importance of broadening college access and completion. The current college completion agenda addresses economic realities, but it also enables a larger proportion of the population to participate in the social and political life of the United States. Community colleges represent a common point of entry to postsecondary education for immigrant and undocumented students, along with millions of other potential degree completers. These institutions prepare graduates for further college work or for joining the workforce and also serve as foundations for personal opportunity.

Member institutions of the CCCIE and many other postsecondary institutions serving high proportions of immigrant and undocumented students are reservoirs of expertise on addressing education issues particular to those student communities. This expertise and the opportunities for engaged scholarship it opens have much to offer broader national reform initiatives supporting a degree and certificate completion agenda. By leveraging this expertise, community colleges can offer a historically underserved student population the opportunity to make their American dreams a reality.

References

American Association of Community Colleges. (2014). *About AACC*. Retrieved from http://www.aacc.nche.edu/About/Pages/default.aspx

Bluegrass Community and Technical College. (2014). Office of Latino Outreach and Services. Retrieved from http://bluegrass.kctcs.edu/en/multiculturalism_and_inclusion/latino_hispanic_outreach.aspx

Boggs, G. R. (2010). *Democracy's colleges: The evolution of the community college in America*. Washington, DC: American Association of Community Colleges. Retrieved from http://www.aacc.nche.edu/AboutCC/whsummit/Documents/boggs_whsummitbrief.pdf

Britz, E., & Batalova, J. (2013). *Frequently requested statistics on immigrants and immigration to the U.S. Migration Information Source, American Community Survey, U.S. Census Bureau (2011)*. Migration Policy Institute Data Hub. Retrieved from http://www.migrationpolicy.org/article/frequently-requested-statistics-immigrants-and-immigration-united states

Carnevale, A. P., Smith, N., & Strohl, J. (2010). *Help wanted: Projections of jobs and education requirements through 2018.* Washington, DC: Georgetown University Center on Education and the Workforce. Retrieved from http://www9 .georgetown.cdu/grad/gppi/hpi/cew/pdfs/state-levelanalysis-web.pdf

Casner-Lotto, J. (2011). *Increasing opportunities for immigrant students: Community college strategies for success.* Valhalla, NY: Community College Consortium for Immigrant Education, Westchester Community College. Retrieved from http:// www.cccie.org/images/stories/pdf/Increasing_Opportunities_for_Immigrant_ Students_2011.pdf

Casner-Lotto, J. (2012). *Dreaming big: What community colleges can do to help undocumented immigrant youth achieve their potential.* Valhalla, New York: Community College.Consortium for Immigrant Education, Westchester Community College. Retrieved from http://www.cccie.org/images/stories/DREAMING_ BIG_CCCIE_Report_9-2012.pdf

Century Foundation Task Force on Preventing Community Colleges from Becoming Separate and Unequal. (2013). *Bridging the higher education divide: Strengthening community colleges and restoring the American dream.* New York, NY: Century Foundation Press. Retrieved from http://tcf.org/assets/downloads/20130523-Bridging_the_Higher_Education_Divide-REPORT-ONLY.pdf

Charles A. Dana Center, Complete College America, Inc., Educational Commission of the States, & Jobs for the Future. (2012). *Core principles for transforming remedial education: A joint statement.* Retrieved from http://www.ecs.org/docs/ STATEMENTCorePrinciples.pdf

Community College Consortium for Immigrant Education. (2014). *Mission & objectives.* Retrieved from http://cccie.org/immigrant-education/mission-vision-guiding-principles

Development, Relief, and Education for Alien Minors (DREAM) Act. (2001). Retrieved from www.congress.gov/bill/107th-congress/senate-bill/1291

Erisman, W., & Looney, S. (2007). *Opening the door to the American dream: Increasing higher education access for immigrants.* Washington, DC: Institute for Higher Education Policy. Retrieved from http://www.ihep.org/%5Cassets%5Cfiles%5C/ publications/M-R/OpeningTheDoor.pdf

Gelatt, J., Batalova, J., & Lowell, B. L. (2006). *Immigrants and labor trends: The future, past, and present.* Washington, DC: Migration Policy Institute. Retrieved from http://www.migrationpolicy.org/research/immigrants-and-labor-force-trends-future-past-and-present

Hankin, J. (2012, October 10). Federal program offers hope for undocumented students. *Community College Daily.* Retrieved from http://www.ccdaily.com/Pages/ Campus-Issues/New-federal-program-offers-hope-for-undocumented-students .aspx

Horn, L., & Nevill, S. (2006). *Profile of undergraduates in U.S. postsecondary education institutions, 2003–04: With a special focus on community college students (NCES*

2006-184). U.S. Department of Education. Washington, DC: National Center for Education Statistics. Retrieved from http://nces.ed.gov/pubs2006/2006184_rev.pdf

Immigration Equality. (n.d.). *Deferred action for childhood arrivals (DACA).* Retrieved from http://immigrationequality.org/issues/immigration-basics/daca/

Immigration Policy Center. (2013). *A guide to S.744: Understanding the 2013 Senate immigration bill.* Retrieved from http://www.immigrationpolicy.org/special-reports/guide-s744-understanding-2013-senate-immigration-bill

Institute on Taxation and Economic Policy. (2013). *Unauthorized immigrants' state and local tax contributions.* Retrieved from http://www.itep.org/pdf/undocumentedtaxes.pdf

Learner Web. (2010). *The LearnerWeb Partnership: A multi-state support system for broadband adoption by digitally marginalized adults.* Portland State University. Retrieved from http://www.learnerweb.org/btop

Lumina Foundation. (2013). *A stronger nation through higher education: Visualizing data to help us achieve a big goal for college attainment.* Indianapolis, IN: Lumina Foundation. Retrieved from http://www.luminafoundation.org/publications/A_stronger_nation_through_higher_education-2013.pdf

Mui, Y. Q., and Jayakumar, A. (2013, September 6). Unemployment dips to 7.3 percent, but only 63% of Americans are in labor force. *Washington Post.* Retrieved from http://articles.washingtonpost.com/2013-09-06/business/41816402_1_labor-force-labor-department-job-market

National Conference of State Legislators. (2014). *Undocumented student tuition: State action.* Retrieved from http://www.ncsl.org/research/education/undocumented-student-tuition-state-action.aspx

National Immigration Law Center. (2014). *Basic facts about in-state tuition for undocumented immigrant students.* Washington, DC: National Immigration Law Center. Retrieved from http://www.nilc.org/basic-facts-instate.issues/education/

Nodine, T. (2010). *College success for all: How the Hidalgo Independent School District is adopting early college as a district-wide strategy.* Boston, MA: Jobs for the Future. Retrieved from http://www.jff.org/sites/default/files/publications/college_success_for_all.pdf

Papademetriou, D. G. (2013, March 12). The fundamentals of immigration reform. *The American Prospect.* Retrieved from http://prospect.org/article/fundamentals-immigration-reform

Passel, J. S., & Cohn, D. (2011). *Unauthorized immigrant population: National and state trends, 2010.* Washington, DC: Pew Hispanic Center. Retrieved from http://www.pewhispanic.org/files/reports/133.pdf

Pérez, W., Cortés, R. D., Ramos, K., & Coronado, H. (2010). "Cursed and blessed": Examining the socioemotional and academic experiences of undocumented Latina and Latino college students. *New Directions for Student Services, 131,* 35–51.

Pew Research Center. (2011). *Unauthorized immigrant population: National and state trends, 2010.* Retrieved from http://www.pewhispanic.org/2011/02/01/unauthorized-immigrant-population-brnational-and-state-trends-2010/

Pew Research Center. (2013). *Second-generation Americans: A portrait of the adult children of immigrants.* Retrieved from http://www.pewsocialtrends.org/files/2013/02/FINAL_immigrant_generations_report_2-7-13.pdf

Plyler v. Doe, 457 U.S. 202 (1982).

Teranishi, R. T., Suarez-Oroco, C., & Suarez-Oroco, M. (2011). Immigrants in community colleges. *The Future of Children, 21*(1). Princeton University and Brookings Institution. Retrieved from http://futureofchildren.org/futureofchildren/publications/docs/21_01_07.pdf

TheDream.US. (2014). *About our partner colleges.* Retrieved from http://thedream.us/colleges/about-our-partner-colleges/

8

ORGANIZATIONAL TRANSFORMATION FOR CATALYTIC SOCIAL CHANGE

Lara Kovacheff-Badke

Detroit, Michigan, was once a thriving metropolis of nearly two million people with the highest per capita income in the United States, a racially diverse residential composition, and multiple global influences (Humbad, 2007; Sugrue, 2014; U.S. Census Bureau, 1951). Located on 53 wooded acres in Detroit's northwest section, Marygrove College enjoyed a reputation of establishing educational programs and services that not only advanced its own institutional goals but also addressed societal and community interests. As signs of social and economic distress began to emerge in Detroit, Marygrove grappled with how its commitment to build a more just and humane world could translate into a positive impact for its students—and for the city that Marygrove called home.

Guided by strong convictions of social responsibility to serve both students and the Detroit community, Marygrove adopted an urban leadership vision focused on developing students' abilities to lead in urban communities. Unknown to us at the time, the mobilization of this new initiative would coincide with the largest national economic collapse since the Great Depression. As the ink was drying on the board of trustees' ratification of Marygrove's urban leadership strategic vision, Detroit lay on the cusp of increasingly devastating economic and social crises (Sugrue, 2014). Grappling with institutional and regional tensions, contradictions, and confusion of purpose, Marygrove forged ahead with its plan to connect urban leadership development, institutional culture, and community-university partnerships in an effort to support and foster positive community change (Marygrove College, n.d.a).

Marygrove's story offers new insights into how organizational transformation, centered on urban leadership development, occurred in a relatively small private college affected by the same challenges that engulfed its community. I tell the story from the lens of an external partner with the college. From 2012 to 2014, I was a member of the National Forum on Higher Education for the Public Good's consultation and research support team with Marygrove College's urban leadership development initiative. As a member of the Building Our Leadership in Detroit (BOLD) Council and one of the initiative's founding Teaching and Learning Leadership Team (TLLT) contributors (Core Values and Principles of Leadership), I was actively involved with the college's organizational transformation, most notably by exploring the integration of urban leadership principles into the curriculum. The lessons and pitfalls I raise in this chapter have application to all faculty, students, and administrators struggling to carry out educational change reforms involving multifaceted dimensions of higher education, especially when those efforts reach outside the institution and into the community. Understanding how the vision was championed amid administrator-faculty tensions (including inherent power dynamics and debate between supporters and naysayers) and organizational complexities (e.g., issues of leadership, change, curricular reform, university-community partnerships, and sustainability) is important to similar efforts. Readers will not only gain an understanding of how Marygrove integrated institutional and community engagement around a shared goal—producing meaningful community change that contributes to the public good—but also benefit from its lessons to adapt to their own context.

This chapter is organized as follows. A brief historical background of Marygrove College and the city of Detroit are presented. Marygrove's model of urban leadership development is then described. The bulk of Marygrove's story is offered in the section that follows on organizational transformation, where I set out the stages of BOLD's mobilization, implementation, and institutionalization. Finally, challenges and directions arising from Marygrove's undertaking are discussed and concluding remarks are presented. This chapter is offered as a reflection in order to help support other organizational transformation efforts confronting the multiple dimensions of education, leadership, and community change.

Historical Background: Marygrove College and the City of Detroit

Marygrove College

Marygrove College is a private, faith-based liberal arts college that has served increasingly varied and diverse constituencies for nearly 100 years, observing its commitment to holistic education that encourages students to act on behalf of justice. Scarce opportunities for women in higher education at the turn of the twentieth century inspired pioneering religious women affiliated with the Sisters, Servants of the Immaculate Heart of Mary (IHM), to establish Marygrove College in 1905 with the goal of advancing a curriculum of speaking, writing, and collaborative learning. The original mission was clear: To educate women in an environment that encouraged the development of the Christian values of love, compassion, justice, reconciliation, and concern for the poor. In 1927, the college moved from Monroe, Michigan, to Detroit and began to build what was to become a legacy of urban leadership.

Marygrove's evolution continued in the tumultuous decades leading up to the civil rights movement of the 1960s. In the late 1960s, significant middle-class flight to the suburbs raised questions about Marygrove's competitiveness and financial viability if it were to remain in the city of Detroit. Leaders at Marygrove rejected pressure from their own trustees to move out of Detroit.

Throughout the 1970s and 1980s, the college faced serious declines in enrollment. Demographically, the area surrounding Marygrove had changed from largely Caucasian to almost entirely African American. Over about two decades, Marygrove's student body changed to reflect these demographic changes, with African American single mothers in their 20s and 30s who attended school part-time making up the majority of the student population. In response to this new student population, Marygrove expanded to offer night and weekend courses, in order to appeal to working adults. In the late 1980s, Marygrove was invited to merge with two other Catholic colleges located in the city. Although there were brief talks to explore the possibilities of consolidation into a comprehensive Catholic city institution, Marygrove remained independent. By the mid-1990s, the college found itself on more secure financial footing and expanded its programs in teacher education, social justice, and performing arts (Bailey, 2003; Burkhardt, 1994; Deuben, 1992; Garsten, 1997; Marygrove College, n.d.f).

By 2006, Marygrove was strengthening its institutional dedication to social justice by systematically connecting leadership development and community change. Through a new integrative leadership development model, Marygrove proposed steeping leadership principles within the entire general education and discipline-specific curriculum by way of content, active learning pedagogy, and experiential learning. By infusing an urban leadership focus into the whole undergraduate curriculum and combining this focus with experiential learning requirements, students would not self-select into an optional leadership program. By connecting leadership development with community change, Marygrove announced its intention to serve as an institutional leader that not only offered degrees and programs that expanded students' understanding of contemporary issues, but also built the leadership skills necessary to lead urban communities similar to Detroit (Andreoli, Hammang-Buhl, & Badke, 2014; Marygrove College, n.d.f, n.d.k; Overton-Adkins, Hammang-Buhl, & Badke, 2014).

The City of Detroit

When Marygrove was first established in Detroit, the city was enjoying a period of great prosperity. The rise of the automotive industry saw Detroit's population soar to over 1.8 million in 1950, a million and a half more people than had resided in the city at the turn of the century (Humbad, 2007). After World War II, affordable mortgages in the suburbs lured Caucasians away from Detroit to own a piece of the American dream. The Big Three automotive manufacturers (General Motors [GM], Chrysler, and Ford Motor Company) that had spurred the population explosion in the first half of the century had run out of space to expand in the city so they built new plants in outlying suburbs where inexpensive land could support their plans for expansion.

Civil unrest throughout the country escalated in Detroit in the summer of 1967. Severe police brutality in African American neighborhoods, racial tensions, and economic problems contributed to a large-scale riot that, though centered in about 20 blocks in the city core, reverberated across the region. Detroit's image suffered a devastating blow, which led to an even greater exodus of businesses and jobs from the city. In the two decades that followed, Detroit experienced racial tensions, damaging housing practices, growing segregation, mass flight to the suburbs, and a plummeting tax base. Each of these factors contributed not only to growing unemployment and financial hardships, but to a glut of abandoned buildings that eventually became magnets for criminal activity (Boyle, 1999; Detroit Riots of 1967, n.d.; Humbad, 2007; Sugrue, 2014).

Detroit experienced a revival in the 1990s, with downtown redevelopment efforts that included restoration of city landmarks, subsidized professional sports with new downtown facilities, three new casino complexes with supporting hotels, and the relocation of GM's corporate headquarters to the downtown core (Sugrue, 2014; Williams, 2007). The downtown and midtown revitalization centered on a young and mostly White populace, however, with the economic and social resurgence largely unfelt in the city's less affluent neighborhoods (Doucet, 2015; Egner, 2012; Gottesdiener, 2014; Sugrue, 2014). On the heels of the downtown and midtown revivals, the first decade of the twenty-first century ushered in an economic and housing market collapse in Detroit neighborhoods (Sugrue, 2014). When Wall Street's financial crisis began sweeping the nation in and after 2008, the Great Recession that ensued resulted in even sharper declines in manufacturing and union jobs around Detroit. An unemployment rate twice that of the national average—21.6% versus 10.2%—rippled through metropolitan Detroit (National Poverty Center, 2012), leading to record home foreclosures, population loss, and growing municipal debt. Vacant properties and closing schools, churches, restaurants, even police stations overtook Detroit's already struggling working-class and poor neighborhoods. The unfortunate epilogue in the city's demise: Detroit filed for bankruptcy in 2013 (Sugrue, 2014).

Catalyst for Change: Urban Leadership at Marygrove College

Despite monumental decline, Detroit residents, visionaries, and supporters remained committed to fueling revitalization. Among the institutions spurring innovation was Marygrove College. Marygrove leaders knew they needed to assure the sustainability of the college's urban leadership development program to create the social change outcome envisioned. To do so, they sought to advance a culture in which faculty and staff held a deep appreciation for the linkages among education, leadership, and community change. The organization also needed to cultivate essential relationships and expand its service as an important community resource. Deliberately transforming itself to live up to its mission of promoting social justice, Marygrove administrators thoughtfully facilitated leadership development to enhance students' abilities to effect positive change in the complex, intertwined communities of metropolitan regions (Andreoli et al., 2014; Marygrove College, n.d.a, n.d.b, n.d.k; Overton-Adkins et al., 2014).

Marygrove's urban leadership model culminated in the integration of three interdependent initiatives. First, it used a distinctive immersion curriculum to develop graduates who understood community service as a civic responsibility. This proactive curriculum incorporated active learning techniques as students learned about leadership and gained a better understanding of the interwoven economic, political, social, environmental, and cultural dynamics that affect urban life (Andreoli et al., 2014; Marygrove College, n.d.a, n.d.k; Overton-Adkins et al., 2014). Second, it built community-based partnerships for neighborhood enhancement and empowerment. Two examples of this dimension are partnerships with St. Dominic and St. Leo community churches to raise awareness of modern civil rights issues shaping urban communities and work with Detroit's Cesar Chavez Academy High School to implement a lesson plan on Michigan's role in the antislavery movement (Marygrove College, n.d.b, n.d.k). Third, Marygrove served as an institutional leader by undertaking projects related to significant issues that affected the city of Detroit, such as increasing high school completion rates or reducing neighborhood blight (Marygrove College, n.d.d, n.d.k).

Organizational Transformation

Rooted in actions that advanced both neighborhood improvement and student leadership, Marygrove's leaders began to contemplate how the college might systematically improve the student learning experience while addressing critical social challenges. Following reasoned hunches based on notions of best practice, Marygrove's model of institutional transformation was largely intuitive in construction. In retrospect, Marygrove's experience can be seen as closely aligning with Curry's (1992) theory of organizational change. In Curry's typology, change occurs though a process of mobilization (in which the system is prepared for change), implementation (in which change is introduced to the system), and institutionalization (in which the system is stabilized in its change state). This section describes Marygrove's organizational transformation process. Though each of these three stages was sometimes interwoven throughout the life of the initiative, preparing, introducing, and internalizing change aptly characterize the transformation process underlying Marygrove's urban leadership initiative (Berman as cited in Lehming & Kane, 1981; Curry, 1992; St. John, 2009).

Mobilization: Preparing for Change

Visioning
Informally underlying its philosophical bedrock for decades, Marygrove's strategic vision of urban leadership had been present and developing momentum on campus for years before its formal adoption in 2006. Its urban location and long-standing commitment to Detroit underscored Marygrove's active role in collaborative social, cultural, political, educational, and economic

efforts designed to generate positive outcomes for Detroit and its citizens. Despite some gains, systemic and sustainable efforts among staunch community supporters were failing to stem the tide of urban decline and the deteriorating conditions that were experienced by residents in many of Detroit's communities. Determined to effect meaningful community change, Marygrove concentrated its efforts where it could have the greatest impact: its students.

Marygrove's leaders appreciated that to realize its urban leadership vision of creating students as agents for social change, it was important to collaborate with external networks committed to achieving positive long-term social change in the metropolitan Detroit region. Although Marygrove's presence in the city clearly presented opportunities to learn, serve, and lead, resident and community voices were integral to shaping the vision of neighborhood revitalization and improved outcomes for Detroit families. As an educational institution, Marygrove had control over curricular and cocurricular leadership development strategies designed to advance pedagogies of urban context, active learning, and community engagement. The college readily undertook the organizational changes that were necessary to develop a distinctive identity in which leadership and leadership development ultimately became part of the college's core values. However, it had less defined influence over the external environment. Working in conjunction with local and national partners whose missions similarly promoted community revitalization through leadership development and empowerment, Marygrove envisioned the creation of a network of institutional partners, each contributing something unique to the overall initiative (Andreoli et al., 2014; Marygrove College, n.d.; Overton-Adkins et al., 2014).

Many questions remained unanswered at this point in the visioning process. For example, resources would need to be invested, but how much and toward what? Where would the money come from? Benchmarks would be necessary to measure progress, yet how would success be determined? Though initially unclear, answers to these questions would begin to emerge as Marygrove's vision of urban leadership moved forward in 2007 with a faculty and staff transformational retreat intended to seek all voices.

Listening
The initial discussions of the proposed vision surfaced a range of responses. Ultimately, a gathering of so many interested and potentially affected people at the 2007 staff and faculty retreat raised more questions than it answered. Marygrove's leadership team listened intently as faculty and staff expressed both support and reservations in regard to the college's newly adopted

strategic vision of urban leadership. Much of the discussion centered on questions of what *urban leadership* would look like at Marygrove, and faculty and staff wondered how their roles might shape leadership development and practice. Participants listened as the new vision of shifting the core foundation of the institution was explained, and how this change in institutional thinking toward a focus on *urban* and *leadership* issues would materialize in a long-term, strategic commitment to positive community social change. Excitement surrounding the visibility and significance the urban leadership program could have throughout the campus and larger community continued to grow among faculty and staff (Marygrove College, n.d.c; Overton-Adkins, 2007).

To develop curricular, cocurricular, and human resource strategies that fulfilled the urban leadership vision, both faculty and staff began to understand that there would be radical shifts in the way they viewed their traditional roles. Forming partnerships with community residents and local organizations that would enable strategically coordinated and sustained community development initiatives would require some faculty and staff to step outside their comfort zones and perceived areas of expertise. Ultimately, Marygrove's urban leadership vision was endorsed by the board of trustees and strongly supported by the campus community because it resonated so deeply with the college's historical commitment to serve Detroit and its demonstrated ability to educate leaders. The college's focus on fostering urban leadership was a clear expression of how it wanted to manifest its mission and values in the twenty-first century (Marygrove College, n.d.c, n.d.k).

The retreat culminated in the formation of a working group to develop a grant proposal and advance a concept paper with an urban leadership development emphasis. BOLD emerged as the centerpiece of the college's innovative, creative, institution-wide initiative. With Marygrove's plans to improve outcomes for Detroit families through its investments in teaching, learning, scholarship, and community engagement for its students, bold measures would indeed be necessary to develop and foster comprehensive urban leadership programming at *all* levels of the college (Andreoli et al., 2014; Marygrove College, n.d.k; Overton-Adkins et al., 2014).

Planning
One of the early events that propelled the BOLD initiative forward was an infusion of funds from small planning grants awarded by the W.K. Kellogg Foundation, John S. and James L. Knight Foundation, and the Community Foundation for Southeast Michigan. Funding from these partners gave Marygrove the resources to formalize how BOLD would transform the

curriculum, connect leadership talent locally and globally, and promote systemic change to sustain leadership development. Guided by the values and beliefs of the college's founding IHM sponsor, all of the strategies implemented were intended to make Marygrove better at living its mission of educating and serving humanity with love, compassion, justice, and concern for the poor. It would now do so by creating a sustained capacity to develop hundreds of present and future leaders from and for Detroit. This growing cadre of distinctive leaders would contribute to social and economic improvements in the lives of Detroit families (Overton-Adkins et al., 2014).

Marygrove's organizational strategy to transform institutional capacity at curricular, faculty, and programmatic levels to create an informed, dedicated cadre of student and community leaders was unavoidably messy. Research into student leadership models in higher education revealed that Marygrove's completely integrative curricular immersion and community engagement model offered a unique urban leadership and social change vision in the field of college leadership development programs. Even though existing best practices and professional norms were taken into account, there were gaps in standards specifically articulated for this emerging area of urban leadership programming existing at *all* levels of college experience (Association of American Colleges & Universities, n.d.; H. S. Astin & A. W. Astin, 1996; A. W. Astin & H. S. Astin, 2000; Badke & Hernandez, 2013; Batchelder & Root, 1994; Calabrese, 1994; Clark, 2004; Connelly, 2009; Dean, 2009; Eyler & Giles, 1999; Finke, Ward, & Smith, 1992; International Leadership Association, 2009; Northouse, 2004; Southern Association of Colleges and Schools Commission on Colleges, 2012; Zimmerman-Oster & Burkhardt, 1999).

As Marygrove prepared the scaffolding necessary to develop a four-year iterative urban leadership experience for all students and meet its BOLD objectives, it concurrently began to align its strategic planning with a quality initiative for institutional improvement that was related to accreditation requirements. A three-year, $1.5 million grant from the W.K. Kellogg Foundation was one of the driving forces behind the end of the BOLD initiative mobilization phase and the beginning of the implementation phase. Applying for the grant had generated communication in preparation of the work and clarity in envisioning the outcomes, but receiving the grant validated the concept and started the clock ticking on executing the BOLD initiative (Overton-Adkins et al., 2014).

To help transition from planning to implementation, a road map of the overall change strategy was created to capture BOLD's comprehensive design and relationship connections. This map is reproduced as Figure 8.1. Providing a visual summary for the leadership team to share with trustees, faculty,

Figure 8.1. Graphic illustration of Marygrove's BOLD initiative.

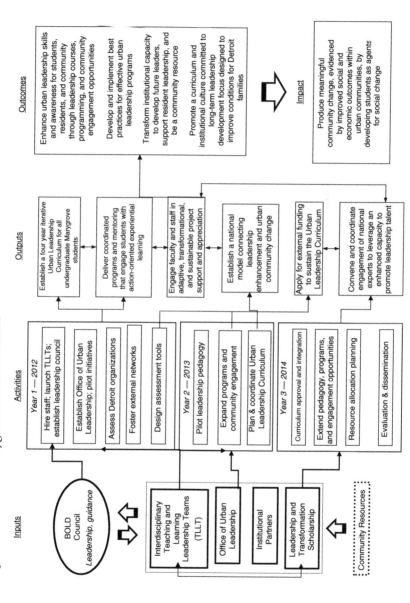

and staff provided not only a means to communicate the initiative's associations but also a framework to track progress and evaluate results. Marygrove embarked on the implementation stage in early 2012, putting into place new organizational structures to spur faculty and staff engagement and cultivate strategic partnerships to anchor neighborhood revitalization.

Implementation: Introducing Change

Once the vision for institutional transformation was in place, interlacing structural, procedural, and cultural change into college policy and behavior lay ahead. The following sections outline Marygrove's process of creating infrastructures and building support to advance the college's strategic initiative.

New Structures During the First and Second Waves of Implementation

Multiple, complex dimensions characterized the first phase of BOLD's implementation stage. Of foremost consideration were efforts to strengthen Marygrove's existing leadership culture across campus constituencies. It was also important to concurrently address how practical leadership skills throughout the general education and discipline-specific courses would be integrated. Expanding the existing curricular design to embody more explicit urban-centric leadership issues demanded not only faculty support but also a conscious integration of the needs and interests of community partners. The end result had to not only support principles that faculty were willing to teach but also link learning outcomes to leadership engagement opportunities that would contribute to positive community change (Overton-Adkins et al., 2014).

To address this first wave of priorities, three new organizational structures were created as catalysts for innovation. First, the BOLD Council, a new executive leadership team, was formed to provide strategic support and guidance for the initiative. Second, an Office of Urban Leadership was established to integrate campus community engagement projects and identify, cultivate, solicit, and steward community, institutional, and philanthropic partners through which internal and external talent and resources could be connected. Third, key proponents of the BOLD vision were selected to participate in faculty and staff TLLTs—interdisciplinary learning teams that would facilitate an understanding of the philosophies, norms, traditions, assumptions, and applications of Marygrove's BOLD ideal—spearheading the design and development of curricular initiatives (Andreoli et al., 2014; Marygrove College, n.d.a; Overton-Adkins et al., 2014).

First-generation TLLTs consisted of four groups. The Core Values and Principles of Leadership team explored the foundational urban values and principles that would guide the initiative, grounding them in best practices and scholarly validity. An Urban Subject Matters team explored urban-focused subject matter to infuse in the four-year undergraduate curriculum. An Artists-as-Activists team explored innovations in leadership pedagogy through which artists and educators could move beyond traditional written and spoken means in order to engage in civic leadership. The Participatory Action Research team rounded out the inaugural collaborative groups. This team explored how the BOLD model would support those most impacted by the intended community change and integrated those experiences and ideas into the design and methods contemplated in effecting change (Marygrove College, n.d.i). The leadership teams conducted most of their work over the summer of 2012, which was the first year of the Kellogg grant. Membership was by invitation and was based on existing expertise and interest. Both faculty and staff were compensated for their time on the TLLTs, although there was some debate regarding compensation equity and power differential of the different voices at the table. For example, faculty compensation was more clear-cut if participation on a TLLT was above regular workload, but the situation was less transparent regarding staff members who needed to negotiate with their supervisors as to whether participation on the committee was deemed part of their regular work. True to its social justice values, Marygrove addressed the inherent institutional contradictions by articulating a fairer compensation structure in time for the second-generation TLLT groups being formed (Marygrove College: BOLD Council, 2013).

The work of the first-generation TLLTs led to system-wide foundational elements that were necessary for BOLD to move forward. Progress was communicated to faculty and staff through workshops, lunchtime learning sessions, receptions, and a BOLD retreat. New proposals were solicited for second-generation TLLTs to design innovative leadership development curricula. In the summer of 2013, four additional TLLTs emerged: Feminist Leadership, Non-Traditional Student Leadership, Social Entrepreneurship, and Sustainability and Ecology (Marygrove College, n.d.i). Notably, as opposed to members being hand selected as had occurred with the first-generation TLLTs, second-generation TLLT members self-selected based on their commitment to the project and interest in strategically coordinating additional curricular and cocurricular programming, enhancing the intergenerational nature and sustainability of the TLLT.

Funding from the grant enabled members to be compensated under the newly revised and fairer compensation model. The revised compensation model alleviated some of the inherent power dynamics between participating faculty and staff, with compensation criteria for TLLT staff (whether participation in TLLTs was part of their regular employment expectations or additional compensable, contributions) more clearly delineated. Work across the eight learning teams led to the creation of pilot courses that were linked to BOLD's urban leadership principles and the college's new BOLD student and institutional learning outcomes. Although pilot courses were successful within their departments, the intentionally focused, iterative, and cohesive infusion of urban leadership experiences across the Marygrove curriculum was not yet a reality.

As the first year of the grant drew to a close with curricular and community change initiatives gaining momentum, administrator-faculty tensions began to mount. Clearly, building internal project support was the next priority to be addressed in order to ensure true institutional transformation and sustainability.

Faculty and Staff Engagement

To achieve BOLD's objectives of enhancing urban leadership to produce meaningful community change, deep and widespread faculty and staff engagement was necessary. Faculty support was essential to both curricular and cultural change. As powerful change agents on campus, faculty were well positioned to initiate transformative leadership, model leadership principles, and establish a change agenda in their classrooms. Active engagement by staff was also crucial to the initiative's overall success as their involvement and expertise was needed to create a sustainable infrastructure of campus-community engagement opportunities, supportive community partnerships, and successful student projects. Bringing people on board as implementation materialized was relatively straightforward. Embedding BOLD's core values into college culture, however, would be more delicate.

During the first year of the Kellogg implementation grant, faculty and staff involved in the TLLTs played an active role in building awareness, understanding, commitment, and action among colleagues. Discussions to inform the campus community of BOLD's developments and to receive feedback occurred in a number of ways. Voluntary and mandatory presentations were offered to share information. Departmental meetings focusing on BOLD expanded support, raised challenges, and facilitated integration of the college's urban leadership design. Dissenting opinions triggered a healthy exchange of ideas concerning the need and methods of integrating urban leadership principles into the curriculum. Some faculty and staff voiced concerns over adopting a so-called trendy program in an area that lacked empirical evidence of long-term success. At the other end of the spectrum, champions of the vision fueled support through newly piloted projects that illustrated practical applications of the initiative's possibilities. Faculty, staff, and students involved in the new projects exhibited a palpable enthusiasm and energy. Open discussions during faculty assemblies, lunch and learn sessions, and surveys enabled faculty and staff to voice opinions, both good and bad, to inform the college's decision makers (Andreoli et al., 2014; Overton-Adkins et al., 2014).

At the beginning of this first year of formal implementation, faculty and staff culture surrounding the leadership principles largely consisted of the belief that the principles would limit course content and would be too onerous to implement. However, opinions began to shift as a result of the faculty engagement work occurring on many levels throughout the college. As understanding and clarity regarding the newly sanctioned urban leadership principles grew, faculty increasingly embraced the use of those principles to enhance the content of their courses. Differentiation between principles that were inherently present in course themes and those that were capable of being integrated at a deeper, explicit level began to take shape. In fact, in a college-wide survey designed to measure faculty self-assessment of urban leadership principles that were most saliently addressed in courses, faculty indicated that they possessed a clear understanding of BOLD's urban leadership principles and were able to implement it in such forms as lectures, activities, and modeling behavior. The results of the survey suggested that by the end of the second year of project implementation, a cultural shift in attitudes had already begun. Marygrove faculty had largely embraced the college's urban leadership direction and were on the right track to fully and explicitly integrating urban leadership principles into the curriculum (Marygrove College, 2014; Overton, Badke & Hernandez, 2014).

The faculty curriculum mapping survey provided baseline information for the college to make important course connections to BOLD objectives, analyze the frequency and extent of urban and leadership matters in the current curriculum, examine course and activity sequencing, explore gaps, and suggest improvements. Evidence of deep and widespread faculty and staff engagement was seen in curriculum mapping and analyses of urban subject matters that were being conducted in academic departments. Curriculum redesign, system-wide integration, and outcome assessment were also formally under way in other college processes (Overton-Adkins et al., 2014). For example, the Curriculum Review Committee and General Education Committee began evaluating and formalizing suggested curricular recommendations. An Assessment Committee proposed urban leadership student learning outcomes and initiated assessment protocols. In collaboration with the Office of Urban Leadership, student development and institutional advancement staff strategized on the community development and sustainability aspects of the initiative. Despite conflicting opinions from some constituents, transformational change was being realized. In fact, a faculty vote to approve the new institutional learning outcomes for BOLD passed with an impressive margin of 58 to 2 in favor of the changes. Such positive developments throughout this process and within other facets of campus life reflected measurable gains in advancing a culture of appreciation among education, leadership, and community change (Andreoli et al., 2014; Marygrove College, 2014; Overton et al., 2014; Overton-Adkins et al., 2014).

The progression of the college's internal goals of embedding an understanding of teaching and learning leadership in order to facilitate the creation of curricular and cocurricular innovation was of paramount importance internally. This internal progress was enhanced by simultaneously strengthening external support and active engagement of a variety of partnerships that were necessary to developing skilled urban leaders capable of effecting social change.

Strategic Partnerships

External support and active engagement with community partners were woven throughout the fabric of the BOLD initiative. Academic partners such as the National Clearinghouse for Leadership Programs and the University of Michigan's National Forum on Higher Education for the Public Good (National Forum) informed Marygrove's understanding of existing scholarship and best practices in higher education leadership programs. Formative Evaluation Research Associates (FERA), an independent evaluator that collaborated with Marygrove, utilized participatory action research methodology to assess faculty engagement and learning opportunities. Survey results from both National Forum curriculum mapping data of urban leadership principles used by faculty and FERA data from project evaluations identified strengths and gaps in curriculum, programming, learning outcomes, project support, faculty engagement, institutional culture, and overall perception of the initiative and its implementation. This information was valuable because it provided not only crucial data on which decisions could be based but also a baseline from which to measure future progress and evidence of success (Andreoli et al., 2014; Overton-Adkins et al., 2014).

Grassroots partnerships between Marygrove and community-based organizations generated alliances to revitalize neighborhoods in and around the college. Collaborations on various educational, empowerment, and nontraditional leadership development programming tackled such issues as academic performance and personal development among Detroit youth and emerging young leaders. Without strong university-community partnerships from community councils, clergy, academic institutions serving the city, advocacy groups, leadership alliances, regional chambers, and data networks, Marygrove's initiative could neither be integrated throughout Detroit as the college had envisioned, nor easily sustained past the initial implementation funding (Marygrove College, n.d.b, n.d.c).

Challenging its students to "BOLD-ly" expand the institution's efforts to positively impact the lives of Detroit youth, the Office of Urban Leadership funded collaborative student-led community projects. Building both urban leadership educational and leadership skills, students developed and nurtured a number of new partnerships and community-campus engagement opportunities, including partnering with urban schools and culturally specific community organizations to promote educational skills and college readiness in area youth. Among other projects, Marygrove students developed and managed microfunding initiatives with area entrepreneurs, conducted fund-raising for global health initiatives, raised awareness of social and political conditions in urban environments, initiated peer-based recovery support networks, advanced professional development opportunities, and fostered new mentoring relationships (Marygrove College, n.d.b, n.d.c).

It was evident that building and sustaining strong community relationships were essential components of Marygrove's BOLD vision. The Office of Urban Leadership provided the institutional foundation necessary to support pedagogies of active learning and community engagement. By connecting leadership development with community change initiatives, this resource proved to be integral to facilitating faculty and student connections to action-oriented urban experiential learning. Coordinating programming over time to benefit and sustain collaborative partnerships and addressing issues of urban change, the Office of Urban Leadership and Department of Academic Affairs began tracking engaged learning through specialized reporting software (Overton-Adkins et al., 2014).

The Community Benefit Inventory for Social Accountability for Education (CBISA) software enabled Marygrove, the first college in Michigan to use the software, to measure the impact its students were having on the community and to share data and stories with its constituents and partners. Moving beyond a series of successful curricular and cocurricular engagements, Marygrove utilized this resource to enrich community collaborations by more explicitly connecting its leadership development scholarship and programming with advancements in community well-being. Tremendous gains were made in purposefully connecting institutional initiatives to neighborhood revitalization and serving the public good during the implementation surge in year two of the grant (Overton-Adkins et al., 2014).

Project momentum was temporarily slowed when two key BOLD leaders departed the college in the beginning of year three. However, given the importance of project champions in sustaining both internal and external relationships and advancing institutional knowledge, this change in personnel created only a short-lived blip as the college ramped up for its final phase of the initial vision: institutionalizing the change in culture and innovations, or risk the initiative coming to an end.

Institutionalization: Internalizing Change

Organizational models, strategies, and processes expounding on the ways institutional change occurs are plentiful (Berquist, 1992; Hearn, 1996; Kezar & Eckel, 2002; Levy & Merry, 1986; Lindquist, 1978; Swindler, 1986; Tierney, 1988, 1991). Marygrove did not adopt a formal theory of change or conceptual model at the outset of its urban leadership development vision. However, as the project unfolded, its evolution began to parallel a simple three-stage typology of change as delineated by Curry (1992).

In the first stage of mobilization, through campus-wide early conceptualization and planning, subsequently infused by seed money that enabled planning to evolve into the creation of a concept paper and articulated vision for the project, Marygrove leaders prepared the system for change. Once the board of trustees approved the urban leadership strategic vision, work progressed through an implementation grant that proved to be a major catalytic influence in moving the initiative forward. The second stage of institutional change emerged through implementation. In this stage, change was introduced into the system through the creation of new infrastructure supports, including interdisciplinary faculty and staff TLLTs, the Office of Urban Leadership, communication supports, and the advancement of strategic partnerships internal and external to the college. As the college's commitment to fostering urban leadership became tangible and visible to key stakeholders, it entered the third stage of institutionalization, in which the system became stabilized in its changed state.

Marygrove's organizational transformation had progressed beyond idea generation and piloted projects to the successful execution of activities that anchored neighborhood revitalization. Institutionalization of the holistic urban leadership vision was now backed by overwhelming faculty support of BOLD's institutional learning outcomes. The final year of the Kellogg grant saw the creation of over 80 pilot projects that purposefully integrated experiential learning with general education and programmatic influences (Overton et al., 2014).

In addition to these projects that bridged curricular and cocurricular experiences, institutionalization efforts permeated the college's culture in other ways. Cocurricular institutionalization, led by the director of the new Success Center, developed services to guide, inspire, and inform students' experiences at Marygrove. Urban leadership basic content for both current and incoming students was advanced through staff and faculty teams providing coaching and skill development. Success coaches were trained in facilitation, mentoring, tutoring, and career achievement. These specialists then worked with students in first-year experience courses, orientation, and bridge programs. Linking awareness of self, awareness of others, understanding of an increasingly urban world, and community leadership with skills development and success coaching, students would increase their competence and effectiveness as urban leaders well prepared for meaningful and impactful careers (Fike, El-Sayed, & Tsukayama, 2014).

Led by the dean of faculty, additional efforts in curriculum institutionalization were seen through advancements in working with division chairs and faculty to build assessment tools and enhance commitments to continuous curricular improvement. In order to ensure sustainability by developing faculty exploration and innovation in pedagogy that connected leadership development with community change, the college created a professional development Center for Excellence in Teaching and Learning. The center not only captured the pedagogies developed through the grant work's piloted initiatives of the TLLTs and participatory action research practices but also supported the development of its faculty's scholarship on urban subject matters and pedagogy, strengthening the college's emergence as a national leader connecting leadership enhancement with urban community change (Fike et al., 2014).

Marygrove faculty and staff have shared insight and knowledge gained through the BOLD project with other local and national higher education professionals, scholars, community, and industry. Presentations at the American Association of Colleges and Universities (Andreoli et al., 2014), Higher Learning Commission of the North Central Association (Overton-Adkins et al., 2014), Yes We Must Coalition (Andreoli & Hammang-Buhl, 2014; McKenzie-Bennett, 2014), Association for Psychological Science (Scher, 2014), and Association for the Study of Higher Education (Badke & Hernandez, 2013) have raised the level of dialogue and action. Having their work well received and generating constructive deliberation on the subject of urban leadership has helped to strengthen the appreciation of faculty and staff in regard to the links among education, leadership, and community change, which has further strengthened Marygrove's transformational change and alignment while simultaneously broadening awareness of BOLD within the academic community.

Future Plans: Challenges and Direction

Marygrove's vision of organizational transformation for catalytic social change is well under way. Faculty and staff have emerged as leaders in advancing the college's iterative undergraduate urban leadership curriculum and guiding the coordinated programming and mentoring necessary to support students' success as urban leaders. Students are becoming equipped with urban leadership skill sets, knowledge, expanded networks, and the desire to succeed as effective leaders in their communities. Having met its initial milestones, Marygrove now looks to focus on other areas that would contribute to advancing the college's strategic urban leadership vision and expand institutional capacity.

Among the biggest challenges Marygrove experienced in mobilizing, implementing, and institutionalizing its urban leadership vision were (a) the time constraints that were imposed by ongoing obligations of existing programs, teaching loads, and serving the administrative needs of its 2,000 students and (b) the financial sustainability of mounting course activity, meaningful opportunities for student engagement, community collaborations, and chances for local organizations and residents to build leadership skills. Given the busy workload faculty and staff balance, with cyclical demands of the academic calendar and professional activities, the "heavy lifting" of the urban leadership initiative occurred during the summer. Sustaining the momentum once the academic year began proved difficult. Marygrove leaders have yet to find an easy organizational solution to the dilemma of having more to do than time allows.

Economically, the Kellogg-funded implementation grant generated clarity for the vision (establishing a national model connecting urban leadership development with community change), subsidized institutional and infrastructure supports (creating the Office of Urban Leadership, Center for Excellence in Teaching and Learning, and Success Center, to name a few), and served as a catalyst in advancing pilot curricular and experiential learning projects (revising First-Year Experience courses, implementing a new summer bridge program for incoming students, and mentoring Detroit youth to expand educational attainment), but the funding period is drawing to a close. Key deliverables of the initial three-year implementation plan have been met and have even been exceeded in some areas. Additional grant support will certainly be sought to maintain momentum, but any such award is uncertain. There could be some allocation of internal funds to sustain the project; however, levels needed to maintain the current initiative and grow into contemplated directions are unknown. What is certain is that the leaders at Marygrove College remain committed to, and have constituent support for, the long-term vision connecting leadership development with positive community change (Fike et al., 2014).

In order to proactively advance the needs of its own constituents and the community it serves, Marygrove's leaders continue to focus on three areas of improvement. The first area it seeks to enhance is communication. Through evaluation feedback loops, Marygrove recognized that its own efforts at communicating internally and externally were deficient. The irony of this gap is that "effective communication" was one of the 14 urban leadership principles adopted by BOLD. As year three of the implementation grant draws to a close, Marygrove is taking steps to improve its communication strategies, especially with faculty and staff (notably through the newly formed Success Center and Center for Excellence in Teaching and Learning), as academic reorganization accelerates (Fike et al., 2014).

A second area to develop involves engaging all faculty, including adjuncts, in curricular review and redesign for continuous improvement and sustainability. Much of the baseline curricular data on urban leadership understanding and integration was derived from the curriculum mapping effort undertaken during year two. Although the mapping results indicated faculty possessed insightful and practical understanding of the principles and their curricular integration, not all faculty participated in the survey. Many of the critical responses from the survey came from faculty already deeply engaged in BOLD work. How best to address different levels of engagement and understanding of the urban leadership vision among academic units and individuals is a challenge Marygrove has begun to address through the dean of faculty's work with division chairs and faculty. Immediate next steps to narrow the involvement gap include increasing workshops on community engagement, curriculum, and pedagogy; increasing exposure to urban leadership subject matter and pedagogy; and continuing to provide professional development opportunities to improve capacity and promote the institutionalization of urban leadership principles (Fike et al., 2014; Marygrove College, 2014).

Finally, despite significant advances connecting student leadership engagement opportunities with BOLD's learning outcomes, the third area is a need to more explicitly integrate urban leadership principles throughout the entire curriculum and coordinate cocurricular activities with them. Great strides have been made in integrating urban leadership values and principles in an array of departments across the college, particularly in political science, social work, business, social justice, performing arts, visual arts, science, math, general education, and discipline-specific capstone courses. Other areas, however, have been slower to embrace the urban leadership focus. Work has been initiated with those departments to consider strategies for improving how principles might be conveyed more purposefully and project support enhanced. Similarly, the important cocurricular work connecting leadership development with community change initiatives can be more explicitly integrated with student learning outcomes. Although significant contributions to neighborhood revitalization are evident, the ways in which students' urban leadership skills are developed are not always explicitly connected to engagement and outcomes. The use of CBISA software tools, as well as the college's Success Center initiatives, will be instrumental in measuring impact both on the community and on student learning (Fike et al., 2014; Marygrove College, n.d.b, n.d.e; Overton-Adkins et al., 2014; Persley, 2014).

Marygrove's organizational transformation has created significant ripples in Detroit, from alleviating blight to encouraging elementary and middle school student engagement and academic enrichment to supporting business development for community entrepreneurs (Fike et al., 2014; Marygrove College: BOLD Projects, n.d., Community/Blight, n.d.; Persley, 2014). Infusing urban leadership principles throughout the general education and discipline-specific curricula for all undergraduate students (as opposed to delivering alternative models to students who self-select or offering limited leadership courses), Marygrove has combined content, active learning pedagogy, and coordinated experiential learning as the cornerstone of its national urban leadership student development model.

The model's goal is clear: To focus on the skills necessary to improve social and economic outcomes within urban communities. By graduating students with such leadership skills, Marygrove has witnessed its alumni creating positive change within the communities they serve. Although Marygrove has always espoused a mission-based commitment to service, this model moves beyond merely providing optional experiential learning components to infusing leadership values and principles into every aspect of the Marygrove College experience. Grounded in standards from the American Association of Colleges and Universities (among them, the rubrics of civic engagement, creative thinking, critical thinking, ethical reasoning, global learning, integrative thinking, intercultural knowledge and competence, teamwork, written and oral communication), as well as those from the Council for the Advancement of Standards in Higher Education's functional area programming and service standards, Marygrove has implemented a backward design process to create rubrics for both student learning and institutional outcomes of urban leadership principles (Andreoli et al., 2014; Association of American Colleges & Universities, 2007; Dean, 2012). As a result, students better understand who they are, how they relate to others, how to understand an increasingly urban world, and how they can lead in their communities. As its students carry their leadership skills into the community to be agents of social change, Marygrove's BOLD program has indeed connected urban leadership development, institutional culture, and university-community partnerships to produce meaningful community improvement.

As one considers this project's connection to the focus of this book, it is possible to miss the *engagement* if defined narrowly. Our conceptualization of engaged research encompasses opportunities for collaboration and mutually beneficial capacity building that has positive outcomes for the community we are working in and with. Marygrove's curriculum work is ultimately about engagement with its community. As researchers interested in connecting to community, it made perfect sense that our joining this work was in many respects working toward our goals. We are learning from this the need to think beyond what we as individual faculty and researchers can do and to see that collaboration may mean advancing someone else's efforts focused on community connections.

References

Andreoli, J., & Hammang-Buhl, J. (2014, April). *Building Our Leadership in Detroit (BOLD): Designing a comprehensive urban leadership curriculum.* Poster presentation at the Yes We Must Coalition, College Success for All.

Andreoli, J., Hammang-Buhl, J., & Badke, L. K. (2014, March). *Building Our Leadership in Detroit (BOLD): Designing a comprehensive urban leadership curriculum.* Poster presentation at the American Association of Colleges & Universities Annual Conference, Chicago, IL.

Association of American Colleges & Universities. (n.d.). *Essential learning outcomes.* Retrieved from https://www.aacu.org/leap/essential-learning-outcomes

Association of American Colleges & Universities. (2007). *College learning for the new global century: A report from the National Leadership Council for Liberal Education & America's Promise.* Retrieved from https://www.aacu.org/sites/default/files/files/LEAP/GlobalCentury_final.pdf

Astin, A. W., & Astin, H. S. (2000). *Leadership reconsidered: Engaging higher education in social change.* Battle Creek, MI: W. K. Kellogg Foundation.

Astin, H. S., & Astin, A. W. (1996). *A social change model of leadership development guidebook, version 3.* Los Angeles: University of California, Los Angeles. Retrieved from http://www.heri.ucla.edu/PDFs/pubs/ASocialChangeModelofLeadership-Development.pdf

Badke, L. K., & Hernandez, E. (2013, November). *Student leadership development programs: Student transformation as agents for social change.* Paper presented at the Association for the Study of Higher Education Annual Conference, St. Louis, MO.

Bailey, L. (2003, July 1). Fay accompli: After leading merger of colleges, University of Detroit Mercy president leaves formidable financial, academic legacy. *Crain's Detroit Business, 3.*

Batchelder, T. H., & Root, S. (1994). Effects of an undergraduate program to integrate academic learning and service: Cognitive, prosocial cognitive, and identity outcomes. *Journal of Adolescence, 17,* 341–355.

Berquist, W. (1992). *The four cultures of the academy.* San Francisco, CA: Jossey-Bass.

Boyle, K. (1999). *After the rainbow sign: Jerome Cavanagh and 1960s Detroit.* Retrieved from http://www.reuther.wayne.edu/exhibits/cavanagh.html

Burkhardt, J. (1994). Getting to yes on a merger. *Planning for Higher Education, 22*(3), 19–24.

Calabrese, R. L. (1994). Teaching students to be part of a democratic society. *The Education Digest, 59*(8), 54.

Clark, D. R. (2004). *The art and science of leadership.* Retrieved from http://nwlink .com/~donclark/leader/leader.html

Connelly, R. J. (2009). Introducing a culture of civility in first-year college classes. *The Journal of General Education, 58*(1).

Curry, B. (1992). *Instituting enduring innovations: Achieving continuity of change in higher education.* ASHE-ERIC Higher Education Report No. 7. Washington, DC: George Washington University, School of Education and Human Development.

Dean, L. A. (Ed.). (2009). *CAS learning and development outcomes* (7th ed.). Washington, DC: Council for the Advancement of Standards in Higher Education.

Dean, L. A. (Ed.). (2012). *CAS Professional Standards for Higher Education* (8th ed.). Washington, DC: Council for the Advancement of Standards in Higher Education.

Detroit Riots of 1967. (n.d.). Retrieved from Rutgers University website: http://www.67riots.rutgers.edu/d_index.htm

Deuben, C. J. (1992). Factors facilitating or inhibiting institutional merger among three Catholic institutions of higher education. *Dissertation Abstract International, 53*(12), 4224A. (UMI No. AAT 9310643).

Doucet, B. (2015, February 17). Detroit's gentrification won't give poor citizens reliable public services. *Guardian.* Retrieved from http://www.theguardian.com/public-leaders-network/2015/feb/17/detroit-gentrification-poverty-public-services-race-divide

Egner, D. O. (2012, April 18). What Turin, Italy has that Detroit needs. *Huffington Post.* Retrieved from http://www.huffingtonpost.com/david-o-egner/detroit-innovation_b_1434807.html

Eyler, J., & Giles, D. E., Jr. (1999). *Where's the learning in service learning?* San Francisco, CA: Jossey-Bass.

Fike, D., El-Sayed, J., & Tsukayama, R. (2014, July 14). *Building Our Leaders in Detroit (BOLD) update.* Oral report to the W. K. Kellogg Foundation. Marygrove College, Detroit, MI.

Finke, R. A., Ward, T. B., & Smith, S. M. (1992). *Creative cognition: Theory, research, and applications.* Cambridge, MA: MIT Press.

Garsten, E. (1997). Detroit's "Great Warrior," Coleman Young, dies. *CNN.* Retrieved from http://www.cnn.com/US/9711/29/young.obit.pm/

Gottesdiener, L. (2014, November 16). How Detroit is splitting into two cities for rich and poor: A journey across a city divided post-bankruptcy. *Alternet.* Retrieved from http://www.alternet.org/civil-liberties/how-detroit-splitting-two-cities-rich-and-poor

Hearn, J. C. (1996). Transforming U.S. higher education: An organizational perspective. *Innovative Higher Education, 21,* 141–151.

Humbad, S. N. (2007). Detroit population history 1900–2000. *Somacon.* Retrieved from http://www.somacon.com/p469.php

International Leadership Association. (2009). *Guiding questions: Guidelines for leadership education programs.* Retrieved from http://www.ila-net.org/communities/LC/GuidingQuestionsFinal.pdf

Kezar, A., & Eckel, P. D. (2002). The effect of institutional culture on change strategies in higher education: Universal principles or culturally responsive concepts? *The Journal of Higher Education, 7*(4), 435–460.

Komives, S., Lucas, N., & McMahon, T. R. (2007). *Exploring leadership: For college students who want to make a difference* (2nd ed.). San Francisco, CA: Jossey-Bass.

Lehming, R., & Kane, M. (Eds.). (1981). *Improving schools: Using what we know.* Beverly Hills, CA: SAGE.

Levy, A., & Merry, U. (1986). *Organizational transformation: Approaches, strategies, theories.* New York, NY: Praeger.

Lindquist, J. (1978). *Strategies for change.* Washington, DC: Council for Independent Colleges.

Marygrove College. (n.d.a) *About BOLD.* Retrieved from http://urbanleadership.marygrove.edu/about-us/bold-building-leadership.html

Marygrove College. (n.d.b) *BOLD projects.* Retrieved from http://urbanleadership.marygrove.edu/about-us/bold-building-leadership/bold-projects.html

Marygrove College. (n.d.c) *BOLDRetreat.* Retrieved from http://urbanleadership.marygrove.edu/about-us/bold-building-leadership/bold-retreat.html

Marygrove College. (n.d.d) *Community/Blight.* Retrieved from http://www.marygrove.edu/home/news/community/1311-blight-targeted-in-the-marygrove-college-campus-neighborhood.html

Marygrove College. (n.d.e) *Community partnerships.* Retrieved from http://urban-leadership.marygrove.edu/about-us/the-office-of-urban-leadership/community-partnerships.html

Marygrove College. (n.d.f) *History of Marygrove.* Retrieved from http://www.marygrove.edu/home/who-we-are/history.html

Marygrove College. (n.d.g) *IHM sponsorship.* Retrieved from http://www.marygrove.edu/home/who-we-are/ihm-sponsorship.html

Marygrove College. (n.d.h) *Our mission.* Retrieved from http://www.marygrove.edu/home/who-we-are/mission.html

Marygrove College. (n.d.i) *Teaching and learning teams.* Retrieved from http://urbanleadership.marygrove.edu/about-us/bold-building-leadership/teaching-and-learning-teams.html

Marygrove College. (n.d.j) *Urban leader.* Retrieved from http://www.marygrove.edu/home/urban-leadership-mainmenu/marygrove-urban-leader.html

Marygrove College. (n.d.k) *Urban leadership*. Retrieved from http://www .urbanleadership.marygrove.edu/about-us/bold-building-leadership.html

Marygrove College. (2012, April 9) *Press Release*. Retrieved from http://www .marygrove.edu/home/news/press-releases/1173-marygrove-college-to-revise-curriculum-to-develop-urban-leadership.html

Marygrove College. (2013, Winter/Spring) *BOLD Council*. Unpublished meeting minutes and council communications.

Marygrove College. (2014, June) *Urban Leadership Principles Faculty Survey*. Unpublished report to Marygrove College's BOLD Council from the University of Michigan Research Team.

McKenzie-Bennett, C. (2014, April). *Building resiliency: The gentleman's roundtable*. Poster presented at the Yes We Must Coalition, College Success For All.

National Poverty Center. (2012, March). *Employment problems in the wake of the Great Recession: Findings from the Michigan Recession and Recovery Study (Policy Brief No. 30)*. Ann Arbor, MI. Retrieved from http://www.npc.umich.edu/ publications/policy_briefs/brief30/NPC%20Policy%20Brief%20-%2030.pdf

Northouse, P. (2004). *Leadership theory and practice*. Thousand Oaks, CA: SAGE.

Overton-Adkins, B. (2007, May 3). *The pedagogy of leadership in an urban context: Re-building an institutional vision of its urban leadership*. Retreat presentation, Marygrove College. Detroit, MI.

Overton-Adkins, B., Hammang-Buhl, J., & Badke, L. K. (2014, April). *Urban leadership as catalytic change: Strategic planning and the quality initiative*. Poster presented at the Higher Learning Commission Annual Conference, Chicago, IL.

Overton, B., Badke, L. K., & Hernandez, E. (2014, August). *Advancing Marygrove's pedagogy of leadership in an urban context: Urban leadership principles survey data and analysis*. Faculty workshop presentation, Marygrove College, Detroit, MI.

Persley, M. (2014, January 29). *The community connections-Marygrove College partnership: A powerful collaboration* [Web log post]. Retrieved from http:// leadershiplearning.org/blog/miriam-persley/2014-01-29/communityconnections-marygrove-college-partnership-powerful-collaboration

Rucker, W. C., & Upton, J. N. (2007). *Encyclopedia of American race riots: Greenwood milestones in African American history. Vol. I: A-M*. Westport, CT: Greenwood Press.

Scher, D. (2014, May). *Embedding urban leadership principles into psychology courses*. Poster presentation at Teaching Conference, Association for Psychological Science, San Francisco, CA.

Southern Association of Colleges and Schools Commission on Colleges. (2012). *The principles of accreditation: Foundations for quality enhancement* (5th ed.). Decatur, GA: Author.

St. John, E. (2009). *College organization and professional development: Integrating moral reasoning and reflective practice*. New York, NY: Routledge.

Stamm, A. (2014, August 28). Detroit is a national model for "a remarkable economic resurgence," *Time* says. *Deadline Detroit*. Retrieved from http://www .deadlinedetroit.com/articles/10265/detroit_is_a_national_model_for_a_ remarkable_economic_resurgence_time_says#.VK6yvkv8tGY

Sugrue, T. J. (2014). *The origins of the urban crisis: Race and inequality on postwar Detroit.* Princeton, NJ: Princeton University Press.

Swindler, A. (1986). Culture in action: Symbols and strategies. *American Sociological Review, 51*(2), 273–286.

Tierney, W. (1988). Organizational culture in higher education. *The Journal of Higher Education, 59,* 2–21.

Tierney, W. (1991). Organizational culture in higher education: Defining the essentials. In M. Peterson (Ed.), *ASHE reader on organization and governance* (pp. 126–139). Needham Heights, MA: Ginn Press.

United States Census Bureau. (1951). *Statistical abstract of the United States, 1951.* Retrieved from http://www2.census.gov/prod2/statcomp/documents/1951-02.pdf

Williams, C. (2007, September 13). Detroit casinos deal city urban renewal. *USA Today.* Retrieved from http://www.usatoday.com/news/nation/2007-09-13-315133439_x.htm

Zimmerman-Oster, K., & Burkhardt, J. (1999). *Leadership in the making: Impact and insights from leadership development programs in U.S. colleges and universities.* Battle Creek, MI: W. K. Kellogg Foundation.

REFLECTIVE NARRATIVE

A View From the Hyphen:
Bridging Theory and Practice

Will Cherrin

My day at University Preparatory High School (UPHS)[1] usually began before I had the chance to put my book bag down. Over my heavy breathing from ascending four flights of stairs I was often addressed with "Mr. Cherrin, do you have another permission slip for the college trip?" or "Mr. Cherrin, I have advisory first period, can we register for the SAT?" My answer was always the same. Maybe it's that I just didn't know how to say no, which is true. Or maybe, like the majority of my peers, my students were the most important part of my life.

For three years I served as the director of the College Preparation and Leadership Program (CPLP) at UPHS. Though my staff and I were employed by a nonprofit, we were completely integrated into the school. We taught college prep classes during the school day, provided extracurricular opportunities after school, and counseled students everywhere in between. We were school staff, we were lunch staff, and we were after-school staff, just like every teacher and administrator there. Breaks consisted of running to the copy machine with a turkey sandwich in my left hand and a stack of financial aid information in my right, all while debating whether LeBron James or Kevin Durant would win MVP with a student who struggled to fit in with his peers.

Spending time on lesson plans, meeting agendas, and even larger programmatic decisions often took a backseat to real life. Finding time to reflect on a class or workshop and make strategic changes to future lessons was rare. What was more common was getting used to everything happening on the fly. In hindsight I realize that the way we worked with our students was reflective of this constant necessity to be in the "now." It was all about following the college application timeline—take the SAT, get the teacher recommendation, fill out the FAFSA—without any attention given as to what to expect on the actual college campus. Sadly, when my former students got there, many of them were not prepared. Ultimately, I left UPHS and the job I loved because I felt I was failing my students. I felt I needed to reeducate myself if I was going to truly be successful as an educator.

My day now usually begins in a seat in a classroom, 15 minutes early with a stomach full of breakfast. Instead of being greeted by urgent students, I engage in a discussion on access and equity in higher education for under-represented students. As a graduate student in higher education working as a research assistant for the National Forum on Higher Education for the Public Good, I have the opportunity to read about and analyze the challenges my former students face from an outsider's perspective. The dialogue we have in class is rich and grounded in theory. Though I am sure it takes me longer than most of my classmates to finish the articles and navigate through the academic language I once knew as an undergraduate, I am finding my work to be extremely mentally stimulating. In my time as a graduate student, I have been moved, intrigued, angered, and empowered by the research I have read and conducted. But after every article I struggle through, I find myself asking the same question: "So now what do I do with this information?" I wonder if my classmates are thinking the same thing. I wonder if the authors thought the same thing.

Recently, in one of my classes, we had a guest speaker who conducted research on African American students in Detroit. When asked what he hoped his research would accomplish, he said that he hoped it would change the negative perceptions that high school teachers have of their African American students. I wondered if this man had ever really spent time talking to teachers and how he planned on getting his research in their hands. Or, if he even cared. Or, if he once cared before the world of "publish or perish" clenched its fist around him. I could not help but think about my peers at UPHS who are working tirelessly to empower their students every day.

During this class I asked myself: What is research really for? How is it possible that with such need for support at schools like UPHS and with the existence of such powerful research institutions and skilled researchers, there exists such a large gap between research and practice?

A friend of mine often makes me aware that, whether I like it or not, I am on the "hyphen" of research and practice. I still identify at heart as a practitioner, but there is no denying that I am now, too, a researcher.

As a researcher I recognize what it means when starting a new project to conform to the demands of the funder or the interests within an academic unit at an institution, especially for young scholars. I recognize the feeling of completion when the writing is done. And, even though I'm not a tenure-track faculty member, I understand the importance of getting published. As a practitioner I recognize what it means to have no time to sit down, let alone read and decode a 30-page document. I recognize what it means to always have to be in the present and not have time to worry about the future. And I recognize what it means to feel like nobody else cares. As someone on the hyphen, I recognize the disservice we do to our students when this disconnect persists.

As my brief time away from direct student work comes to a close, I realize how lucky I am to have experienced both the perspective of the researcher and the perspective of the practitioner. This privilege will make me a better educator not only because I have developed a tool kit of knowledge but also because I know where to go to access more. The work at the National Forum and my course work have also given me a window into what can be, the ability to bring research and practice a little closer together. But what about my peers at UPHS?

When I return to the work that I love, I plan to return as an advocate for closing the gap between research and practice. Although the daily grind will no doubt get in the way, I now realize how important it is to access research to better inform my practice. I hope to create a space where my coworkers and I can reflect on best practices instead of simply "winging it" as a result of time pressure and the always unpredictable needs of our students. I also hope to encourage my fellow researchers to consider bridging this gap as well. How can we make the content of our research more accessible for someone who does not have the money to subscribe to a journal or the time to translate statistical jargon to arrive at data and information that could have been summed up in a few impactful sentences? And how do we ensure that we get these data in the hands of those who need it? Do we have to challenge ourselves to make the extra push? What if we only pursued topics we were passionate about? Would that be enough incentive to go beyond simply getting published in a journal?

I envision a perfect world back at UPHS where teachers sit around a table after school and discuss the findings from a new research study on empowering students through a cultural wealth framework. The study was encouraged and informed by teachers. At its conclusion the study was sent to the teachers by the researcher, who summarized for them the key points and offered to answer any questions they had. Though the teachers have to grade papers, create lesson plans, and interact with the everyday animation the school brings, their passion keeps them there at the table, as they see the potential impact this research could have on their work. They are able to use it, translating some, if not all, from the abstraction of academia to the realities of their students' lives. That, for me, is what research is really for.

Note

1. University Preparatory High School (UPHS) is used as a pseudonym.

REFLECTIVE NARRATIVE

A Journey of Social Consciousness and Action From Teaching Assistantship and Service-Learning Experiences

Megan B. Lebre

During my final year of graduate school at the University of Oklahoma, I participated in a practicum experience serving as a teaching assistant (TA) for the newly funded and developed course entitled University-Community Engagement Toward Social Justice. The course was taught by Penny Pasque. My main role during the course was to serve as a community partner site coordinator, which provided a practical experience for students to serve at agencies in the community. The semester prior to the class, I created connections with agency volunteer coordinators and discussed the logistics of the students' projects. The graduate students worked with six agencies that addressed education for homeless children, human trafficking, food distribution, home renovation for seniors, family clothing and supplies, and children with disabilities. The project details varied for each agency but some examples included tutoring and mentoring children, data entry and information organization, programming, home renovation, and fund-raising. With 6 community partners and more than 20 graduate students in the class, I was tasked with pairing students based on their interest to an agency. Throughout the rest of the course, I ensured that both the students and the community partners had a mutually beneficial experience.

On a larger scale, this opportunity allowed me to examine the intricacies of the university-community relationship beyond our course. Through my role as a TA, I learned valuable lessons regarding open communication, attention to detail, and constructive feedback. In particular, I believe these factors made me successful in the role as I built a bridge between the six service organizations and the students in the class. Through open dialogue, both my graduate student peers and the community partners felt comfortable sharing their successes and concerns with one another and with me.

As the point person for the projects, I aimed to be available for the agency volunteer coordinators and students as questions arose or issues came up during the service-learning experience. Additionally, our in-class group reflection time was helpful in receiving feedback from students about their experiences and allowed me to make adjustments to the projects or advocate for my peers or the agency needs to ensure a positive experience. Looking back, I can identify this experience as influential in teaching me the value of active listening, reliability, and open communication. Today, I intentionally practice these traits in my interactions with students, faculty, staff, and the surrounding community, because I know the difference it makes in the greater relationship between the university and community.

Being the TA for this course was unlike any other opportunity, because it gave me the opportunity to take my passion for community engagement to the next level. For four years, I volunteered at the Center for Children and Families, Inc. (CCFI) during its Neighborhood Centers program, which provides after-school child care for families in Norman, OK. During my time volunteering, I tutored, mentored, and participated in games and activities with students ages 5 to 18. As a TA, I coordinated the site experiences for the students in the class, but I also had the opportunity to serve at one of the locations. With my past experiences volunteering with CCFI, I chose to serve at a school in Oklahoma City for homeless children called Positive Tomorrows.

Positive Tomorrows

The mission and vision of Positive Tomorrows is to provide free education in Oklahoma City for homeless children from kindergarten through fifth grade. Specifically, "Positive Tomorrows is a sanctuary of hope; educating homeless children and their families for life" (Positive Tomorrows, 2015, para. 1). The teachers, social workers, and volunteers are committed to nurturing the children academically, socially, and emotionally, preparing them for success as both students and community members. Volunteers are invited to serve through tutoring, providing afternoon care, and assisting with after-school activities. Positive Tomorrows, a 501(c)3 nonprofit organization, is funded by private donations and is led by a board of directors, 15 staff members, and numerous volunteers. The school is free for its students, and the criterion of enrollment is that a student is struggling academically and/or socially due to homelessness.

The Oklahoma City Mission, domestic violence shelters, motels, houses of friends and relatives, and cars are examples of the places children at Positive Tomorrows call "home." Often, school becomes the most stable aspect of their lives. A life of transience or mobility creates developmental barriers, leaving students one or two years behind their peers. However, the staff and volunteers meet each student at his or her developmental level. In fact, Positive Tomorrows staff are conscious of health, hygiene, and behavioral issues and have the means to address them. For example, if a student does not have a coat on a cold day or looks like he or she may be dirty, staff members assist the students in a sensitive manner and take the young person to the "clothing closet" or provide hygiene essentials. Additionally, Positive Tomorrows has family support services within the school that ensure students are being taken care of both physically and emotionally. The school also provides a counselor for students and includes family members in counseling sessions, if necessary.

The overall program outcome of Positive Tomorrows is that students will be able to transition into a public school. One of the success stories of Positive Tomorrows is about a boy named Edwin. He first attended Positive Tomorrows as a first grader but was soon integrated into the public school system. Years later, Edwin was struggling both academically and socially, so his family requested he reenroll at Positive Tomorrows. Once back with Positive Tomorrows, Edwin received one-on-one attention and attended counseling sessions. After one year, he transitioned into public school as a seventh grader and, because his skills and maturity quickly improved, his teachers moved him up to the eighth grade. Once he was in high school, Edwin's teachers sponsored him for Oklahoma's Promise, a scholarship that, upon high school graduation, awards students college tuition for up to five years as long as they maintain their grades academically. Edwin received the scholarship, giving him the opportunity to move forward and pursue higher education ("Former Positive Tomorrows Student," 2010).

The staff and students at Positive Tomorrows truly made the experience memorable. Additionally, I loved the opportunity to volunteer with two other students from the class and discuss our experiences together as well as share with the rest of the class via online discussion boards and reflective discussion in class. In fact, I firmly believe this was an important reason why this service-learning experience was lasting and impactful. Compared to volunteering at CCFI, I was able to discuss my experiences with my peers who were volunteering with me as well as discuss with my peers in class. These in-depth discussions made the experience more meaningful and nourishing because I was given multiple spaces (online and in person) to discuss what I was learning, how I felt, and what was changing about my perspective of the social issue of homelessness. My peers and I became stable figures for the children on their Tuesday afternoons, and I believe the transformative experiences that occurred with the students, and within each of us, changed us all for the better.

Four Years Later

As I moved on from Positive Tomorrows and graduate school, I discovered a few lessons regarding social change from my course experience that continue in my life. Power, including the artifacts, relationships, and opportunities, provides partnerships between those targeted for injustice and those who consider themselves allies (Chambers & Gopaul, 2010). For me, this continues to be the most important aspect of success for any establishment working for social change on a systemic level. You must have allies in order to be successful. For example, women need men as allies to ensure that progress in the feminist movement occurs.

That course, University-Community Engagement Toward Social Justice, is a testament to the power of learning about the injustices of a community and engaging students in scholarship and service-learning to target those injustices and become stronger allies to a cause. In my past and current professional roles, I am acutely aware of who is in the room, who is being silenced, and if a group or the institution (e.g., students, faculty, administrators, policies, procedures) is oppressing a person or group in any way. I am constantly seeking the answers to these questions: "What do I stand for? To whom am I an ally and how am I demonstrating that through word and action? What am I doing to effect positive change on a micro and macro level?" Had I not been allowed to explore these dynamics in both a theoretical and practical way through the University-Community Engagement Toward Social Justice course, I do not know if I would be the socially conscious professional I am today.

Now, a few years removed from my experience in that course and from Positive Tomorrows, I am still influenced on a conscious and subconscious level from these experiences. Because of my role as the TA and site coordinator, I know how to build trust through communication and consistency in my words and actions to create an inclusive and safe community. In each of my professional roles, I have found myself listening to students share stories of oppression and injustice, and I am able to empathize, listen, and give voice to their community needs. I cannot help but think back to the students of Positive Tomorrows and the social, economic, mental, and physical barriers these students had. Drawing from my experience with Positive Tomorrows, I believe I am more aware when a group or person feels oppressed or unheard, and I then ask questions and find ways to give the group or person space to feel heard. I also make sure to use my voice to support that group or person.

Moreover, I am constantly checking in with myself regarding student interactions. I reflect on what the staff did at Positive Tomorrows and what we learned in our higher education and student affairs programs: to meet students where they are on a developmental level. Wherever they come from or who they are in that moment, I listen as they share their story and assist them as they navigate their academic journey. I work to remove barriers and find opportunities for them to achieve academic and personal success—whatever that looks like for the individual person.

My hope is that courses like University-Community Engagement Toward Social Justice continue to spread across the nation so that other students may have transformative experiences that help shape and mold them as students and influence their professional journey as they and we become lifelong agents of change.

References

Chambers, T., & Gopaul, B. (2010). Toward a social-justice centered engaged scholarship: A public and a private good. In H. E. Fitzgerald, C. Burack, and S. Siefer (Eds.), *Handbook of engaged scholarship: Contemporary landscapes, future directions, Vol. I: Institutional change* (pp. 55–70). East Lansing: Michigan State University Press.

Former Positive Tomorrows Student Prepares for College. (2010, July 19). In *Meet the stars*. Retrieved from http://www.positivetomorrows.org/2010/07/19/former-positive-tomorrows-student-prepares-for-college/

Positive Tomorrows. (2015). *Our mission*. Retrieved from http://positivetomorrows.org

REFLECTIVE NARRATIVE

The Impact of Research Involvement on My Own Understanding of Educational Equity

Briana Akani

W hen I joined the Impact of Shifting Demographics on the Mission of Historically Black Colleges and Universities (HBCUs) project through the Undergraduate Research Opportunities Program (UROP) in the fall semester of 2013, I had not had any significant prior research experience, but the topic drew my interest. Although we would be looking at the impact of changing populations on the campuses of HBCUs in their entirety through surveys of administrators, faculty, and students, I was most interested in the effects that these changes have had on the students themselves.

My prior experience with HBCUs had led me to understand that the culture on these campuses was much different from that of predominantly White institutions (PWIs). At HBCUs, students—and Black students, in particular—were nurtured and mentored in ways they could not be on large PWI campuses, such as the one I attend. The attention these students receive allows them to thrive, and as a Black student I was particularly invested in studying this unique attention. Has the nurturing culture on these historically Black campuses changed as more diverse student populations continued to enroll in increasing numbers? Do Black students now receive less of this critical mentorship and interaction with the faculty, at the expense of their success at these institutions? And, most important, do Black students find themselves left out as these schools change their profiles to match those of bigger PWIs whose fame and large endowments allow them to attract larger numbers of enrollees?

Through my engagement with this research and our attempts to answer these questions, I have gained plenty of new background knowledge regarding minority students in higher education. Before getting acquainted with this field of research, I did not know that minority groups other than African Americans also had institutions dedicated to their academic success, such as tribal colleges and Hispanic-serving institutions. As I learned more about them, I became interested in how other minority students are being served. I began to wonder how the experiences of non-Black minorities compare to those of Black students at HBCUs and whether other minority-serving institutions had similar cultures of nurturing.

I was intrigued by the telephone calls we received from interested faculty members who took our survey and wanted to talk about the project. I was puzzled by one administrator who did not want his institution included in the project. I was frustrated by how hard it is to get people to respond and get involved.

As we move further with this research, I expect that I will continue to learn new concepts regarding higher education and will formulate even more questions to pursue. Of course, in order to begin to explore the questions that I developed in the initial stages of my participation in the project, I would need to become deeply involved in the research; the opportunities for research immersion provided to me by Betty Overton lent greatly to my learning experience. From submitting to the Institutional Review Board and writing grant proposals, to designing of the survey instrument and analyzing the collected data, I was given the chance to be involved at every step. This experience in conducting research through my hands-on involvement has been invaluable to me. My strengths in writing, literature review, analysis, and critical thinking have greatly improved as a result of my involvement in the HBCU project, and I can carry these skills with me well into graduate school and my postgraduate career.

My involvement in this research project has also led me to understand how important research is in solving problems in our society and serving the populations being studied. Without research projects, we would have very little understanding of the very real dilemmas that minorities face in education. Historically, we have seen that poor and non-White students have been systematically disadvantaged regarding access to adequate education and academic success, and through research we can understand exactly how these disadvantages negatively affect their lives.

Specifically, in regard to the Impact of Shifting Demographics on the Mission of HBCUs project, our main goal is to understand how increased numbers of non-Black students at historically Black institutions affect the educational attainment of Black students. Others can put these findings into action. Similarly, research about how other minority students can succeed in higher education can have a direct effect on uplifting those who have been marginalized in society as well as those in the mainstream of the society. The research we are pursuing also helps institutions think about their missions. Our project has direct implications for effecting social change and addressing what we consider to be the public good, ensuring educational equity for all students.

Part Four

ENGAGING POLICY DISCUSSIONS AT THE
STATE AND NATIONAL LEVELS

9

UNDOCUMENTED STUDENT ACCESS TO HIGHER EDUCATION
Focused Efforts at the Federal and Institutional Levels

Kimberly A. Reyes, Aurora Kamimura, and Kyle Southern

At the National Forum on Higher Education for the Public Good (National Forum) engaged research has taken many forms. For almost 10 years, one of the major research agendas for the National Forum has been a focus on access to higher education for undocumented and immigrant young people. The National Forum began this focus when the immigration issue was just a small murmur in the public media. Increasingly, however, as immigration policy and opportunities for undocumented students have gained attention as polarizing issues in the public arena, the National Forum has found itself dynamically positioned to provide information and to influence institutional and public policy.

Each year in the United States, approximately 65,000 students graduate from high school without legal documentation of their residence in this country (Gonzalez, 2009). This population of undocumented students either entered the United States without legal authorization or entered legally and remained in the country without authorization (Suro, Suárez-Orozco, & Canizales, 2015). Many undocumented students first learn of their immigration status as they prepare for rites of adolescence, such as applying for a driver's license or obtaining a first job. Most undocumented students come to the United States under the compulsion of their parents or other guardians.

Upon graduating from high school, many undocumented students find their ability to access higher education inhibited by state laws, institutional policies, and federal laws that restrict admissions or financial aid to U.S. citizens and legal residents. Although some states have adopted policies with more inclusive postures toward undocumented students, others have no stipulated policies on the issue at all (Burkhardt et al., 2011). In the absence of comprehensive federal action, state policies reflect a patchwork of inclusive, restrictive, and unstipulated environments for undocumented students seeking to pursue postsecondary educational opportunities. The difficulties undocumented students face in obtaining access to higher education largely result from the complexity of conflicting state, system, and institutional policies and practices, which is further exacerbated by the failure of the federal government to address immigration reform in a comprehensive manner.

Without a national policy to guide admissions and financial aid for undocumented students, states and institutions have pursued decision processes as diverse as the system of American higher education. This chapter details the work of the National Forum both to anticipate changes in state and federal policies on the issue and to advocate for inclusive practices on the part of postsecondary institutions. Specifically, in this chapter we examine the strategic activity of the National Forum's immigration initiative, which has operated under a change strategy that acknowledges the domains of (a) federal and state policy, (b) institutional practice, and (c) public will in improving access to higher education for undocumented students.

Since its inception in 2007, the National Forum's immigration initiative has been at the center of a unique convergence of scholars, graduate students, policymakers, advocacy organizations, philanthropic entities, and postsecondary institutions. These entities have played critical roles in shaping how the National Forum has framed the issue of undocumented student access to higher education, and have oriented the National Forum's scholarly and programmatic work to reflect their conception of this complex legal, political, and institutional challenge.

As our work has evolved over recent years, our strategic direction has reflected a noticeable shift from a focus on changing federal and state policy to one of changing institutional practice. We attribute this shift in direction to our model of engaged scholarship, which exemplifies the critical role of partnerships with actors within and outside of the academy. By inviting these diverse constituencies to participate in our theorization of mechanisms by which barriers to undocumented student access operate, the National Forum has been able to describe more accurately the complexity of the issue.

With a collaboratively constructed understanding of the issue, we have better equipped ourselves and our network with the ability to identify context-specific solutions and build momentum for broad social change that serves the public good.

In order to advance this public good framework for the issue of undocumented student access and success, this chapter

- describes the overarching vision of the National Forum's immigration initiative;
- provides a historical case study of the National Forum's immigration initiative;
- presents the key driving factors of the immigration initiative's important developmental shift toward a focus on institutional practice; and
- offers points for further consideration by communities interested in using models of engaged scholarship to advance a public good argument for broadening educational opportunity for our nation's undocumented youth.

The National Forum's Immigration Initiative: A Vision for Access and Success

In 2007 the National Forum, in cooperation with a wide range of partners across the country, launched a broad effort to focus attention on access to educational opportunities for undocumented students, with a particular emphasis on the educational gaps created by inconsistent federal, state, and institutional policies. Key stakeholders from across the field of higher education identified the University of Michigan as the base for this national initiative. This decision recognized the university's visibility in the area of educational diversity and its location in the center of the country. The initiative's leaders intended to signal that this was a national issue and a public concern inherently connected to the principle of expanding college access for all capable students as a public good. The National Forum's advisers contended that establishing an initiative at the University of Michigan, an institution far removed from the country's southern border, would enhance the profile of the issue on a national scale.

Efforts over the ensuing seven years led to the adoption of an overarching goal and a corresponding set of guiding principles that inform our model of change, which is depicted in Figure 9.1.

Figure 9.1. Project overview and theory of change.

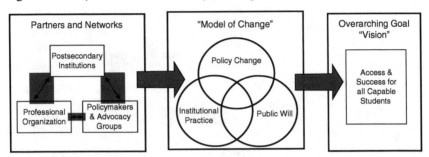

Our statement of goals and assumptions is as follows:

- At the National Forum, we share an overarching goal to ensure all undocumented students have the opportunity to receive a college education.
- Consistent with this goal, we are committed to the passage of appropriate federal and state laws that pave the way for access, success, and full participation. This is not a partisan commitment, but a reflection of our core professional values that relates directly to our belief in the public good mission of higher education.
- For purposes of strategy, we assume that informed public policy will eventually create a framework for leaders to follow. However, we also recognize that favorable legislation—isolated from other changes—will not completely address the challenge of educating Latin@, immigrant, or undocumented students. We base this recognition in our observation that court cases, civil rights laws, and affirmative action programs have yet to eliminate systemic barriers to opportunity.
- We believe the problems associated with access for undocumented students are closely related to and result in part from inconsistencies across institutions and political jurisdictions, uncertainties in practice, mixed or unclear messages sent to these students and their families, and a polarized public discourse.

The National Forum has developed a collective vision of a country in which all capable individuals have access to postsecondary education in order to create a nation where more of our future citizens are prepared to contribute to our social, civic, and economic prosperity. Based on our assessment, we believe that creating the conditions described will depend on a sophisticated network of postsecondary institutions, professional organizations, policymakers, and advocacy groups working toward the alignment of three key factors: appropriate policies, changes in institutional practices, and the continued cultivation of public will to support inclusive policies and practices (see Figure 9.1).

The immigration initiative undertaken by the National Forum and its partners has stressed the fundamental interdependence of all three of these conditions for change. This initiative represents a long-term, multiproject, multiorganizational agenda involving several partners and diverse stakeholders. The focus of the immigration initiative has transformed over time from a primary interest in advocating for federal legislative change to a strategy that directs attention toward institutional practices and decision patterns that prohibit access to higher education for undocumented students. To advance this aim, we support the creation of an environment in which campuses may implement relatively quick policy changes in order to provide immediate access and promote success for undocumented students despite their difficult political circumstances.

By shifting the focus to institutional practices, we have not ignored policy issues or underestimated the importance of building public will. On the contrary, in consultation with our coalition of partners and professional networks, we continue work to bring change to all three of the key factors designated in our change model. We rely on strategy throughout the efforts of this initiative by calling on the differentiated strengths across our network and assigning roles as appropriate to advance our mission, capacity, and spheres of influence. In our work at the National Forum we have found that four primary domains support this shift in emphasis: evidence, legitimacy, key relationships, and environmental influences. The intersections shared by each of these domains provide for this initiative's successful outcomes to date. We will better describe and give examples of how these domains developed in importance over time and contributed to the success of the project by providing the historical context for the immigration initiative.

Historical Case Study of the Immigration Initiative

In 2006, two key members of the National Forum's advisory board encouraged its founding director, John C. Burkhardt, to place the issue of undocumented student access at the forefront of the organization's commitment. At the time, the organization was focused on addressing community and state policy issues shaping access to education. An immigration agenda would change many aspects of the National Forum's work and require new approaches to staffing and funding.

Tomás A. Arciniega, who was then a member of the governing board of the Hispanic Association of Colleges and Universities (HACU), and Jaime Chahin, treasurer of the American Association of Hispanics in Higher Education (AAHHE), agreed to consult with the National Forum in organizing a new immigration effort. Burkhardt and these two important leaders provided the organization with strong direction and afforded the burgeoning initiative both a wide network of contacts in major philanthropic circles and valuable insight into how foundations approached projects centered on civic engagement, immigrant integration, and higher education access, even around politically contested issues. The importance of this will become clear.

The political context was foreboding: There had been no serious immigration reform legislation at the federal level in almost 20 years, and Congress could not muster the votes to formally take up the Development, Relief and Education for Alien Minors (DREAM) Act which had been first proposed in 2001. The DREAM Act, while it took a number of different forms over many versions and repeated introductions, was designed to provide a conditional path to citizenship for undocumented young people, contingent on the completion of a college degree or two years of military service. Research and advocacy groups in states bordering Mexico—the country of origin for 58% of undocumented residents (Passel & Cohn, 2011)—including California and Texas, had already established an agenda around the goals of the DREAM Act.

Focus on Federal Policy Change: 2007 to 2008

The National Forum launched the immigration initiative in June 2007 by hosting "Challenges and Opportunities: Conversations About Immigration and Higher Education," a three-day convening held at the University of Michigan–Ann Arbor and funded primarily by the W.K. Kellogg Foundation, the Lumina Foundation, the Carnegie Corporation of New York, and the College Board State Services Office. The decision to involve several different funders from the outset of the initiative was strategic and important, as will be seen. National Forum staff involved in the project also designed the conference to engage a diverse group of stakeholders across the fields of immigration policy and higher education in "reframing and reorienting the discussion on immigration, encouraging leadership, prompting action, and strengthening collaboration among individuals having a stake in the outcome of this historic debate" (National Forum, 2007, p. 10).

At this convening, 150 educators, policymakers, and community organizers committed to situating the issue of access for undocumented students in the forefront of professional and constituency dialogues. Participants also inspired the creation of a powerful network of well-situated educators and advocates across the United States that could come together in order to advance policy and practice toward improving undocumented students' access to higher education.

Following the success of the Ann Arbor conference, the University of New Mexico and California State University–Fullerton hosted comparable convenings in June 2008. These convenings brought together students, advocates, professional association leaders, system and institutional leaders, and policymakers from across the nation to create new diverse networks and policy initiatives that were aimed at raising awareness and garnering, commitment for the passage of the DREAM Act. At the time, the National Forum and its partners saw great potential for higher education stakeholders to create momentum for supporting the passage of federal immigration policy, including the DREAM Act. Furthermore, the mobilization inspired by these early convenings indicated to the National Forum that examining this national issue in terms of opportunities for local action, in particular, could be a powerful organizing principle.

The National Forum's approach was further legitimized when, in 2008, the American Council on Education (ACE) featured the National Forum's work on immigration and higher education as a "nationally significant" approach. ACE considered the National Forum's approach distinctive because of its emphasis on building networks and partnerships that engage multiple levels of policymakers (institutional, state, and national) working toward the common goal of building "public will" in support of improving educational opportunity for immigrants as a fundamental civil rights issue. Recognizing the power of the partnerships that were forming through this convening strategy, the National Forum sought additional philanthropic support to continue building a national conversation on immigration issues.

Shifting Focus to Higher Education Associations: 2009 to 2010

Following the initial set of convenings, National Forum colleagues began to consider how research activities might play a more strategic and intentional role in the immigration initiative. With Burkhardt's encouragement and with guidance from the U–M faculty, senior graduate researcher Noe Ortega became a key architect in constructing the immigration initiative's research strategy over the next several years. When he arrived in the summer of 2009, Ortega brought a wealth of professional experience in student services, a multiregional knowledge of Latin@ interests across the higher education landscape, and several professional connections to national higher education organizations and associations. Coupled with his professional experience, Ortega's doctoral course work in the areas of public policy and organizational theory brought a unique sophistication to the work of the immigration initiative.

AAHHE commissioned Ortega to write a paper examining the support for the DREAM Act within the higher education community. Ortega's

(2011) findings indicated that although the majority of the most influential national higher education associations[1] had publicly endorsed passage of a federal DREAM Act, the failure of Congress to pass this legislation had entangled undocumented student access in a web of complicated federal and state mandates. Consequently, the policies and practices of postsecondary institutions did not necessarily align with the inclusive policy positions of the national higher education associations (Ortega, 2011). Findings from this study proved a critical turning point for the National Forum's immigration work after Ortega presented them at the 2010 AAHHE annual meeting.

Until 2009, the National Forum had based its immigration initiative on the traditionally held assumption that professional associations could influence institutional behavior at the local level through the interpretation of federal access policies for undocumented students. However, Ortega's findings directly challenged that assumption and suggested that there were more powerful pressures than national associations dictating the actions of individual institutions. Following the findings from this research and the successful networking activities in Michigan, California, and New Mexico, the National Forum focused intently on outlining a comprehensive model of change that would reflect the interconnectedness of three important domains and associated goals: policy change, institutional practice, and public will as depicted by Figure 9.2.

Supported by funding from the Marguerite E. Casey Foundation, the Carnegie Corporation of New York, the New Partnerships Foundation, and the University of Michigan's National Center for Institutional Diversity, the National Forum organized and cohosted four critical strategy meetings designed to integrate the perspectives of policymakers, institutional practitioners, and other relevant stakeholders on the issue. In October 2009, the National Forum participated in the First Triennial Conference on Latin@ Education and Immigrant Integration at the University of Georgia. This conference gathered educators, foundation representatives, scholars, elected officials, and community leaders to discuss how immigration-related effects on education could be effectively addressed in a heavily politicized climate. Participants focused their discussions on how the research agendas of Latin@-focused centers from around the country could be utilized to inform public policy and to create strategies for closing the Latin@ student achievement gap in environments that were apathetic or even hostile to immigrant issues.

Two months later, the National Forum invited Juan Sepúlveda, director of the White House Initiative on Educational Excellence for Hispanic Americans, to facilitate a public forum entitled "The State of Latin@s in U.S. Education" at the University of Michigan–Ann Arbor. Information gathered at this event served to inform the Department of Education's national initiative for Hispanic educational success and engage the National Forum's

Figure 9.2. National Forum change strategy.

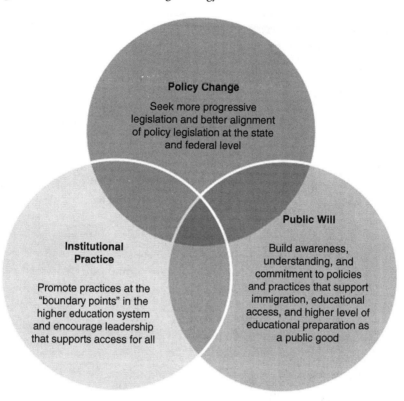

partner institutions and associations in identifying potential stakeholder sites in new regions and within key institutional groups. This gathering functioned as a planning meeting to design the last of the three major meetings to design a future gathering that was to serve as a capstone event: a National Summit in Washington, DC that was held in April 2010. With the passage of the DREAM Act increasingly doubtful and legislation queued up in several states to further restrict access, a new strategy was needed.

The National Summit, organized in partnership with the Kellogg Fellows Leadership Alliance (KFLA), convened college presidents, researchers, professors, student activists, higher education association representatives, and legal professionals to resituate access for undocumented students as a central civil rights issue within the context of contemporary educational values, practices, and responsibilities. After an opening session facilitated by Sepúlveda, Burkhardt proposed the National Forum's new change strategy, which focused on state and institutional policy change. This was followed by responses and thought-provoking presentations from Jamie P. Merisotis, president and CEO of the Lumina Foundation; Jonathan Rochkind, vice president and director of research at the nonprofit public engagement organization Public Agenda; Jonathan Alger, then senior vice president and general counsel at Rutgers University; Kent Wong, director of the UCLA Center for Labor Research and Education; and Susan Sturm, professor of law and social responsibility at Columbia University.

During the meeting the National Forum also secured commitments for future collaborative work with Justin Draeger, then vice president of public policy, advocacy, and research for the National Association of Student Financial Aid Administrators (NASFAA); Barmak Nassirian, then associate executive director for external relations for the American Association of Collegiate Registrars and Admissions Officers (AACRAO); Manny Frias, president and CEO for the Sereno Alliance for Higher Education; and William Flores, president of the University of Houston–Downtown. In short, the National Summit demonstrated the National Forum's convening power as an organization and its ability to blend research, practice, and advocacy in a vision for change.

Following the National Summit, the Lumina Foundation provided its support to the National Forum's initiative with a major grant that enabled it to sponsor mobilizing efforts across the country to focus on the role that student narratives and undocumented student activists could play in addressing the issue of how best to increase postsecondary opportunities for immigrant and undocumented students. The Lumina Foundation also committed to work in partnership with the National Forum in planning a strategy summit at their Indianapolis headquarters in May 2011 as the culminating event in this series of meetings. The National Summit helped the National Forum establish strong footholds in federal and state policy circles, philanthropy, senior-level university leadership, and the academy. Collectively, these connections represented a strong step forward in aligning the domains outlined in the National Forum's change strategy.

The National Forum team had also pivoted within an increasingly unfavorable political climate for policy reform regarding greater access to postsecondary education for undocumented students. In April 2010 (the very week of the Summit in Washington, DC), Arizona Governor Jan Brewer signed SB 1070 into law, making Arizona home to the country's strictest anti-undocumented-immigrant legislation when it went into effect that July. Hopes for passing the DREAM Act were further dashed when, in December 2010, the Senate failed to clear the procedural hurdle of cloture with a vote of 55 to 41. These developments forced the National Forum to confront the dubious prospects for federal and state policy reform and to imagine new possibilities for how local action might better serve to cultivate public will for federal, state, and institutional policies.

Embracing an Institutional Perspective: 2010 to 2012

Following the National Summit and the recognition of the unlikely prospects for federal policy reform, the National Forum initiated an effort to conduct original research that could extend and build upon Ortega's (2011) findings. Scholars in the National Forum's network of partners urged it to provide empirical evidence of the effects of the varying state policies on institutions as they engaged the issue of undocumented student access.

Ortega and the rest of the graduate student team, guided by the National Forum's director and advisory board, set to work designing a national survey of financial aid officers and admissions professionals that would compare inclusive, restrictive, and unstipulated policy environments with the actual practices that shape access, participation, and graduation. To frame the study, the team drew on theories of legal ambiguity, which generally assert that "ambiguities in laws and regulations are open for interpretation and not always known or fully understood by those who implement them" (Edelman, 1992; Edelman & Suchman, 1997, as cited in Burkhardt et al., 2011, p. 6). With the understanding that different interpretations of state law would have different effects on institutional policy, the study explored how colleges and universities reconcile laws that constrain undocumented students' educational access with institutional values, governance arrangements, and local circumstances. The National Forum capitalized on the relationships that had been solidified at the National Summit and secured the partnerships of both NASFAA and AACRAO to provide participants for the survey. Generously funded by the Texas Guaranteed Student Loan Corporation, the study demonstrated that

1. institutions in inclusive state policy environments are more likely to have campus policies that admit, extend in-state tuition, and offer financial assistance to undocumented students;
2. private and for-profit institutions are more likely to offer financial assistance to undocumented students, with four-year colleges being more likely to provide financial assistance than two-year colleges;
3. the higher the percentage of undocumented immigrants in the state, the more likely it is to offer in-state tuition to undocumented students, and
4. the more aware that institutional professionals are of their association's access-oriented position, the more likely their respective institutions are to act inclusively toward undocumented students. (Burkhardt et al., 2011, p. 12)

The National Forum presented preliminary findings of the study, *Reconciling Federal, State, and Institutional Policies Determining Educational Access for Undocumented Students: Implications for Professional Practice*, at the AAHHE Annual Meeting in March 2011. The study's findings sparked animated

conversation among AAHHE attendees and continued to be a major point
of discussion later that summer during meetings at the Lumina Foundation
headquarters and the NASFAA annual meeting in Boston, Massachusetts.

The National Forum also secured funding from the Carnegie Corporation of New York to conduct institutional case studies that examined the
role of institutional decision makers in setting practice guidelines regarding admissions and financial aid awards for undocumented students. The
National Forum studied patterns of reporting in college newspapers on
this issue and examined several cases in which local controversies revolved
around the rights of undocumented students. This research, first presented at
a University of Michigan convening in March 2011, provided attendees with
the opportunity to dissect and talk through real examples of the complexity that institutional leaders confront when they are mediating the tensions
among federal and state policies, institutional missions, and local contexts.
The feedback from this convening surfaced a nascent desire for a space in
which institutional leaders and practitioners could talk with and learn from
each other as they confronted these issues on their respective campuses.

As National Forum researchers conducted this work, they also fulfilled
their commitment to the convening strategy that was funded by the Lumina
Foundation following the National Summit. Throughout 2010 and 2011,
the National Forum sponsored and helped organize programs and speakers
for five convenings that were planned to incorporate the collaborative ideas
developed at the National Summit with a particular focus on highlighting
the narratives of undocumented students and DREAM activists. Through
this effort, the National Forum sought to reposition the immigration issue
in order for higher education to have greater agency in efforts to expand
educational access for Latin@, immigrant, and undocumented students. The
five convenings were held at the University of New Mexico, the University
of California–Los Angeles, Rutgers University, the University of Michigan,
and the Lumina Foundation headquarters. With support from HACU,
AAHHE, KFLA, and the Annie E. Casey Leadership Fellows, these convenings provided a platform for the National Forum's broad network of partners
to examine multifaceted influences on policy changes that support access and
also identify and disseminate institutional best practices.

The series of convenings in 2010 and 2011 served as important dissemination platforms for the National Forum's sponsored research studies
and provided an opportunity to demonstrate to its network of partners
how rigorous research has significant implications for policies and practices that affect higher education's commitment to inclusion, access, and
equity. The National Forum's unique model of combining action-oriented

research with dialogue allowed it to unify concern for the issue by building a shared narrative across institutions in regard to the urgent needs of undocumented students and the practitioners who serve them. The convenings also brought together a network of several hundred partners that the National Forum had cultivated over four years, including policymakers at the state and federal levels, college and university leadership, "boundary function" administrators,[2] higher education scholars, immigration and education attorneys, and professional associations. This network is an expansive community of well-informed and engaged educators who could draw upon each other for creative strategies, accurate information, and courage. The culminating convening at the Lumina Foundation headquarters was particularly pivotal in drawing new, highly influential actors into the National Forum's network.

By this time, the National Forum had established a clear framework that emphasized taking a closer look at the boundary organizations of institutions and their influence on shaping institutional policy and practice. Lumina participants expressed great interest in this approach and helped the National Forum to secure a research and dissemination partnership with the National Association for College Admission Counseling (NACAC) and to begin talks with the National Association of College and University Attorneys (NACUA). These partnerships marked an important milestone in terms of the National Forum's position as a legitimating agency on the issue of immigration and higher education and as an indicator of the success of our mobilization strategy. A new question presented itself as we reflected on the significant progress to date: *How could we continue to expand this network of educators and strengthen their ability to take a stand in support of undocumented immigrant student issues?*

In May 2011, with support from the Ford Foundation, the immigration initiative capitalized on the energy shared by national partners to begin the development of an online network for college and university leaders dedicated to the support of undocumented students. The original vision for this national network was for it to serve as a so-called Storm Center, a resource for campus leaders seeking support and guidance for action on the undocumented student issue amid a "storm" of external pressures. As opportunities opened for the development of this site, national partners suggested that a website that was focused on providing proactive solutions to the problem would be beneficial. In response to this expressed need, the original vision for a Storm Center quickly transitioned to a network site that would house all of the immigration initiative's research projects and practice-based tools aimed at broadening access and supporting the success of undocumented students.

This network site was named uLEAD (University Leaders for Educational Access and Diversity).

Design for uLEAD began immediately due to the urgent need for alternative models for action on campuses across the country. uLEAD would be a site not only for creating and sustaining professional networks, but also would serve as a repository for reliable information and resources to assist campuses searching for ways to take proactive stances on access for undocumented students. The goal of the immigration initiative was to infuse these practical resources with evidence grounded in research.

The Strategic Transition Plays Out: Focus on Changing Campus Behaviors: 2012 to Present

Throughout 2012, the National Forum's immigration initiative gained significant momentum as it garnered national attention for the resources it provided to campuses focused on providing access for all capable students. The immigration initiative had definitively changed its early focus on efforts to change federal policy to an institutional focus in which all research and networking were concentrated on providing the necessary support to those campuses exploring how to implement favorable action toward undocumented students. With plans for infusing existing research into uLEAD, the National Forum returned to the Lumina Foundation to support further action from boundary function professionals through a series of national convenings. The Lumina Foundation pressed the National Forum to consider a broadened perspective that included access and support of Latin@, immigrant, and undocumented students, which aligned with their national agenda on Latin@ student success. These funded convenings aimed to enhance the developing partnership with NASFAA and AACRAO, encouraging support for the next stage of access for Latin@, immigrant, and undocumented students. In addition, the immigration initiative's increasing emphasis on the role of professional practice intensified the need to put its budding partnerships with NACAC and NACUA to work.

The role of the college admissions community, including high school counselors and college admissions officers, is critical in broadening the access path for all students, particularly undocumented students. Equally critical is the role of a campus team of general counsel, who work with university leaders to interpret laws and guide campus policies on such issues as admissions and access for traditionally excluded communities. As a function of what the National Forum had learned from its institutional case study research, attention had also turned toward working with the extensive community of U.S. Catholic universities and colleges whose historic missions predisposed them to be potential sites of opportunity for undocumented students nationwide. These institutions shared an ethical calling to serve *all* students equally, and this principle framed the National Forum's pursuit of their engagement.

With the projects supported by the Ford and Lumina Foundations underway, 2013 proved to be a year of substantial progress. In March 2013, at the AAHHE Annual Meeting, the immigration initiative launched uLEAD as a resource and accessible site for all practitioners across the nation, including the various constituents and partners throughout the process. The uLEAD site was launched with several resources that the National Forum created with campus practitioners in mind, including teaching modules that were developed from qualitative case studies, a historical timeline of the undocumented student movement, research reports and briefs developed by the National Forum, and an interactive national map that highlights each state's legislative history and resources regarding undocumented students. uLEAD has become an important resource for practitioners seeking support and tools for serving undocumented students.

In an effort to reach broader audiences and ensure that the necessary resources were reaching the boundary function professionals who work with undocumented students on a daily basis, the National Forum engaged in the use of webinars to convene national constituents on critical topics. The inaugural online convening in partnership with NASFAA was launched through a webinar in April 2013 and was titled "Federal Policy Implications for Higher Education Professionals in Broadening Access for Undocumented Students." The second webinar, titled "Supporting the Success of Undocumented Students: Implications of Federal Policy for Student Affairs," conducted in partnership with the National Association of Student Personnel Administrators (NASPA), focused on support services necessary for undocumented students to reach their academic goals. These virtual convenings attracted between 400 and 600 viewers each and served to enhance awareness within the financial aid, admissions, and student affairs professional communities. These recorded webinars immediately became new resources on uLEAD to allow continued access to and supplement the in-person national convening scheduled to take place the following academic year (2014–2015).

A new project with NACAC launched in June 2013. It was a brief survey designed to explore the collaborative strategies and processes, both formal and informal, by which the college admissions counseling community exchanges and authenticates information needed to serve undocumented students in the college choice process. The results of this research pointed to the prevalence of informal networks that high school counselors form with admissions officers to ensure access for their undocumented students. Furthermore, the results of this study point to the personal and professional investment that admissions community members need to make in undocumented students and their families, and the value that these networks possess for supporting undocumented student access. The National Forum is currently developing practice briefs from the results of this study that will be widely disseminated and made available on uLEAD.

As is evident by the focus of the most recent efforts, the immigration initiative has shifted focus onto developing resources and tools for college and university professionals as campuses are indeed the windows of opportunity for student access. This change in focus does not diminish the efforts that are secondarily aimed at working toward federal policy changes in support of undocumented students. Through enhanced mobility and a more directed need on campuses, the immigration initiative has continued to solidify its support of campuses that express interest in broadening access for undocumented students and also in providing the necessary evidence and information for campuses who have not engaged in this movement to date.

Key Factors That Enabled a Shift in Strategy

As the historical case study carefully outlines, it was not a transformational moment at which the National Forum strategically decided to change direction; rather, it was an evolutionary change that took shape over several years. Reflection on the key areas that positioned the immigration initiative to shift its strategy from a focus on federal policy change to changes at the institutional level revealed that three major factors influenced this shift: legitimacy, relationships, and environmental context. These three factors, equally balanced within the context and well supported by collaborative results, have paved the way for the change that was necessary for continuing to broaden access for all capable students, as depicted by Figure 9.3. The following sections highlight the prominent developments within each factor that led to the pivotal shift in strategy.

Legitimacy: Garnered in Partnership With Key Actors

Evidence alone could not have moved the immigration initiative forward, much less made the dramatic shift that was necessary to effect immediate change for undocumented students. From its inception, the immigration initiative recognized the value of key partnerships and the strength of the legitimacy that several national partners could provide for expanding access

Figure 9.3. Model for strategic change of the National Forum.

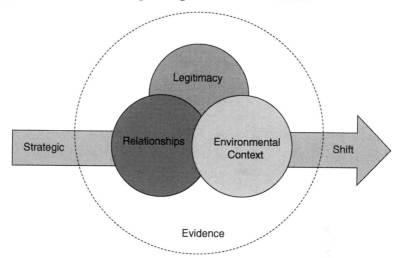

to higher education for undocumented students. The National Forum sought and garnered support from key national leaders in higher education, public policy, and philanthropy such as Jaime Chahín, Tomás A. Arciniega, Jaime Merisotis, Geri Manion, Jeannie Oakes, Kent Wong, Jacob Fraire, Juan Sepúlveda, and others throughout the years in order to provide the initiative with the legitimacy necessary for success in fulfilling the vision of national change. The level of leadership that each of these actors held within their respective national associations, foundations, and political appointments lent legitimacy to the unified voice and narrative of the initiative's network. In turn, their support and the urgency they expressed provided the symbolic leadership at a national level that was needed to enact the change strategy at pivotal moments. Despite the fact that several of these key actors were actively pressing the National Forum to remain focused on providing the evidence necessary to influence federal policy change, they, too, recognized the immediate value in ensuring that institutions and their leaders have the required tools and resources to actively support and broaden access for undocumented students.

Each of these actors represented the National Forum's agenda at key moments, both within their organizations and as in public arenas. It was primarily the legitimacy they provided to the immigration initiative that afforded the National Forum the ability to obtain the crucial funding necessary to conduct research and develop the evidence to move forward. Furthermore, their influence also created the opportunity for national dissemination of this important and collaborative work. Through these opportunities, the National Forum was able to better understand and respond to the needs of its many constituents, which in essence, catalyzed the trajectory toward the strategic shift. As noted in the historical overview, during key moments of the initiative each of these key leaders contributed to the progress of the movement, either through dedicated financial resources, through providing outlets for research to be conducted and shared, or through representation as a national leader.

Relationships: National Networks in Support of the Initiative

The legitimacy that was built throughout the history of the immigration initiative would not have been possible without well-established relationships. Visionary colleagues within the National Forum drew from their professional networks to cultivate the support necessary for the initiative to have a national impact. Because of the potential risks that many foundations faced by investing in the contentious nature of this initiative's work, the immigration initiative leaders were forced to lean heavily on their professional and personal relationships with foundation leaders and national leaders to provide the legitimacy and voice for the initiative. They called on partners from previous professional experiences and secured their support in framing the undocumented student movement as a major civil rights issue of our time.

The strength of these long-standing relationships opened the door for these leaders to support the agenda and bring legitimacy to the effort. Without these key relationships, it would not have been possible to signal to an array of diverse stakeholders that this work was critical in supporting the public good and worth investing in to create socially responsible national change. It was solely through these relationships with such visible partners that the initiative garnered the necessary national attention.

Environmental Influences: The Context in Consideration

The National Forum's efforts to build legitimacy in this policy and research area, coupled with the strength of its external and internal relationships, enabled it to shift the focus of its immigration initiative to an institutional context. Environmental influences originating from the federal, state, and local levels, however, continued to affect the National Forum's approach to understanding the contentious issue of undocumented student access in a state of evolving and ambiguous legal conditions. Despite the failure of Congress to enact comprehensive immigration reform, the topic of immigration and undocumented students remains politically relevant in the public sphere. In fact, the public attention on undocumented students and its increasing relevance for the public service mission of higher education allowed the National Forum to acquire a reputation as a national leader in undocumented student issues. Further, restrictive policies such as Arizona's SB 1070 had polarized the national conversation in many ways, as the fear that these restrictive policies would diffuse to other states had become very real (Holley-Walker, 2011). Therefore, though federal policy discourse was focused on undocumented student issues, so was the state context. The dysfunction of the federal government and patchwork approach of state policies highlights the need for further empirical work on the effects of policy and institutional practice on undocumented student educational attainment.

At the local level, at the University of Michigan's Center for the Study of Higher and Postsecondary Education, many of the researchers working on the immigration initiative have received research training by proximal scholars in the field. As the immigration initiative began to shift the strategy from federal policy change toward changes in institutional practices and behaviors, researchers for the initiative began to shape the scholarly inquiry and interpretation of findings according to the theoretical frameworks that they were learning through doctoral study. The research agenda quickly applied an organizational lens for institutions undergoing change in response to external political pressures situated within a legally ambiguous context. The advice and teaching of these renowned scholars highly influenced the frameworks that were applied to the research conducted for the initiative.

Finally, the expertise and scholarly interests of the individual researchers on the team heavily influenced the direction of the research for this particular agenda. Each scholar shaped the work from his or her own professional and personal experience, bringing a new perspective from political and legal contexts. These distinct critical lenses provided for a more comprehensive view on how to provide the best tools and evidence necessary to create national change.

Implications for Researchers and Practitioners

The National Forum's immigration initiative bears several important implications for others who wish to participate in and create spaces for engaged research aimed at advancing access for undocumented immigrant students and other underrepresented populations. As already noted, this type of work requires giving constant attention to both collaboration and introspection. Dialogue and partnership with the various constituencies that are uniquely involved with or informed on the population of interest must occur throughout the life of the work. These constituencies provide resources that are essential not only for implementing a successful research agenda (e.g., funding, personnel, access to influential networks), but also for creating and refining the direction of any such initiative.

Intentional efforts at convening these constituencies for feedback and new information can also identify what kinds of tools are needed for supporting the students of interest and what types of research questions and designs might help to construct such tools. Constituencies from both policy arenas and practitioner communities were vital in order to maximize the utility of research that aims to better understand the social phenomenon of college access and ultimately to advocate for the students who were without that access. This is particularly true in the case of engaged research on undocumented immigrant students whose educational opportunities lie in a web of state and federal policy, institutional practice, and ideological debate. Two other factors might be considered in understanding how this effort could inform future research and advocacy initiatives: setting and appropriate staffing. The decision to situate the national effort within an organization located in the upper Midwest, at a research university that had not yet considered a change in its own admissions and aid policies related to undocumented students and at a center known more for scholarship and teaching than for advocacy was not arrived at casually. The immigration issue had become politicized and regionalized. Organizing the effort at the University of Michigan benefited from its national reputation for taking on contested issues related to student access; its commitment to diversity; and to the fact that, even if its state legislature attempted to intervene, there would be ample defense given the effort based in institutional history and autonomy. The National Forum's close affiliation with the prestigious Center for the Study of Higher and Postsecondary Education also ensured that there would be a pipeline of well-trained and disciplined researchers available and that the scholarship surrounding the project would be given serious consideration.

In 2006, at the outset of the effort, the number of Latin@ graduate students affiliated with the National Forum was too small to mount the effort that would be needed. During the next 10 years, however, a pipeline was built, and soon doctoral and master's degree students were enrolling at CSHPE or coming from other academic programs across the campus. This cohort of committed individuals, leaving Texas, California, Arizona, Florida, and North Carolina to brave the cold winters in Ann Arbor, transformed the project as they changed the schools and colleges in which they enrolled and, indeed, the National Forum itself.

The National Forum's Immigration Initiative as Engaged Research

At the National Forum, our ongoing efforts with the immigration initiative were conducted in the spirit of engaged research, in which a variety of stakeholders with practical expertise are consulted in the construction, design, dissemination, and ongoing evaluation of the inquiry and its findings. In retrospect, we called upon the principles of what the field terms *action-based research*. Action-based research centers on a practice-based problem and then uses systematic data collection and analysis to produce actionable findings for the community it intends to serve (Gall, Gall, & Borg, 2015). Accordingly, the studies, convenings, and research-based tools for practice that collectively make up the work of this initiative (as discussed previously) required thoughtful methodology that engaged our national community partners at all major junctions along the way. From the initiation stages of selection of focus to data collection and analysis, followed by action, reflection, and modifications (Gall et al., 2015), our partners were not merely involved in the research process but were actively constructing and making meaning of the emergent knowledge being produced.

As each study was designed to build on the findings of previous studies, the goal at hand was focused on developing research-based tools to provide the resources that higher education professionals needed to broaden access and success strategies in support of undocumented youth. With this practice-based objective in mind, we consulted with our advisory board as the studies progressed and frequently shared preliminary findings to help us better understand how to adapt the results to best benefit our higher education constituents. Upon refinement, our team would annually present at two major national association conferences (i.e., HACU and the AAHHE) to reflect with our national partners and gain insight on modifications that were necessary in our conceptual thinking and dissemination strategies. Had we not been actively engaging in reflection with these constituencies, it may not have occurred to us to change the aims of the research from a focus on changing policy to a focus on supporting institutional practice. Ultimately, this iterative process with our national partners and constituents molded our research into action-based tools that continue to serve the needs of higher education professionals who serve undocumented youth.

Conclusion

Established and emerging scholars, including many talented graduate students, have contributed to the transformational research, convening, and advocacy agenda of the National Forum's immigration initiative. As reform efforts led by United We Dream and other advocacy organizations persisted, the National Forum's efforts exemplified both the need for broad reform and the ability of higher education leaders to embrace and articulate the compelling educational interests of the nation's undocumented youth.

Speaking for the majority in the Supreme Court case affirming the right of undocumented students to a free public education in grades K–12, Justice William Brennan wrote, "Paradoxically, by depriving the children of any disfavored group of an education, we foreclose the means by which that group might raise the level of esteem in which it is held by the majority" (*Plyler v. Doe*, 1982). More than 30 years later, restrictive policies toward undocumented students in their pursuit of postsecondary education pose as existential a threat to the young undocumented population's social contribution and advancement as restrictions on access to K–12 education at the time of Justice Brennan's writing. In the higher education sector, however, undocumented students do not seek special treatment—only a level of recognition for their potential and respect for their aspirations on par with those enjoyed by their peers.

The National Forum's work on this issue has evolved to reflect the dynamics of shifting political and policy environments and the interests and perspectives of its team members, funders, partners, and advisers, all of whom have also strongly influenced the direction and focus of the effort. The collaborative and integrative nature of the National Forum makes room for all of these influences, but the work remains grounded in the fundamental compulsion to advance the public good mission of American higher education. Although the personnel and priorities of the immigration initiative have shifted over time, the principle of the public good that compels the work remains constant. The National Forum continues to believe that in time public policy will move toward reflecting the reality of the undocumented population's place as a contributor to the nation's economy and enabling the possibility of this population's potential to contribute fully to democratic society. As the National Forum continues to anticipate needed policy reforms, it will continue to develop resources for and pursue a research agenda to further enable institutional leaders supporting undocumented students on their campuses. The nation will continue to wait for a comprehensive approach to reforming an immigration system all interested parties appear to agree is broken.

In order to advance progress for this deeply personal and political policy matter, faculty, researchers, and policymakers must continue their scholarship even as they play an active part in the national discourse. Access to higher education for undocumented students has become increasingly commonplace in classroom discussions, course reading lists, and faculty research agendas. Scholarship on immigration issues in education has advanced significantly, but there are still large gaps to be filled through multiple disciplines, methodologies, and perspectives. The changing political landscape on issues of immigration complicate progress, but this should not slow the role of higher education researchers and practitioners in forging a path for undocumented student access and success.

Notes

1. These associations include those known as the "Big Six": the American Association of Community Colleges, the American Association of State Colleges and Universities, the American Council on Education, the Association of American Universities, the National Association of Independent Colleges and Universities, and the National Association of State Universities and Land-Grant Colleges.

2. "Boundary function" administrators are campus leaders responsible for specific activities closely affiliated with areas that determine access conditions for identified populations (e.g., Latin@, immigrant, and undocumented students). During this period of time, the immigration initiative was primarily focused on partnerships with admissions officers, financial aid officers, registrars, and general counsel.

References

Burkhardt, J. C., Ortega, N., Vidal-Rodriguez, A., Frye, J. R., Nellum, C. J., Reyes, K. A., & Hernandez, J. (2011). *Reconciling federal, state and institutional policies determining access for undocumented students: Implications for professional practice.* Ann Arbor: University of Michigan, National Forum on Higher Education for the Public Good.

Edelman, L. B. (1992). Legal ambiguity and symbolic structures: Organizational mediation of civil rights law. *American Journal of Sociology, 97*(6), 1531–1576.

Edelman, L. B., & Suchman, M. C. (1997). The legal environments of organizations. *Annual Review of Sociology, 23,* 479–515.

Gall, M. D., Gall, J. P., & Borg, W. R. (2015). Case studies in qualitative research. *Applying educational research: How to read, do and use research to solve problems of practice* (7th ed.). New York, NY: Pearson.

Gonzalez, R. G. (2009). *Young lives on hold: The college dreams of undocumented students.* New York, NY: The College Board.

Holley-Walker, D. (2011). Searching for equality: Equal protection clause challenges to bans on the admission of undocumented immigrant students to public universities. *Mich. St. L. Rev.*, 357.

National Forum on Higher Education for the Public Good. (2007). Program from *Challenges and opportunities: Conversations about immigration and higher education.* Ann Arbor: University of Michigan, National Forum on Higher Education for the Public Good.

Ortega, N. (2011). The role of higher education associations in shaping policy that connects immigration to educational opportunity: A social capital framework. *Journal of Hispanic Higher Education, 10*(1), 41–65.

Passel, J. S., and Cohn, D. (2011). *Unauthorized immigrant population: National and state trends, 2010.* Washington, DC: Pew Hispanic Center. Retrieved from http://www.pewhispanic.org/files/reports/133.pdf

Plyler v. Doe, 457 U.S. 202 (1982).

Suro, R., Suárez-Orozco, M. M., & Canizales, S. L. (2015). *Removing insecurity: How American children will benefit from President Obama's executive action on immigration.* Los Angeles: University of Southern California, Tomas Rivera Policy Institute. Retrieved from http://trpi.org/pdfs/research_report.pdf

10

"THE PROBLEM WITH OUR STUDENTS . . . IS THAT THEIR FAMILIES DON'T VALUE EDUCATION"

Magdalena Martinez

In the spring of 2012, I collaborated with a nationally respected scholar on a project that sought to help public postsecondary leaders use student data to create interventions designed to close the college completion gap between different ethnic groups. At the time, I served in a leadership role at a state agency for higher education, and I was the main liaison to the project. The lead scholar, who was a woman of color, worked with colleges and universities around the country and had developed a theoretically sound approach to examine institutional data to engage postsecondary leaders so that they could find solutions appropriate for their departments, courses, or campuses. A central principle of her research was that campus leaders be meaningfully engaged in defining the problem, understanding data, and finding solutions.

Our project culminated in a daylong workshop for four of the seven public postsecondary institutions in the state; participants included faculty, deans, chairs, and vice presidents. All were employed at emerging Hispanic-serving institutions (HSIs) with at least a 15% Latino student population. During the workshop, as the facilitator encouraged participants to examine their institutional data, a faculty member observed: "The problem with our students, in particular Latinos, is that their families don't value education." The facilitator, somewhat taken aback, attempted to continue the workshop, but another participant exclaimed, "I agree; all the Latina students I know either have kids or are pregnant. Or they are told they have to stay home to care for their siblings." No longer able to ignore the comments, the facilitator responded, "I am a Latina, and in this room there are at least three other Latinas who all have PhDs and whose parents did encourage them to attend and complete college." As the day continued, additional negative perceptions about Latino students, in particular males and undocumented students, were shared. The faculty comments, although initially difficult, opened the door to a deeper conversation about race, ethnicity, and gender.

These attitudes are likely more common than we care to admit, especially considering the lack of ethnic diversity in faculty and executive leadership on postsecondary campuses. The lives of students, in particular those from communities of color, are often misunderstood, generalized, or oversimplified. The faculty members who made the remarks had been at their colleges for about a decade; they were sincere but misinformed. As I reflected on this exchange, it underscored for me the reality that engaged research with specific communities (in this case college faculty and administrators) was not sufficient to gain a deep understanding of policy and practices that affect students; in this circumstance, Latinos. Rather, as illustrated in the example opening this chapter, there was a need to challenge assumptions about what we know about the students we teach. The faculty who spoke up had a reduced and likely incorrect understanding of their Latino students. The workshop's primary purpose was to examine and use institutional quantitative data to improve course and college completion for their students, but such data need to be contextualized for them to be truly meaningful and transformative.

In this chapter I offer an example of how critical qualitative data can help inform community partnerships and research that seek to understand the college experiences of Latino students, specifically for undocumented males, in order to improve college outcomes. The college completion agenda has almost exclusively relied on quantitative data to shape policy and practice decisions at the institutional and state levels. For the last two decades researchers have examined Latino experiences in the context of their campus environment and climate, social and academic integration, and relationships with faculty, but far less research has focused on Latino students' stories of how their lived experiences affect their college experience. Quintero (2010) reminds us that

> telling our own stories is intricately related to survival. We construct meanings as spiders make webs. And surviving is a complex task. There is physical survival. There is emotional survival. And, of course, there is historical and cultural survival. It may be that the only way to delve into survival is through personal story. (p. 136)

Quintero adds that telling stories represents a "means of expression, interpretation and/or transformation of our lives and the lives of those around
us" (p. 137). These narratives can not only help transform students' college
experiences but also alter faculty's perceptions about them and inform interventions, curriculum, and campus programs.

Research on the college experiences of undocumented Latino students
is virtually nonexistent. With the exception of Perez's (2009) book, *We ARE
Americans: Undocumented Students Pursuing the American Dream,* education
researchers and practitioners have little information about the more than 2.4
million children and youth under the age of 24 who are undocumented in
the United States. Simultaneously, scholars are questioning why the number
of Latino males in higher education is decreasing and are proposing national
and institutional approaches to improve their outcomes (Saenz & Ponjuan,
2009; Saenz, Ponjuan, & Figueroa, 2015). Undocumented Latinos are often
labeled but mostly misunderstood, existing under the radar of researchers
because they are reluctant to reveal their immigration status and discuss
their identities. Recently, however, because of discussions about reforming
immigration policy, this group of students is growing more visible. We can
expand our understanding of undocumented Latino males in higher education with critical theories and frameworks that incorporate cultural resources
and knowledge of their communities.

This chapter includes abbreviated data from a larger study that examined
first-year college experiences. Participants were recruited from three public
postsecondary institutions in a western state. Of the 24 individuals who participated, half were males. I use case study methodology (Stake, 1995; Yin,
1984) and present shortened case studies for three males who were undocumented at the time of the data collection. I use Yosso's community cultural
wealth model as a foundation to examine how Latino male students use cultural resources and knowledge in educational settings. Yosso's (2005) model
focuses on how people of color develop ways to counter systemic, material,
and social inequalities. Community cultural wealth in marginalized groups,
she argues, often goes unexamined or misinterpreted in educational research.
Yosso's model and the cultural resources and knowledge framework introduced in this chapter are based on the theoretical underpinnings of critical
race theory (CRT).

For educational researchers CRT offers a way to examine responses to
conditions from specific racial and ethnic perspectives. The theory critiques
educational practices purported to be motivated by the interests of students
of color.[1]

In CRT, racism is assumed to be a permanent fixture in U.S. society, and
the aim is to expose racism within educational structures. CRT scholars use

stories, poetry, fiction, and revisionist histories as important analytic tools to examine educational inequities and reveal multiple types of knowledge. This type of experiential approach is recognized as legitimate knowledge (Parker, Deyhle, & Villenas, 1999; Yosso, 2006) and uses a transdisciplinary approach to research. The goal of any research from this perspective is to create a socially just society. Similarly, Latina/o critical theorists (LatCrit) argue that any analysis must consider not only the realities of racism but also the intersections of other forms of subordination, such as sexism and discrimination based on language, immigration, phenotype, and sexuality (Solórzano & Delgado Bernal, 2001).

Latina/o critical race theorists, for instance, recognize that students of color confront campus microaggressions daily (Solórzano, 1998). Regardless of their theoretical orientations, researchers have documented how students of color often face racially hostile and unwelcoming environments at dominantly White institutions (Clements, 2000; Haro, Rodriguez, & Gonzales, 1994; Hurtado, 1994). Critical race researchers center their analysis on student perspectives, experiences, and understandings of race, ethnicity, gender, community, and self-empowerment (Delgado Bernal, 2001, 2002; Fernández, 2002; Solórzano, 1998; Solórzano & Delgado Bernal, 2001; Yosso, 2006). Although researchers have examined Latino college experiences using critical perspectives (e.g., Delgado Bernal, 2001; K. P. Gonzalez, 2002; Maldonado, Rhoads, & Buenavista, 2005), the role of immigration status has not been central.

Introduction of Students and Their Immigration Status

The three students in this analysis, Moroni, Tomas, and Chico (pseudonyms), were academically high-achieving, traditional-aged college students enrolled full-time at a two-year public college. Their undocumented immigration status was a source of strength and inspired them to have high academic goals.

Moroni and his family were active members of the Church of Jesus Christ of Latter-Day Saints (LDS).[2] Moroni was a shy 18-year-old who artfully communicated his beliefs about education, life, and religion. His extensive reading on issues related to integrity, values, and ethics separated him from many of his peers. Moroni and his family were from Mexico and arrived in the United States when he was 8 years old. Moroni did not see a pathway to change his immigration status. When asked where he saw himself in the future, he stated, "If I don't have my citizenship papers by like 25, I'm just gonna go [to Mexico] cause I don't want to live like this." When asked why he chose 25 as his deadline, he explained:

I just think I was going to wait 10 more years, but I can't go back to Mexico when I'm 28 or older than that 'cause I need to be young enough to, . . . like before I get married. I can't take a whole family over there. I don't know that much about how the economy is or how to work and live over there.

The ambiguity of his immigration status and the fear of deportation constantly weighed on how Moroni proceeded with his academic and life goals. There was no question he wanted to continue living in the United States, yet he did not want to "be hiding [his] whole life." He was keenly aware that his undocumented status would limit his work options, his ability to apply for financial aid, the type of postsecondary institutions he could attend, and his career choices. But he was undeterred; Moroni aspired to obtain a bachelor's degree in architecture and eventually a doctorate.

Chico was born in Mexico and arrived in the United States at the age of seven with his parents and older sister. He felt lucky that his family did not have to endure a difficult border crossing; they arrived by plane on a visitor's visa and overstayed their visa. In the sixth grade Chico became aware of his immigration status. His parents advised him that if someone asked him about his nationality to state that he was a U.S. citizen. By his junior year of high school he understood his immigration status limited his career and college options. He was enrolled in a magnet school and was unable to complete the selective program because the vocation certification required legal immigration status. At the time he also realized he could not apply for federal financial aid to attend a four-year institution. Chico lowered his voice when he spoke about his immigration status and sadly admitted that his "immigration status has placed a lot of barriers" to his education.

Chico carefully followed the legislative debates about the DREAM Act[3] and was "really, really hoping it would happen." Initially he was optimistic, but as time passed and Congress failed to pass any meaningful immigration reform laws, he felt less hopeful that his immigration status would change. Returning to Mexico was not an option. Chico had attended only American schools, and his primary language was English. When asked if he felt an allegiance to a country he quickly answered, "The U.S. because I've lived here for so long that I feel that this is my home. I don't feel that Mexico is my home."

Tomas had been in the United States for less than five years. Tomas, his mother, and his younger brother were reunited with his father, who had lived in the United States for more than 10 years. Unlike Moroni and Chico, Tomas had left and reentered the United States at different points in his life. Tomas spent considerable time living and attending school in Mexico. His life in Mexico framed his academic and life goals. He was critical of the Mexican government and saw little economic and social mobility there regardless of the amount of education he could obtain. Tomas found it difficult to relate to U.S.-born Latinos and felt youth in this country did not understand the economic and social advantages here compared to other countries, such as Mexico. In his view, U.S.-born Latinos had many educational doors open to them but often did not take advantage of these opportunities. Tomas lamented the fact that he and other undocumented immigrants did not have the same opportunities, although he admitted he had more opportunities in the United States than in Mexico. He saw issues of language and immigration status as barriers he could eventually overcome. He had no intention of returning to Mexico.

Moroni, Tomas, and Chico faced myriad challenges their first year in college, including financial difficulties, confronting campus microaggressions, adjusting to course work expectations, family responsibilities, and concerns with immigration status. Within four years of beginning college Moroni transferred to a research university in another western state and graduated, Tomas also graduated, and Chico's college status was unknown. In the following section, I highlight the role of cultural resources and knowledge and how the three used these resources to navigate their first year of college.

Cultural Resources and Knowledge

Critical theorists suggest that cultural resources enable students to participate in academic settings and construct strategies for adaptation and survival (Delgado Bernal, 2002; N. Gonzalez, Moll, & Amanti, 2005; Orellana, 2003). Students' perceptions of campus climate are considered important analytic frames to understand their postsecondary decisions and strategies for success (K. P. Gonzalez, 2002; Maldonado et al., 2005; Solórzano, 1998; Tierney, 2000). Equally important are students' perceptions and understanding of their culture within the context of their educational experiences and how their culture is used as a resource to achieve their postsecondary goals.

In this analysis I use Geertz's (1973) interpretation of culture to mean a system of shared values, beliefs, norms, assumptions, and ideologies constructed in groups through various practices (e.g., verbal and nonverbal communication, rituals, artifacts, traditions, and myths). As such, culture gives significance to groups and provides members with frameworks by which to construct systems of meaning and ways of organizing behavior.

A cultural resource is a culturally based asset, material, or value that can enhance a student's undergraduate experience. The student draws on such a resource during difficult times or when handling a new situation. A resource can provide relief or bring resolution to a difficult situation. These resources are often derived from life lessons, experiences, and interactions; for instance, immigration status, gender, religion, economic status, and ethnicity. The Latino males in this analysis drew from three central resources as they navigated their first year of college: (a) their sense of ethnic, racial, or regional identity; (b) narratives and *consejos* (advice or counsel) shared by family; (c) relationships and networks; (d) cultural knowledge of social inequities; and (e) cultural knowledge of bilingual and bicultural practices. Their identities were context driven yet always encompassed the role of ethnicity and race within U.S. culture and society. The students also saw their parents as knowledgeable, valued their experiences, and drew from their examples to make educational decisions. The relationships and networks they developed were often an expression of their identity and drew on interpretations of important narratives and *consejos* shared by significant individuals in their lives.

Identity

Tajfel's (1981) social identity theory assumes individuals' self-concepts derive from knowing that they are members of particular groups. Tajfel hypothesized that the formation of social identities is the consequence of three social psychological processes: categorization, comparison, and distinctiveness. Social categorization refers to nationality, language, race and ethnicity, skin color, or any other social or physical characteristic meaningful in particular social contexts. Social comparison involves the characteristics of individual groups, such as status, that become significant in relation to a perceived difference from other groups. Social distinctiveness involves the desire to achieve a positive distinction. From this perspective, ethnic and racial identities are equivalent to other forms of identities. Individuals draw on these identities depending on the context and on the other group identities present. For this study, racial and ethnic identities were considered along with other identities (e.g., gender, religion, immigrant status, socioeconomic status) students deem important.

Moroni's identity was primarily connected to his religion and his Mexican ethnicity. At times the two intersected; his religious education and involvement had been largely in Spanish and with other Mormons of Mexican origin. He often admitted that religion was the "most important" part of his identity, saying

> I think that's the most important one of all. Like being Mormon, like I think it dictates in what I believe in basically. How I act, the people I hang out with. My political stance is pretty much based on my religion too. So I think that's the biggest part of my life.

Although his religion played a central role in his identity, his ethnicity was also important. He preferred to identify as a Mexican immigrant rather than Latino or Hispanic: "'Immigrant' is something I would use. But Hispanic and Latino, I don't like those labels." In his academic work, Moroni often drew from his Mexican and Mormon experiences. Topics for class papers and discussion often concerned his religion, such as morality and mortality, and his ethnic and religious identities.

Chico was also vocal about his ethnic identity in educational settings and with his peers. He rarely spoke Spanish in high school and was a part of the "Asian group" of students on campus. A turning point for him was attending a Latino precollege leadership program geared to prepare students for college. Chico described himself as a "Latino Mexican American."

> Latino because I speak Spanish. . . Mexican because I was born in Mexico, my *familia* is Mexican, *teniendo sangre mexicana en mis venas* [having Mexican blood in my veins], and I grew up in Mexico until I was 7 years old; and American because I speak English, I studied in American schools since second grade, now graduated from one, and grew up with the American culture.

Chico was involved in the Movimiento Estudiantil Chicano de Aztlan (MEChA), which shaped his student and ethnic identity. He said, "If you are involved with MEChA, people automatically have an assumption about you being politically active, very intelligent, knows what happens around." Chico further differentiated his view of ethnic identity by social class as he explained that he liked the *fresa* (strawberry) talk. Among Latino youth *fresas* are Latinos who are middle to upper class and described as "preppy" or mainstream. Often these individuals have an easier time in mainstream institutions and settings (Moje & Martinez, 2007). Chico explains, "I don't know why, but I like the way certain Mexicans talk. I like change, the way I dress, the way I talk. I am constantly changing. When I heard them [other MEChA students] talk, I said 'I'm going to try that.'" Like Moroni, Chico incorporated his sense of ethnic identity into his classroom learning and was often a source of inspiration and motivation.

Tomas did not identify with Latino, Hispanic, or even Mexican labels; rather he preferred to identify with the city where he was born and raised, Guadalajara. He explained,

Me identifico con la ciudad en la que nací, en donde viví. . . . Yo no me considero como parte de todo México, se me hace muy distinto. La manera de ser de la gente y la actitud y todo me gusta más de la ciudad donde vivo. Y porque las otras ciudades no me agradan, por eso me considero de mi ciudad.	I identify with the city in which I was born, where I was raised. . . . I don't consider myself part of all of Mexico, I think it is very distinct. The way that people are and the attitude, and I like everything more about the city where I lived. And because other cities do not please me, that's why I identify with my city.

Tomas admitted that most of the time in educational spaces it is necessary for him to identify as Latino or Hispanic. Unlike Chico he does not necessarily look to student ethnic organizations to validate his identity or experiences of growing up in the United States. The fact that Tomas entered and left the United States at different points in his life played a significant role in how he interpreted his identity. In fact, he identified more often as an international student in educational settings and was not conflicted about U.S. assimilation, like Moroni and Chico. All three males held a fluid interpretation of their identity and labeled themselves depending on situations they were in, yet it was clear their identities were a resource for classroom assignments that allowed them to incorporate their reflections on social structures. Their social identities were often shaped by counter-stories and *consejos* shared by family.

Counter-Stories, Narratives, and Consejos

Narratives and counter-stories are a means to sustain and circulate cultural resources and knowledge within groups. Latino families pass on to their children important *consejos* and culturally based *educación* to help them succeed; these constructs are also referred to as pedagogies of the home (Villenas & Moreno, 2001), funds of knowledge (N. Gonzalez, et al., 2005; Vélez-Ibáñez & Greenberg, 1992), and community cultural wealth (Yosso, 2005). Valdés (1996) described *consejos* as "spontaneous homilies designed to influence behavior and attitudes" (p. 125) that go beyond providing advice to solve a particular problem. Valdés also considered *la educación de los hijos* (education of the children) in a much broader sense to include personal development beyond academic learning. According to Espinoza-Herold (2007), "Education in the Latino family includes manners, moral values, and rules of conduct, in addition to aspirations and expectations for the future" (p. 262). All families, regardless of race, engage in similar practices; however, mainstream educators and researchers historically have interpreted Latino family practices as counterproductive to the academic motivation and success of their children. In the case of the Latino males in this chapter, counter-stories and *consejos* shaped their social identities and were an integral ingredient in academic success.

Narratives and counter-storytelling in education research is a method of recounting the experiences and perspectives of racially and socially marginalized people. Yosso (2006) suggested that such an approach raises critical consciousness about social and racial injustice that directly affects communities of color. Researchers have found that storytelling is an important component in learning about structural inequality, teaching children how to handle difficult situations, and countering negative images in the dominant media and society (Flores, 2000; Gándara, 1995; Olmedo, 2003; Villenas, 2001). Within this tradition of critical theories (López & Parker, 2003; Parker et al., 1999) stories are treated as valid and valuable knowledge that "merit serious attention as forms of social analysis" (Renato, 1993, p. 143). Flores (2000) suggested that narratives and counter-stories offer a "dimension of oppositionality" (p. 691) that allows marginalized and disenfranchised communities to create discourses about themselves. In doing so, stories provide a "means of 'historical correction,' sharing power within a culture, and have the resistive power and liberating potential in their shifting of insider/outsider boundaries" (Flores, p. 692). In effect, counter-stories offer critical reflection on the experiences and histories of individuals whose voices are often excluded in research.

Moroni's father often shared stories about his involvement in a "Communist group" and how he once had to hide from authorities because of his protests to have running water in underserved Mexican villages. Another time, his father and friends in college hijacked a bus to bring attention to their social justice causes. Moroni believed that his father "knows a lot," and he liked "discussing politics and religion with him." Both Moroni and his father shared stories about each other. Moroni explained the "American version" of history he was taught as compared to his father's version:

> He went to college and stuff, so he knows a lot about history. He knows history, but the way he was taught in Mexico, so that's another thing we discuss. The Mexican–American War—like I was taught the American version, and he was taught the Mexican version. So I have fun discussing it.

Another form of sharing narratives and *consejos* is through music. Moroni's father often wrote and sang *corridos*.[4] His father wrote about love, relationships, and famed lawbreakers or *narcotraficantes* (drug traffickers).

THE PROBLEM WITH OUR STUDENTS. . ."   225

The ballads are about things . . . like soap operas, people loving each other, girlfriends . . . There's one about a girl that likes her brother's friend, and there's one about a guy who *es un narcotraficante*, and the police get his son and tells [sic] him that if he doesn't give up they'll kill his son and stuff. And he wrote one to my mom and one when my sister was born. And he wrote one when they were 10 years married. I read that one. I liked that one.

His father's *corridos* were often laden with moral lessons and *consejos* on disposition and persistence, in particular about education.

Chico's parents had high expectations of him and communicated these through stories about their own lives. His mother completed a vocational career training program in Mexico and was a physical education teacher for seven years, then worked at an airline for about five years before immigrating to the United States. Chico's mother often shared stories of her life in Mexico and her high expectations and standards, which were encouraged by her father. Through his mother's stories Chico became conscious of the gender inequalities in society. He attributed his feminist identity to his mother and told the following religious story to illustrate the importance of women.

Well, she told me the story that Eve was not made up of Adam's feet to get stepped over. She wasn't made out of his skull to be put over. She was made out of his rib cage, you know, close to the heart, an essential part of the body; below the shoulder for protection but right next to the heart for love. So that's one of the things that stuck with me.

Chico drew on stories for classroom assignments and would often highlight the important role of strong women in his life. For instance, in an English assignment, he wrote about Anita, a Chicana professor:

Anita, a Chicano/Chicana professor at [the university], has been someone I've looked up to for close to three years now. Anita is politically conscious, a feminist, a Chicana, and a very dear friend of mine. When a question swims in my conscience, she always knows the exact words to better help me understand. Anita is my unofficial *persontor* [a feminist term derived from *mentor*], whom I can look up to no matter the question or subject.

Chico explained how his father taught him to be compassionate and loving toward himself and others, despite his father's difficult childhood. "It's amazing to me," said Chico. "He comes from a life which he is able to step out [of]. He's given me a very different life than his." Like Moroni, Chico's parents offered *consejos* on how to succeed and pointed to the opportunities afforded to them in the United States, yet they were critical of the political environment, especially related to immigration reform.

Tomas's father played an important role in his life and shared stories and *consejos* on life and achieving his goals. In particular, Tomas's father often pushed him to finish what he started. Like Chico's father, Tomas's father grew up under very difficult circumstances without much adult supervision, yet he was able to remake his obstacles into lessons on how to raise his own family. Consequently, intelligence in his family was measured not only by academic achievement but also by resourcefulness in sustaining a family. In Tomas's view, his father's life in the United States was a model of endurance and persistence in the face of significant economic and social obstacles. Tomas translated this into his own educational ambition, feeling it was possible to succeed despite his linguistic and immigration hurdles.

Relationships and Networks

Their relationships provided all three young men with cultural nourishment (K. P. Gonzalez, 2002). These support networks included family members, mentors, friends, and role models who also served as cultural translators and brokers, passing on information about their personal experiences and their knowledge of the dominant, White, middle-class culture to help students in mainstream schools and colleges (Maldonado et al., 2005; Moje & Martinez, 2007).

Moroni's central relationships and networks were connected to the LDS Church. A church member encouraged his father to immigrate to the United States. In their local church other immigrant Latinos shared their ethnic culture, rituals, and language within the context of their faith. Moroni's relationships and networks in and outside of college were always connected to his church. Before college, these were primarily with Latinos, but after college he was invited on a mission, and his network expanded. Only a few members from his local church went on to college, and even fewer served church missions, mostly for financial reasons. Moroni's decision to go on a mission exposed him to non-Latino networks and relationships with high-ranking White church leaders and members. He then was invited to attend other meetings and presentations outside of his regular Latino LDS ward and was encouraged to consider other career options. For instance, he said he attended an "LDS General Conference, and somebody talked about the importance of education and mentioned some things about agriculture. I wanted to major in landscape architecture, but now I want to see what I can do in agriculture."

Moroni's mission was the beginning of a new circle of networks and relationships with other Mormon men. Few males in his Spanish-speaking ward were called on missions; Moroni received more attention than other young missionaries and felt a sense of pride and responsibility to represent not only his family but also his Latino ward. Other Latino members with whom he regularly attended church provided affirmation of his immigrant identity and experiences on a day-to-day basis, and White LDS members provided him a bridge to mainstream culture. Moroni drew from both these networks in his academic career.

Like Moroni, Chico's relationships and networks were an extension of his identity. His first-year involvement in the Chicano student group played a central role in his college experience. He attended weekly meetings, volunteered for student activities and programs, demonstrated for social justice causes, and socialized with others in the group. In addition, Latino faculty and administrators serving as advisers to the student group helped him access campus resources. Chico knew them on a first-name basis and often spent time with them outside the classroom and in social settings. Chico also knew Latino academic advisers whom he met his first year.

Tomas's network of support primarily included his family and other Latino immigrant students on campus. In particular, his parents played an important role in grounding his U.S. educational experiences, including his first year of college. For instance, although it was difficult for him to adjust to college socially, he interpreted such isolation from a broader societal perspective of living in the United States and felt his isolation was what many immigrants experienced as a result of being in a new country and learning a new culture. A strong family unit was critical to his social survival. Other immigrant Latino students also served as an extension of his support network and often provided encouragement. Tomas met a Latino academic counselor at a precollege leadership program. He often consulted him. Toward the end of his second semester Tomas considered another major, but his counselor encouraged him to stick to a science-related degree.

Cultural Knowledge of Social Inequalities

Moroni, Chico, and Tomas viewed their culturally based knowledge of social inequalities as a strength when confronting first-year college challenges. Consistent with previous research, their life experiences and family stories provided them a filter for their campus experiences (Delgado Bernal, 2001). Their parents often shared knowledge of social inequalities through stories, *consejos*, and other cultural modes of communication. Delgado Bernal (2001) reminds us that

> Community and family knowledge is taught to youth through such ways as legends, *corridos*, storytelling, and behavior. It is through culturally specific

ways of teaching and learning that ancestors and elders share the knowledge of conquest, segregation, labor market stratification, patriarchy, homophobia, assimilation, and resistance. This knowledge that is passed from one generation to the next. . . can help us survive in everyday life. (p. 624)

Moroni, Chico, and Tomas translated their cultural knowledge about social, political, and economic inequalities into college survival skills.

Moroni's father often shared stories with his son about social unrest in Mexico and his own socialist ideals. Stories of social justice and economic inequality were common themes in many of these narratives. In fact, his father saw immigrating to the United States as an act of resistance against an oppressive Mexican government. Moroni recognized inequalities existed in the United States, yet his frame of reference was the social and economic injustices in Mexico learned through family stories. For instance, Moroni's father completed a college degree in Mexico but was unable to support his family there. It was *necesidad* (necessity) and *hambre* (hunger) that forced Moroni's family to leave Mexico. Consequently, Moroni was very critical of the Mexican system but felt a strong "responsibility" to "go back and help people" in Mexico. Specifically, he said, "I feel I have a responsibility to go back and help people. I think there's a lot of bad things going on [in Mexico]. If more Mexicans were to go back from the U.S., things would change." When asked for an example, he replied,

Like the way the police behave, politicians. The more people who live in the U.S., when they go to Mexico it's like taking [the] U.S. to Mexico. There are some principles and values that apply to all countries, like working with transparency, when government accounts for what it does.

Even though Moroni recognized there were inequalities related to his immigration status and postsecondary options, he felt these were barriers he could overcome through persistence and resilience. Moroni did not "blame" the United States for "protecting its borders"; instead, he hoped "good citizens" like him would eventually be rewarded with a pathway to legal residency. Moroni did not see himself as a victim of his immigration status or barriers faced during his first year of college; rather, these experiences prompted him to feel he could help solve social inequalities.

Unlike Moroni, Chico was very critical of the United States and its xenophobic culture. Chico's mother taught him about how race, gender, religion, and sexual orientation injustices intersected within social institutions. She encouraged him to be analytical about widely accepted views in academia, popular culture, and the media. Chico's knowledge of social inequalities came from his mother's stories of her life and the female immigrant experience. This helped him confront difficult classroom conversations on race, gender, and immigration.

Cultural Knowledge of Bilingual and Bicultural Practices

Yosso (2005) describes linguistic capital as more than just knowledge of an additional language; rather, it recognizes individuals as "engaged participants" who gain "intellectual and social skills attained through communication experiences in more than one language and/or style" (p. 78). Linguistic or cultural translation and teaching or tutoring family members are seen as enriching students' overall knowledge (Orellana, 2003).

In the classroom and on campus, the students' bilingual and bicultural knowledge played a significant role. Moroni, Chico, and Tomas consciously used their linguistic capital to acculturate new knowledge. Moroni used his bilingual and bicultural skills to help him achieve his academic goals and to help his family navigate mainstream culture. In college he joined Latino student groups to sustain his Mexican identity. In class assignments he often used his spoken language and the cultural language familiar to him to make sense of assignments and theories. For instance, based on his bilingual experiences he was motivated to research the role of language acquisition in early childhood development for one of his courses. He viewed his knowledge of multiple languages and his Mexican culture as strengths he could use to assimilate and understand his course assignments.

Moroni's bilingual and bicultural knowledge was further reinforced in his LDS ward, where Spanish was the primary language for religious readings and text discussions. LDS practices and rituals, such as meals, were adapted to Latino cultural practices.

Chico also used his bilingual and bicultural skills in educational settings. Although he did not often speak Spanish in high school, in college he sought out opportunities to incorporate his linguistic and bicultural knowledge in course assignments. In one example, Chico told his professor why he wanted to focus on a Latino artist, Gerado Mejia, for a class assignment:

> I did [the assignment on] a song called *Sueña* [Dream]. It's really cool. He [the artist] is talking to a younger person, telling them not to give into everybody's negative influence and just believe, keep on going. That song is very powerful, and that's why I chose it. And it's in Spanish. At first I asked him [his professor] if I could do the song. And he said it would be best in English, and then I told him it's a very good message, and I'd like to present it. I will translate it. At first he was skeptical. He was saying "no" because he said that everybody else won't be able to feel the power. And then I was

telling him, "If I translated it and people actually read it, the message will get through no matter what." And so I did do the presentation. The whole time he was skeptical, and, from me feeling his doubt, it just kind of motivated me. And my two friends said, "You know you should just do a song in English *para que no estés peleando con el* [so you won't be fighting with him]." But I was, "No." It just motivated me so much that that was the best presentation that I've done.

Chico was discouraged from presenting his chosen artist, yet he insisted and prevailed. Mejia is an Ecuadorian American rapper turned recording executive, known for his *reggaeton* (Spanish hip-hop, rap) music. Chico did not see his language and cultural knowledge as in conflict with his educational goals; when allowed, he drew from these resources.

Reflections

As illustrated in this chapter, engaged research needs to incorporate multiple levels of critical analysis in order to challenge embedded assumptions; in this case about students we serve. In this chapter I discuss how a well-intended research project and subsequent workshop on how to improve college completion revealed the assumptions college faculty and administrators held about students they served. I suggest that multiple methods be incorporated as part of engaged research to present a contextualized understanding of undocumented Latino male college students. I illustrate how critical qualitative methods can be used to reveal a richer and complex picture of students. I present abbreviated case studies of three undocumented Latino male students with a focus on the students' stories and how they used their cultural knowledge and resources during their first year of college. Had such data been available as part of the college completion research project, they may have encouraged faculty, administrators, and/or community partners to reframe their understanding of the students they served.

There is no denying that students benefit from access to basic college culture knowledge throughout their education. For example, knowing how to apply for admissions, get financial assistance, and interact with faculty, peers, and advisers are all important to succeed in college. For the three young men who are highlighted in this chapter, culturally based resources and knowledge were equally important. Yosso's (2005) community wealth capital framework provided a critical lens to understand how they interpreted their families' stories and created meaning. Latino families and communities intentionally encourage, teach, and advise their children on how to succeed in college by passing along knowledge of their native language, customs, and rituals. Strong commitments to ethnic communities and critical awareness of social, economic, and political inequalities and intergenerational relationships were key to these students' first-year experience. In many instances, their social identities and family backgrounds mitigated challenges and helped connect them to other students, faculty, and college personnel. Specifically, ethnic student groups served as sites where college knowledge, resources, and peer advice circulated in a place where ethnic and social identities and cultural knowledge were validated. Employing critical qualitative methods to understand students' stories can provide a deeper understanding of why students attend college, how they overcome challenges, and how faculty and administrators can meaningfully engage them in and outside the classroom.

In his seminal book on social analysis, Rosaldo (1993) states, "Stories often shape, rather than simply reflect, human conduct" (p. 129). He quotes psychologist Jerome Bruner, who argued, "stories shape action because they embody compelling motives, strong feelings, vague aspirations, clear intentions, or well-defined goals" (p. 129). It was clear that the stories, as narrated and understood by the young men in this chapter, shaped their academic aspirations, intentions, and goals. By encouraging students to critically reflect on their experiences and interpret their material, social, and political challenges and how they overcome barriers, researchers and faculty can open the door to critically reflect on their perceptions of their students and engage in a deeper conversation about race, ethnicity, and gender as understood and narrated by students themselves.

Notes

1. Ladson-Billings (1998) illustrates how this is done in school curriculum by describing the way that White supremacist master scripts silence multiple voices and perspectives by reducing, for instance, Martin Luther King Jr. to a "sanitized folk hero" who fought for a race-neutral society. This script, she argues, "presumes a homogenized 'we' in a celebration of diversity. . . . Thus, students are taught erroneously that 'we are all immigrants,' and, as a result, African American, Indigenous, and Chicano students are left with the guilt of failing to rise above their immigrant status like every other group" (p. 18).

2. Latino membership has increased 35% since 1995, and Spanish speakers now account for 130,000 of the 5.5 million U.S. members of the Church of Latter-Day Saints, according to church figures. It is estimated that by 2020 the Latino population will make up 50% of the Mormon membership in Utah (Solórzano, 2005).

3. The DREAM Act would permit certain immigrant students who have grown up in the United States to apply for temporary legal status, obtain permanent status, and become eligible for citizenship if they go to college or serve in the U.S.

military. The Act would also eliminate a federal provision that penalizes states that provide in-state tuition without regard to immigration status.

4. A *corrido* is a Mexican ballad or folk song in the form of a narrative. Various themes are featured in Mexican *corridos*, and *corrido* lyrics are often old legends about a famed criminal or hero in the rural frontier areas. Some *corridos* may also be love stories. Contemporary *corridos* written within the past few decades feature much more modern themes (Hernández, 1999).

References

Clements, E. (2000). Creating a campus climate in which diversity is truly valued. *New Directions for Community Colleges, 28*(4), 63–72.

Delgado Bernal, D. (2001). Learning and living pedagogies of the home: The *mestizo* consciousness of Chicana students. *Qualitative Studies in Education, 14*(5), 623–639.

Delgado Bernal, D. (2002). Critical race theory, Latino critical theory, and critical raced-gendered epistemologies: Recognizing students of color as holders and creators of knowledge. *Qualitative Inquiry, 8*(2), 105–126.

Espinoza-Herold, M. (2007). Stepping beyond *Sí Se Puede: Dichos* as a cultural resource in mother–daughter interaction in a Latino family. *Anthropology & Education Quarterly, 38*(3), 260–277.

Fernández, L. (2002). Telling stories about school: Using critical race and Latino critical theories to document Latina/Latino education and resistance. *Qualitative Inquiry, 8*(1), 45–65.

Flores, L. A. (2000). Reclaiming the "Other": Toward a Chicana feminist critical perspective. *International Journal of Intercultural Relations, 24*, 687–705.

Gándara, P. (1995). *Over the ivy walls: The educational mobility of low-income Chicanos*. Albany, NY: State University of New York Press.

Geertz, C. (1973). *The interpretations of culture*. New York, NY: Basic Books.

Gonzalez, K. P. (2002). Campus culture and the experiences of Chicano students in a predominantly White university. *Urban Education, 37*(2), 193–218.

Gonzalez, N., Moll, L. C., & Amanti, C. (2005). *Funds of knowledge: Theorizing practices in households, communities, and classrooms*. Mahwah, NJ: Erlbaum.

Haro, R. P., Rodriguez, G. J., & Gonzales, J. L. (1994). *Latino persistence in higher education: A 1994 survey of university of California and California State University Chicano/Latino students*. San Francisco, CA: Latino Issues Forum.

Hernandez, G. E. (1999). What is a *corrido?* Thematic representation and narrative discourse. *Studies in Latin American Popular Culture*. Retrieved from http://www.chicano.ucla.edu/center/events/whatisacorrido.html

Hurtado, S. (1994). The institutional climate for talented Latino students. *Research in Higher Education, 35*, 21–41.

Ladson-Billings, G. (1998). Just what is critical race theory and what's it doing in a nice field like education? *International Journal of Qualitative Studies in Education, 11*(1), 7–24.

López, G., & Parker, L. (Eds.). (2003). *Interrogating racism in qualitative research methodology*. New York, NY: Peter Lang.

Maldonado, E. Z., Rhoads, R., & Buenavista, T. L. (2005). The student-initiated retention project: Theoretical contributions and the role of self-empowerment. *American Educational Research Journal, 42*(4), 605–638.

Moje, E. B., & Martinez, M. (2007). The role of peers, families, and ethnic identity enactments in educational persistence and achievement of Latino and Latina youth. In A. J. Fuligni (Ed.), *Contesting stereotypes and creating identities: social categories, social identities, and education participation* (pp. 219–238), New York, NY: Russel Sage Foundation.

Olmedo, I. M. (2003). Accommodation and resistance: Latinas struggle for their children's education. *Anthropology & Education, 34*(4), 373–395.

Orellana, M. F. (2003). *In other words: Learning from bilingual kids' translating experiences*. Evanston, IL: School of Education and Social Policy, Northwestern University.

Parker, L., Deyhle, D., & Villenas, S. (Eds.). (1999). *Race is . . . race isn't: Critical race theory and qualitative studies in education*. Boulder, CO: Westview Press.

Perez, W. (2009). *We are Americans: Undocumented students pursuing the American dream*. Sterling, VA: Stylus.

Quintero, E. (2010). Learning from children's and teachers' stories. In L. Diaz Soto & H. Kharen (Eds.), *Teaching bilingual/bicultural children (pp. 135–144)*. New York, NY: Peter Lang.

Rosaldo, R. (1993). *Culture and truth: The remaking of social analysis*. Boston, MA: Beacon Press.

Renato, R. (1993). *Culture and truth: The remaking of social analysis*. Boston, MA: Beacon Press.

Saenz, V. B., & Ponjuan, L. (2009). The vanishing Latino male in higher education. *Journal of Hispanic Higher Education, 8*(1), 54–89.

Saenz, V. B., Ponjuan, L., & Figueroa, J. (2015). *Ensuring the success of Latino males in higher education: A new national perspective*. Sterling, VA: Stylus.

Solórzano, D. G. (1998). Critical race theory, race and gender microaggressions, and the experience of Chicana and Chicano scholars. *International Journal of Qualitative Studies in Education, 11*, 121–136.

Solórzano, D., & Delgado Bernal, D. (2001). Critical race theory, transformational resistance and social justice: Chicana and Chicano students in an urban context. *Urban Education, 36*, 308–342.

Stake, R. E. (1995). *The art of case study research*. Thousand Oaks, CA: SAGE.

Tajfel, H. (1981). *Human groups and social categories*. New York, NY: Cambridge University Press.

Tierney, W. G. (2000). Power, identity, and the dilemma of college student departure. In J. M. Braxton (Ed.), *Rethinking the student departure puzzle* (pp. 213–235). Nashville, TN: Vanderbilt University Press.

Valdés, G. (1996). *Con respeto: Bridging the distances between culturally diverse families and schools: An ethnographic portrait*. New York, NY: Teachers College Press.

Vélez-Ibáñez, C., & Greenberg, J. (1992) Formation and transformation of funds of knowledge among U.S.-Mexican households. *Anthropology Education Quarterly, 23*(4), 313–335.

Villenas, S. (2001). Latina mothers and small-town racisms: Creating narratives of dignity and moral education in North Carolina. *Anthropology & Education Quarterly, 32*(1), 3–28.

Villenas, S., & Moreno, M. (2001). To *valerse por si misma* between race, capitalism, and patriarchy: Latina mother-daughter pedagogies in North Carolina. *International Journal of Qualitative Studies in Education, 14*(5), 671–688.

Yin, R. (1984). *Case study research: Design and methods.* Newbury Park, CA: SAGE.

Yosso, T. J. (2005). Whose culture has capital? A critical race theory discussion of community cultural wealth. *Race Ethnicity and Education, 8*(1), 69–91.

Yosso, T. J. (2006). *Critical race counterstories along the Chicana/Chicano educational pipeline.* New York, NY: Routledge.

11

LINKING STATE PRIORITIES WITH LOCAL STRATEGIES
Examining the Role of Communities in Postsecondary Access and Success in Michigan

Nathan J. Daun-Barnett

A
ccess to an affordable, high-quality postsecondary education is one of the most compelling public priorities in the twenty-first century. Policymakers and education advocates increasingly call for a more highly educated workforce to compete in a global knowledge economy. Jobs that once required a high school diploma or vocational certification increasingly require some postsecondary education and a sustained commitment to lifelong learning. Unfortunately, throughout the latter part of the twentieth century, the cost of college has risen much faster than inflation, and family wages have not kept pace, which has made the dream of a postsecondary education increasingly difficult for low-income, first-generation, and underrepresented minority students to achieve.

Historically, states have assumed much of the responsibility for providing affordable postsecondary education in the United States, and the federal government has expanded its role providing financial assistance to low- and middle-income students and families over the past 50 years, but support for higher education is competing for scarce taxpayer dollars, and public support has not kept pace with increased demand. Local communities have played a role in higher education since the expansion of community colleges in the 1940s and 1950s, but they are beginning to play a more prominent role as catalysts for postsecondary opportunity.

This chapter examines the development of the community-based college access strategy in Michigan from the work of the Statewide Commission on Higher Education and Economic Growth in 2004 through the announcement of the Kalamazoo Promise to the proliferation of local college access networks (LCANs) and Promise Zones through the second decade of the twenty-first century. The National Forum on Higher Education for the Public Good (National Forum) played an important role in the early stages of developing local strategies to address college access in Michigan, and it laid the foundation for what has become a model for other states. From this point on, I refer to the National Forum as "we," because I was part of the National Forum during this work. Michigan is not the only state to connect local assets and initiatives (grassroots) with state-level policies and priorities (grasstops), but it is the first to elevate communities to such a prominent role in postsecondary access. The seeds of innovation from Michigan are beginning to take root in other states, and their experience is instructive for others.

In this chapter, I examine the development and evolution of a community-based strategy to improve postsecondary opportunity across the state. I focus on recent developments from the announcement of the Lieutenant Governor's Commission on Higher Education and Economic Growth in 2004 to the establishment of more than 50 local college access networks in communities across Michigan. I use a multidimensional framework of social change to examine how communities develop unique solutions to complex social challenges and respond to state incentives to conform to a set of identified "best" or "promising" practices. The framework illuminates why it can be so challenging to align local practices with state policies. In the process of tracing the evolution of local access strategies in Michigan, I also describe three critical developments in Michigan that have framed contemporary debates around college access and success. The first critical developments in the college access debate in Michigan I describe are the two University of Michigan affirmative action cases—*Grutter v. Bollinger* and *Gratz v. Bollinger*—which upheld the principle of race-sensitive college admissions and called for a holistic review of each application but sparked a conversation about affirmative action that eventually resulted in a ballot initiative to change the state constitution. Those cases continue to reverberate throughout the higher education community. The second critical moment for college access in Michigan was the announcement of the Kalamazoo Promise, which has become the model place-based tuition guarantee program—scores of communities across the country have considered or attempted to replicate its work. Its success has reverberated across the country, and as many as a dozen communities have similar initiatives in place. This chapter looks at anticipated outcomes

In the first section of this chapter, I consider briefly the barriers known to influence students' chances for postsecondary participation in order to understand how local access strategies have evolved. In the second section I discuss the multidimensional framework for social change as a way to conceptualize the evolution of local solutions to the college access challenge. This framework was developed to understand the role community foundations play in the establishment and development of LCANs, but it is applicable to the broader contours of social change initiated at the local level. The third section examines the evolution of local initiatives in Michigan, and the final section considers the role of engaged research in the social change process.

Strategies to Address Barriers to Postsecondary Access

College access is one of the central issues facing educators, researchers, and policymakers, and the challenges are complex. A good deal of work has been done examining the effects of academic preparation (Allensworth, Nomi, Montgomery, & Lee, 2009; Perna, Rowan-Kenyon, Bell, Thomas, & Li, 2008), college affordability (Heller, 1999; Long, 2007; St. John, Daun-Barnett, & Moronski, 2012), and access to information and support on the choices students make about whether or where to attend college (Conley, 2005; Daun-Barnett, & Das, 2013; Venegas, 2006). One strand of the college access literature suggests that misalignment of K–12 and higher education systems results in confusing and contradictory signals sent to students and families about the path to and through postsecondary education (Kirst & Venezia, 2004; Vargas, 2004). Researchers have developed comprehensive conceptual models to make sense of this complex terrain. For example, St. John and Asker (2003) use the balanced access model to argue that in order to increase college participation, policymakers must attend to both the academic preparation students receive in high school and students' ability to afford the cost of college. Further, Perna (2006) proposes a four-level conceptual model that recognizes college access operates at the individual, school and community, higher education, and broader sociopolitical levels. Her model recognizes that the effects of policies, practices, and intervention strategies depend upon the situated context of each student, extending Bourdieu's conception of *habitus* to both organizational and system levels.

Even though theory suggests that the local context may influence students' opportunities for postsecondary education in unique ways, little work has been done that focuses on college access at the community level. There is a body of literature considering the role of precollege outreach programs, which typically operate in communities. Research on these programs is largely descriptive (Gandara & Maxwell-Jolly, 1999; Swail & Perna, 2002; Tierney, Corwin, & Colyar, 2005), but a limited number of studies have examined whether these interventions affect students' postsecondary opportunities (Avery & Kane, 2004; Constantine, Seftor, Martin, Silva, & Myers, 2006; Seftor, Mamun, & Schirm, 2009). The initiatives are promising for those who participate, but these programs are difficult to bring to scale and serve a relatively small proportion of the eligible population.

The recent emphasis on community-based strategies can be traced, at least in part, to the success of the Kalamazoo Promise (Miller-Adams, 2008). The 2005 announcement of a place-based tuition guarantee program for all graduates of the public high school system created a good deal of interest in developing locally based strategies rather than focusing on state or federal policy levers (Daun-Barnett, 2011). These programs are most commonly known for eliminating cost as a barrier to college access, but as organizers in Kalamazoo note, the strategy could not be successful if services did not exist to help students and families take full advantage of the Promise. Another community-based strategy that has received some attention in recent years is the National College Goal Sunday Initiative, sponsored by the Lumina Foundation for Education (Institute for Higher Education Policy, 2007). A recent study linking tax preparation with Free Application for Federal Student Aid (FAFSA) completion support (Bettinger, Long, Oreopoulous, & Sanbonmatsu, 2009) renewed interest in developing community collaborations to increase both tax filing and FAFSA completion in low-income communities (Daun-Barnett & Mabry, 2013).

All of this work on college access is instructive; certainly, it addresses the full array of potential barriers students face as they consider whether or not to attend college. What is typically missing from this body of literature, however, is the connection between what occurs in the local community and the broader sociopolitical contexts. Most of the work to date examines barriers and interventions at a single level—financial aid programs at the state or federal level, high school graduation requirements at the school or state level, access to information in precollege outreach programs, or alignment of systems at the state level. Some studies attempt to account for these effects at multiple levels (Musoba, 2004; Perna et al., 2008) but they do not describe how linkages are made between local practices and initiatives and state policy priorities. More directly, little has been done to examine the process by which social change agendas operating at multiple levels are aligned to address the complexities of increasing postsecondary access. The next section provides a framework for examining these connections, drawing on literature describing the structure of social change initiatives.

The Multidimensional Framework for Social Change

In this chapter, we draw on literature examining how networks influence social change in relation to local pathways to college. For example, Vandeventer and Mandell (2007) synthesize the literature on the work of networks designed to effect social change. Their work notes that networks vary depending upon the nature and complexity of the problem being addressed, the level of trust in relationships among network participants, and the amount of risk partners are willing to assume to leverage the assets of the network to effect social change. The issue of trust is particularly salient in the context of education, given its importance as a condition for successful school reform (Forsyth, Adams, & Hoy, 2011). Successful networks take time at the beginning of the process to determine whether a network is feasible and how the network will accomplish its aims.

Recently, the collective impact framework has received a good deal of attention as a way to think about how to facilitate social change on complex issues of social import. Kania and Kramer (2011) build upon the work of effective networks by more formally articulating how successful large, complex social change initiatives are organized to leverage the time, energy, and resources of the collective to achieve an agreed-upon set of outcomes. Kania and Kramer (2011) note

> *Collective impact,* [unites] a group of important actors from different sectors to a common agenda for solving a specific social problem. Unlike most collaborations, collective impact initiatives involve a centralized infrastructure, a dedicated staff, and a structured process that leads to a common agenda, shared measurement, continuous communication, and mutually reinforcing activities among all participants. (p. 1)

The collective impact model suggests that there are five conditions for successful social innovation and change (Hanleybrown, Kania, & Kramer, 2012). The first—and perhaps most important—condition is setting a common agenda among network collaborators. Kania and Kramer (2011) claim the goal is not to develop consensus but rather a shared understanding and a collective vision for the intended change such that partners agree upon the goals. Second, partnering agencies agree upon a set of shared measures, by which the success of the work will be evaluated. Even if there is no consensus on the means to effect change, a collective impact process results in clarity on the anticipated outcomes. Shared measurements allow partner organizations to hold one another accountable for progress on those outcomes.

Third, Kania and Kramer (2011) suggest that "the power of collective action comes not from the sheer number of participants or the uniformity of their efforts, but from the coordination of their differentiated activities through a mutually reinforcing plan of action" (p. 40). As such, the call for mutually reinforcing activities implies some coordination but expects partners to maintain discretion over how the goals will be achieved. The fourth condition of an effective collective impact initiative is continuous communication to develop trust among the principal leaders and to allow for the expectation of accountability among partners. Consistent with Vandeventer and Mandell's (2007) work on networks, communication is critical to establish trust among partners. They also recognize that developing trust takes time, and it requires an intentionally structured process of continual engagement for that trust to develop. The fifth and final condition is the establishment of a backbone organization. According to Kania and Kramer (2011), "the expectation that collaboration can occur without a supporting infrastructure is one of the most frequent reasons why it fails" (p. 40). The backbone organization in the collective impact model appears to operate in a manner consistent with Vandeventer and Mandell's (2007) conception of the facilitator role in networks.

In the context of examining the roles community foundations play in effecting social change, at least two other frameworks have been utilized in the literature. The first is the linear transformation model, frequently referred to as a logic model (Frumkin, 2006; W.K. Kellogg Foundation, 2004). Logic models are used to link resources to activities, outputs, and outcomes and are most useful when the problems being addressed are clearly articulated and the change strategy is relatively simple. In this model, the community foundation provides support to the lead agency responsible for achieving its intended outcomes. Kremers (2011) presents a second model when he argues that a key to large-scale, transformational change is the ability to align or layer agendas vertically from the local community practice to state and national policy priorities. Where collective impact focuses on horizontal alignment of partnering agencies and agendas, it does not attend to the range of grassroots influences at the community level and the competing pressures to conform to best practices at the state or national level.

Daun-Barnett, Wangelin, and Lamm (2013) build upon both the collective impact and the layering models to examine the role community foundations played in the establishment and evolution of LCANs in Michigan. Their work suggests that effective social change strategies must attend to both the horizontal alignment emphasized by collective impact and the vertical alignment of agendas emphasized in layering (see Figure 11.1). Consider, for example, the federal Promise Neighborhood grants administered by the U.S. Department of Education (USED). Communities are expected to develop local solutions at the neighborhood level to improve educational opportunities. At the local level, they will coordinate with all relevant service providers with a stake in the neighborhood (horizontal integration), and they will be expected to develop solutions that conform to prescriptions in the USED call for proposals (vertical integration).

Daun-Barnett and colleagues (2013) also argue that in order to understand the roles of community foundations or any set of lead agencies, it is important to account for the evolution of the network or collective over time. As networks mature and relationships evolve, the structure by which a community organizes its activities toward social change may also evolve. One of the particular challenges they note is that there are competing priorities influencing the agenda both horizontally and vertically, as is the case in the Promise Neighborhood example. USED recognizes the value of developing local solutions to complex problems but also wants these initiatives to conform to the promising practices that informed the creation of the grant program itself. Both Vandeventer and Mandell (2007) and Kania and Kramer (2011) note the importance of horizontal alignment—the establishment of a

Figure 11.1. Multidimensional model for social change.

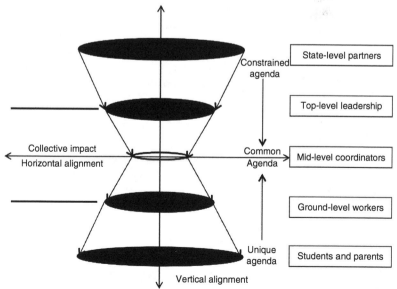

common agenda and the importance of continuous communication underscore this emphasis. The multidimensional framework (Figure 11.1) notes that pressures to create unique solutions tailored to the assets and challenges in local communities may be at odds with incentives and pressures from above to adopt promising practices irrespective of their applicability in a new context.

The multidimensional framework is instructive for thinking about the role of community foundations in the formation of LCANs because, in many cases, they provided the structure around which the agenda was set and managed. In this chapter, we adapt the framework to consider the role researchers can play linking grassroots voices with grasstops action. The National Forum played a critical role linking "grassroots" and "grasstops" perspectives to address college access and success, and the National Forum's experience underscores the challenge of finding common ground from which to move forward.

The College Access Context in Michigan

Michigan has been a visible leader in the evolution of community-based strategies to improve postsecondary access and success, and that local approach has deep roots. Michigan's higher education is nationally unique because its public universities have been granted constitutional autonomy, meaning that each institution operates under the guidance of its own board of regents. The state has no higher education coordinating board, and when collaboration occurs, it is facilitated through the Presidents Council, State Universities of Michigan—a voluntary member organization whose chief responsibility is to lobby on behalf of higher education. Community colleges operate in a similarly independent way, even without the same formal constitutional protections of autonomy. Until 2006, Michigan was one of five states that left high school graduation requirements to the discretion of the local education agency. In short, education in Michigan has a rich history of local control.

In addition to the local control afforded education at all levels, Michigan is home to a robust network of community foundations and other philanthropic organizations. The Council of Michigan Foundations (CMF) provides some coordination and support for the entire network of foundations, including the W.K. Kellogg Foundation, the Kresge Foundation, and the Charles Stewart Mott Foundation, whose combined total annual giving approaches $550 million. Additionally, 65 community foundations operate throughout Michigan, with assets ranging from $1 million to more than $600 million. Education is a key part of community foundations' missions, and the recent evolution of college access strategies represents the most recent iteration of that work for many community foundations. This robust network of community-based philanthropy is an important catalyst for social innovation and change in their local communities, and college access is among the priorities of many of the foundations.

Local Solutions to the College Access Challenge in Michigan

In March 2004, Governor Jennifer Granholm announced the formation of a statewide commission in higher education and economic growth to be chaired by her lieutenant governor, John Cherry. The so-called Cherry Commission convened at a time in Michigan when public support for higher education was at a low point. In a listening tour around the state conducted by the governor's staff, the people of Michigan ranked higher education among the lowest priorities for policymakers. Tax revenues were declining in the midst of a recessionary period that predated the national collapse in 2008—a consequence of a deteriorating automotive manufacturing industry at the time. Scarce resources forced policymakers to choose among competing priorities; as a result, state support for public higher education was cut in three successive legislative sessions, and public universities increased tuition levels by as much as 10% annually. This period of scarce public resources for higher education provided the backdrop for the creation of the Cherry Commission—which is entirely consistent with research on the role of states in terms of financing public higher education (Delaney & Doyle, 2007).

In the following sections, I discuss the Access to Democracy project, which was designed to engage communities in deliberative dialogue on the question of "Who is college for?" Then, I discuss the work of the Cherry Commission and the announcement of the Kalamazoo Promise. The former recognized the potential for developing community compacts to address postsecondary opportunity, and the latter became the first local access strategy launched in Michigan. Finally, I examine the development of Promise Zone legislation, which attempts to replicate the Kalamazoo model in 10 other communities around the state, and the development of LCANs under the statewide college access network (MCAN) umbrella.

Access to Democracy and the Deliberative Dialogue Process

One plausible method for aligning community priorities with state and national initiatives and policies is to include partners in a social change process that operate at multiple levels simultaneously. Community foundations play this role routinely in their local work as Daun-Barnett and colleagues (2013) demonstrate, but any number of partners may operate in similar ways. In the context of college access work and the Cherry Commission, we served as a critical link between community solutions and state policy priorities through engaged scholarship that sought to understand how communities understand the college access challenge and how to infuse that perspective into the state policy discourse. In particular, two initiatives were undertaken simultaneously that allowed for researchers to engage in local community dialogues around college access and to influence the policy agenda—the Access to Democracy and the Cherry Commission. It is important to recognize that these two initiatives were intended to be complementary, allowing the National Forum to serve as the conduit between the grasstops policy-making process (Cherry Commission) that would shape public priorities for higher education and grassroots, community-based deliberations (Access to Democracy) around the trade-offs associated with alternative strategies for supporting higher education. Access to Democracy began about six months prior to the Cherry Commission and was linked to national debates over college access, particularly in relation to the use of affirmative action in the admissions processes at selective institutions.

The Kettering Foundation and others (e.g., Public Agenda) have been actively engaged in the promotion of deliberative dialogue on issues of public importance (Mathews & McAfee, 2003). Deliberative dialogue is a process of framing public issues for deliberation among community members that recognizes that issues are frequently more complex than public debates recognize and that all responses to questions of public importance involve trade-offs that must be weighed for communities to make informed judgments (Doble, 1996). Deliberative dialogue is not designed to move communities toward consensus building—rather it is intended to frame conversations that allow individuals to clarify their own priorities, to weigh the trade-offs of a number of strategies, and to more actively engage individuals in the decision-making process.

We initiated the process of framing the issue of college access for deliberative dialogue in partnership with the Kettering Foundation. Specifically, the Kettering Foundation asked "Who is college for?" as a way to engage residents of communities across Michigan in an important conversation about college access and affirmative action. At the time the Access to Democracy campaign was being launched, the University of Michigan was in the middle of defending its use of race-based affirmative action in college admissions at the U.S. Supreme Court, and public discourse on the issue was too frequently dichotomized in support of or opposition to affirmative action as a public policy. We recognized that the issues surrounding the use of affirmative action were far more complex than was portrayed in public debate and that people's responses were based upon deeply embedded assumptions about fairness and equity that shaped how individuals responded to the question.

The first step in framing deliberative dialogue was to identify the right question and to frame possible responses to that question in ways that illuminated the tensions and trade-offs. The discussion guide identified the following general responses to the question of "Who is college for?": (a) those willing to work for it, (b) those most academically qualified, and (c) everyone. After a six-month process of framing the issue of college access in this way, community dialogues were held in communities across Michigan from Grand Rapids and Ann Arbor to Lansing and Flint. These dialogues provided us a window through which to view how Michigan residents felt about issues of access to postsecondary education and how they weighed the trade-offs of each response. In several communities, these dialogues served as a starting point for more sustained conversations around college access for local residents.

Deliberative dialogue was one mechanism by which we could engage people across Michigan in a conversation about the value of postsecondary education—a strategy to understand what residents of the state thought at the grassroots level. At the time Access to Democracy was initiated, there was a national discussion surrounding affirmative action that polarized the state of Michigan, but there was no broader state conversation about the larger issues of postsecondary access and success. This changed in March, 2005, with the announcement of the State Commission on Higher Education and Economic Growth (Cherry Commission) by Governor Jennifer Granholm.

The Cherry Commission on Higher Education and Economic Growth

Twenty-eight education, community, and policy leaders from across the state of Michigan convened to provide recommendations to the governor on how best to accomplish the following key goals: (a) double the number of adults in the workforce with a postsecondary credential, (b) improve alignment between institutions of higher education and the emerging employment opportunities in the new economy, and (c) build a dynamic workforce with employees equipped for success in the global knowledge economy (Lt. Governor's Commission on Higher Education and Economic Growth, 2004). The work of the Cherry Commission was divided into four work groups addressing students' preparation for postsecondary education, participation in college, degree completion, and the economic benefits of college in the new economy. The National Forum played a critical role in the work of the Cherry Commission. John C. Burkhardt, founding director of the National Forum, served as a consultant to the organization of the commission, and a graduate student research team was selected to provide research support for the four separate work groups. The Cherry Commission provided a window of opportunity for us to assist in the process of connecting what graduate students were learning in communities through Access to Democracy (grassroots) with the key policy conversations influencing how the state might act to address issues of college access and success (grasstops).

The Cherry Commission was convened for a total of six months, and the final report presented 19 recommendations to the governor to address her three goals. The commission's final report became a blueprint for the governor's education agenda. Some of the recommendations—such as adopting the ACT college admissions test for all students and building a P–16 data tracking system—were already underway prior to the creation of the commission. A few of the recommendations were unexpected because they were not a part of the initial commission agenda. For example, the commission recommended the adoption of high school graduation course requirements, which Michigan had previously left to the discretion of local education agencies and had been attempted several years earlier. One recommendation, in particular, was described by the lieutenant governor as a "sea change" in the commission's thoughts about how to improve postsecondary opportunity in Michigan. Recommendation Number Seven called for the creation of Community Compacts for Educational Attainment (Governor's Commission on Higher Education and Economic Growth, 2004). The text supporting this recommendation called for local policymakers to link with business, labor, and education leaders to develop local solutions to the barriers preventing some students from attending college and other students from achieving success upon arrival. The sea change as described by the lieutenant governor was the insistence of commissioners that any strategy to double the number of college-educated adults in the state would require local solutions addressing the unique challenges of each community and leveraging the assets each has at their disposal. It also implied that, in order for local solutions to work, state policymakers had to recognize the importance of connecting local innovations with state policy priorities. Recommendation Number Seven may have been one of the commission's most innovative recommendations, but it was also one of the last that was acted upon in a meaningful way.

Kalamazoo Promise and the Proliferation of Place-Based Tuition Guarantee Programs

Prior to 2005, there was little discussion of place-based tuition guarantee programs. The Georgia HOPE program may be an exception, though it operated at the state level and was primarily designed to incentivize and reward academic achievement (merit). Eugene Lang began the I Have A

Dream Foundation in response to a promise of free tuition that Lang made to a classroom of sixth-grade students if they completed high school and attended college. Many similar initiatives have grown from Lang's early work, but these initiatives operated on a much smaller scale than the Kalamazoo Promise (I Have A Dream Foundation, 2008). George Weiss built Say Yes to Education on a similar model, working with sixth graders in 1987, and began working with schools in Hartford, Philadelphia, and Harlem by 2004 (Say Yes to Education, 2013). In 2005, the city of Kalamazoo launched a program that would serve as a model for communities across the country (Miller-Adams, 2008).

The Kalamazoo Promise was announced by the superintendent of Kalamazoo Public Schools (KPS), and the most notable feature of the Promise was the guarantee of full tuition to any two-year or four-year public college or university in the state of Michigan. Students were simply required to finish high school and gain admission to an eligible institution. The longer students attended school in KPS, the higher the percentage of tuition and fees they were eligible to receive, equaling 100% for students who spent their entire career in KPS schools. The guarantee was first dollar, meaning that the Promise would pay the full cost of tuition and fees directly to the institution, irrespective of whether students received other forms of aid. In fact, students were not even required to apply for other aid. Though the tuition guarantee was the feature that received the most attention, the Promise was actually part of a much larger economic development strategy for southwest Michigan (Kitchens, Gross, & Smith, 2008), and it was done in partnership with Communities in Schools to provide the comprehensive supports students would need to take advantage of the Promise.

The success of the Kalamazoo Promise as an educational intervention and as an economic development engine is well documented (Miller-Adams, 2008; Miron & Cullen, 2007). The city experienced early gains in housing values, and school enrollments increased by more than 10% after decades of slow declines. Participation rates rose, though early assessments of degree completion suggest that a number of students—particularly those choosing two-year colleges—are no more likely to earn their degree than students prior to the Promise. As an economic engine, however, 70% of these students attend either Kalamazoo Valley Community College or Western Michigan University, meaning those tuition subsidies remain local (Miller-Adams, 2008).

The Kalamazoo Promise was not connected in any way to the work of the Cherry Commission, but it was certainly informed by the same conditions both locally and statewide. As Kitchens and colleagues (2008) note, local leaders in southwest Michigan recognized they were falling behind as an industrial rust belt city entering into a global knowledge economy and that the only way to attract more people and employers to the city was to expand their stock of human capital—in other words, train more people for the jobs of the future. These were the same conversations happening within the Cherry Commission. The economic development community, in partnership with civic, business, and education leaders, chose to develop its own solution to the problem and—with the help of anonymous donors—created a model for the state of Michigan and beyond. At first, the influence of Kalamazoo was indirect—communities across the state, in partnership with their local community foundations and philanthropic organizations, assessed whether similar strategies were feasible for their respective communities. A few began community-based college access initiatives in response to these conversations, but none developed a tuition guarantee. In 2008, the influence of Kalamazoo was formalized as the governor announced the creation of 10 Promise Zones across the state of Michigan.

Promise Zones and the LCAN

Political scientists study the spread of innovation across a range of policy issues, and they view communities or states as laboratories of innovation (Cohen-Vogel, Ingle, Albee Levine, & Spence, 2008; McLendon, Heller, & Young, 2005). Consider, for example, the passage of No Child Left Behind in 2001—it was an extension of existing federal education policy but informed by work happening in the home state of George W. Bush. Texas served as the laboratory for a set of ideas that were incorporated into federal policy. Harlem Children's Zone has served as another more relevant policy laboratory. The success of the comprehensive community-based strategy to support students and families from the time they are born through their successful completion of postsecondary education or entry into the workforce became the model for the Federal Promise Neighborhood grant competition funded by the USED. In a similar vein, the Kalamazoo experiment served as a laboratory for the state.

Promise Zones

In 2008, Governor Jennifer Granholm proposed and signed into Michigan law a state initiative to create 10 Promise Zones in eligible communities (Michigan Senate Fiscal Agency, 2008). The legislation allowed communities to apply for the designation but stipulated that in order to qualify, they must serve a higher proportion of low-income students than the state average. The designation as a Promise Zone allowed communities to access a potential funding mechanism—a tax capture of a portion of the additional tax revenues generated by attracting more residents to a particular place and increasing property values. As Daun-Barnett and Holohan-Moyer (2013) noted, this funding strategy was far less stable and substantial than the funding secured for Kalamazoo. Participating communities were required to create a coordinating board of community leaders and educators and establish a plan to raise funds for the tuition guarantee. Additionally, the law set the minimum tuition guarantee at the rate of tuition and fees for the community college and required that all students exhaust publicly available sources of financial support before being eligible for the Promise.

It is too early to examine whether this strategy increased chances for students to attend college from these communities, but, given that communities must raise initial scholarship funds before the tax capture is initiated, Promise Zones are unlikely to be as robust as the Kalamazoo Promise. Equally, although the 10 identified communities were in need of the additional resources for college participation, a major concern arose. There were many more communities across the state that could be served, based upon eligibility criteria, and the tax capture was designed to redistribute resources for the K–12 school aid fund, meaning that some schools may have received less when those resources were redistributed.

One of the important limitations of the Promise Zone specifically, or the policy laboratory generally, is the lack of attention paid to adapting tested innovations to local conditions. The Promise works in Kalamazoo precisely because it was crafted by local community leaders in response to the challenges they faced and the assets they had at their disposal. Attempts to replicate an innovation like the Promise cannot neglect those conditions as they attempt to adopt the strategy. Equally, agencies that attempt to develop policies and programs to replicate these innovations, whether they are the USED or the Michigan legislature, should provide time and flexibility for communities to adapt. In some cases, evaluators serve as the linkage between state priorities (grasstops) and local efforts at design and implementation (grassroots), but the important insight from the multidimensional framework for social change is that vertical alignment is critical and should be the responsibility of one or more partners in the social change process.

The Michigan College Access Network (MCAN)

One of the catalysts for the local development of college access strategies across Michigan was the federal College Access Challenge Grant (CACG) administered by the USED. In 2008, governors were invited to identify agencies within their states to administer block grants to increase postsecondary opportunities for students. States approached the CACG in very different ways—some used the money to expand opportunity by growing their financial aid programs, and others used it to develop comprehensive college access web portals, professional development opportunities, and statewide college access networks. Under the federal CACG program, governors in each of the 50 states; Washington, DC; and the territories were eligible to receive grants of $66 million or more, allocated according to the proportion of children living below poverty in the state (U.S. Department of Education, 2011). In 2009, the total program expanded to $150 million, and Michigan's share rose from $2.1 to $4.2 million. The governor's advisers on education convened a small planning group of interested state agencies and nongovernmental organizations. During the first year, those resources were utilized to explore the existing college access assets across Michigan and to extend the community-based dialogues to better understand how communities understood the role of higher education in society. The first year of CACG also gave collaborators an opportunity to consider a variety of state and local strategies.

The CMF, in partnership with the Office of Foundation Liaison (OFL) in the governor's administration, sought out state-level strategies to address the college access challenge and turned their attention to the state of Ohio. The Ohio College Access Network (OCAN) had been established in 1999 to coordinate the efforts of local college access initiatives across the state (Ohio College Access Network, 2014). In 2008, it was a well-established network of community providers with a balance of state-level supports to ensure the continuity of the college access work across the state. OCAN was a part of the larger National College Access Network (NCAN, 2014), which shares a similar history but has been in existence since 1995. During the second year of the CACG, the state of Michigan revised its college access strategy and focused its energy on developing a state college access network (MCAN) and creating a comprehensive college access web portal (Michigan College Access Portal [MiCAP]).

MCAN was modeled on its Ohio predecessor with at least one important exception. Instead of the network emerging from the needs of the college access programs—as was the case in Ohio—MCAN provided seed funding to establish local networks to coordinate existing services, identify gaps based upon community needs, and develop local solutions to the college access challenge. By 2014, MCAN expanded its network of LCANs to more than 50 communities across the state. The local networks build upon Recommendation Seven of the Cherry Commission report, and nearly a decade after the commission issued its recommendations, Michigan has developed a concrete strategy to create community compacts. Many of the early LCANs were also identified as Promise Zones by the state.

The success of the MCAN model is predicated on effective alignment vertically from state priorities to local solutions, and it relies heavily on horizontal alignment of key stakeholders and partners across communities. In 2011, MCAN reshaped its funding strategy to create incentives for communities to employ collective impact as an organizing model for social change. Collective impact focuses primarily on horizontal alignment, dealing with the complex challenges within a given place and across the leadership of relevant agencies, organizations, and interest groups (Kania & Kramer, 2011). At the heart of the collective impact model is the establishment of a common agenda, whereby all partners enter into collaboration and engage in consistent and sustained communication, particularly among principal leadership empowered to make decisions and commitments on behalf of their respective organizations (Hanleybrown et al., 2012). Agenda setting from this perspective takes a great deal of time, and it requires that partners commit to a process and potentially redefine the nature of the problem or array of solutions that will be brought to bear. Each partner may continue to maintain an organizational agenda broader than the agenda of the collective, but partners are committed to the common agenda, both in principle and frequently in terms of dedicated resources.

Collective impact places the backbone organization at the center of the social change model, which assumes responsibility for managing partners, ushering the common agenda under the guidance of partners, and providing administrative support for the array of partners involved in the project. As such, the community foundation serves as one of many key organizational partners in the collective impact model. The collective impact model was first described by Kania and Kramer (2011) in their examination of successful social change strategies, and the model was popularized for the college access arena through the experience of STRIVE in Cincinnati, Ohio. Foundation Strategy Group highlighted their experience as an exemplar of collective impact, and since that time, STRIVE has consulted with others to implement collective impact in other communities. MCAN has partnered with STRIVE to provide technical support to incorporate collective impact into the work of LCAN.

At first glance, the MCAN-LCAN structure attends directly to the need for vertical alignment of state priorities and local solutions. From the perspective of the multidimensional framework for social change, this is critical to the eventual success of a community change strategy. However, two factors complicate this model. First, although MCAN is a prominent state actor with an eye toward vertical alignment, it is not the only actor that plays this role. At least two other entities also attend to alignment between state opportunities and priorities, on one hand, and local needs and community solutions, on the other. The Promise Zones began as an initiative under the

Granholm administration, and though no formal office was charged with this responsibility, one of the governor's senior advisers assumed the role of consulting with the 10 Promise Zones to develop their organizing structures, raise seed money for the initial tuition guarantees, and plan for the eventual tax capture. This person also interprets the law, navigates the state apparatus, and works with communities to develop their local solutions.

At the heart of many of these LCAN strategies is the local community foundation. As Daun-Barnett and Lamm (2012) discovered, community foundations have assumed critical roles in the formation of their respective LCANs, from serving as the primary convener of community partners to providing resources and serving as fiduciary agents to hiring staff and developing programs. Community foundations across Michigan have historically been committed to education, and access to college has frequently been a part of that role. The community foundations also collaborate under the umbrella of the CMF. Like the MCAN-LCAN dyad, CMF works with local community foundations and serves, in this case, to link local members to the state agenda. One of the important linkages at the center of the LCAN model is coordinated in collaboration between MCAN and CMF—the infusion of support from the Kresge Foundation. The Kresge Foundation has recently committed itself to the college access agenda and has provided resources to encourage community foundation investments in the long-term sustainability of the LCAN as well as in the programmatic priorities identified by MCAN to place college advisers in high-need high schools.

The second complicating factor, from a vertical alignment perspective, is that priorities at the state level may impose constraints on communities that have been charged with responding to the access challenge given their unique assets and challenges. Recommendation Number Seven from the Cherry Commission recognized the importance of empowering local actors to develop strategies that can respond directly to the conditions they face. From a grassroots perspective, each set of community strategies should be uniquely tailored and may include a variety of programs and interventions. In contrast, MCAN and other state-level actors seek to identify promising models and then replicate those models in an effort to accelerate the social change process. In short, they use other communities as laboratories of innovation, and they attempt to bring those ideas to scale in new contexts. The challenge for communities is that these innovations may or may not fit, given the unique circumstances of each individual community, but they are tied to resources that are critical during the early stages of organizing around a college access agenda.

The most recent iteration of this constraint was MCAN's collective impact grant. MCAN has offered three levels of grants: a planning grant to start the conversation and begin the agenda setting process, a start-up grant to begin testing and refining local strategies, and a continuous improvement grant for communities that choose to adopt the STRIVE version of collective impact. Each grant has a set of conditions for eligibility. The planning grant, for example, requires new communities to commit to 11 conditions, including support of the MiCAP and the Know How 2 Go social marketing campaign. Both are potentially useful and powerful tools, but they were not created to address the specific challenges in each community. The continuous improvement grant is only by invitation and requires eligible communities to commit to two key conditions. First, they must adopt the collective impact framework and participate in the technical support provided by STRIVE. Second, they must commit to raising matching funds of 100% the first year ($25,000) and increases each year after. Both of these conditions are informed by best or promising practices from the field and are consistent with the laboratory approach, but they may operate at odds with the notion that locally tailored solutions are best to address the unique conditions in communities.

Currently, any community could choose to develop its own college access strategy and do so without the constraints or the resources of MCAN or the Kresge Foundation. We have not observed a community that has chosen to do so. Communities across the state value the opportunity to bring external dollars into their initiatives and most appreciate the expertise from MCAN, Kresge, and others. The paradox this set of conditions introduces is that accelerating the process of social change may actually be at odds with the very social change strategy MCAN is promoting. According to Kania and Kramer (2011), setting the common agenda takes time, and defining the agenda broadly and being inclusive of the full array of partners requires a comprehensive strategy. Communities and partners have to develop sustained and continuous communication and identify complementary activities to achieve their shared goals as measured by an agreed-upon set of metrics. Kania and Kramer also note that funders must be committed to supporting a longer term process rather than funding the development of individual solutions.

The incentives introduced through the laboratory model call for swift and decisive adoption of strategies and may encourage communities to act in very specific ways before community partners have coalesced around a common agenda. Placing specific strategies ahead of the common agenda may slow down the agenda-setting process, which is predicated on developing relationships and establishing trust among key partners. For example, MCAN has developed a partnership with the National College Advising Corps (NCAC) to fund the placement of college advisers into high schools across the state. The initial plan called for the placement of 16 advisers with a plan to scale up gradually. MCAN saw the value added to those communities and quickly expanded the effort by growing the corps to 64 members. That represents substantial growth in a two- to three-year period with the potential to provide tremendous benefits to many more students across the state. However, even with 64 members, most high schools that need additional support will not receive it. Communities frequently will have to decide to compete for these scarce resources before they know how this strategy might fit into their common agenda, and, even then, community leaders may need to contend with providing resources to some schools and not others. To be sure, that is a very difficult choice to make when collective impact sets a broad table and multiple schools and/or districts may want the same resources. Consider the implications for a city such as Detroit. Currently, there are 21 public high schools within the city limits. Nearly all of those high schools would benefit from the presence of a college adviser, but that would account for a third of all positions available from NCAC and MCAN. Across the state, there are nearly 800 high schools serving more than 452,000 students, and many of those high schools serve high proportions of low-income students and families who could also benefit from the support of one of the 64 college advisers.

The Kalamazoo Promise is similarly instructive as a policy laboratory. When observers from around the country look at Kalamazoo, they see an amazing and unique program that began in 2005 with the announcement of the tuition guarantee. When Janice Brown, executive director of the Kalamazoo Promise, discusses the process by which the Promise came to fruition, she is clear on two points. First, the Promise was a part of a much larger and more complex social change initiative for regional economic development. Second, the Promise was the result of more than five years of conversations among principal leadership across education, business, and local government. A similar story could be told of the Harlem Children's Zone; it has become the model for federal investment in neighborhood strategies to improve opportunities for low-income families, but it took nearly 20 years for a modest initiative on a single block of Harlem to grow into the significant social change effort it is today (Tough, 2008).

The Complementary Role of Engaged Scholarship in College Access

One of the important, but frequently overlooked, influences on the social change process is engaged scholarship. At nearly every point in the Michigan experience, education researchers were actively engaged in the college access conversations. Researchers developed the Access to Democracy deliberative dialogue process and engaged communities across the state in conversations to weigh the trade-offs of college access strategies. A research team provided critical support to the Cherry Commission as it considered how best to double the number of college graduates in the state and to better align higher education with workforce development. Both the Upjohn Institute and Western Michigan University have been instrumental research partners for the Kalamazoo Promise as they evaluate whether or not the initiative has had the intended effects on educational opportunities and regional economic development. Further, researchers have been involved in the various stages of development for the Promise Zone legislation, the development of MCAN, the evaluation of state efforts to increase postsecondary access and success, and the expansion of the MCAN network of LCANs.

The multidimensional framework emphasizes both horizontal alignment of community partners around a common agenda and vertical alignment of complementary agendas operating at multiple levels. Responsibility for alignment has been assumed by various state-level actors such as MCAN and CMF as well as local partners such as community foundations. In the collective impact model, the backbone organization would be charged with coordinating the alignment of agendas, but as our experience in Michigan has suggested, this function frequently has fallen to community foundations, school districts, or entities that form at the intersection of the two. We discuss the role of engaged scholarship as part of the alignment function in the context of the Access to Democracy Initiative and the infusion of public deliberation into the Cherry Commission. We conclude, consistent with Overton's explication of engaged scholarship earlier in this volume, that researchers have the potential to make important contributions to both horizontal and vertical alignment in a social change process.

Translating Research to Practice

Educators, policymakers, and change agents are motivated to act; researchers attempt to understand. Frequently, that means a gap remains between what researchers have come to understand and what practitioners should do to effect change. Researchers must pay closer attention to the practical implications of their work and communicate their findings and recommendations to the appropriate audiences. Both are critical to social change, but researchers are reluctant for at least four reasons. First, researchers are acutely aware of the limitations of their knowledge. As such, they tend to make more modest claims that are defensible theoretically or empirically. Second, high-quality research takes a long time to complete, and it may not always move at a pace sufficient to inform conversations happening among educators and policymakers seeking to solve problems. Third, the incentive structure prioritizes publishing findings in venues whose primary audience is the research community rather than the communities of practitioners and policymakers. These top journals and academic publishers establish high standards for quality and are rated to have a high impact on the field. For researchers who are tenure-track faculty, these publishing venues are most important in terms of promotion. What is significant to another researcher is often different from what might be valued by a policymaker or practitioner, meaning that engaged scholars must either write for two separate audiences or find alternative strategies for translating research into practice.

Fourth, there is a related debate regarding whether or not researchers should set their own research agenda or if they should seek to align their interests with the questions and research needs as they are presented among practitioners and policymakers. In short, researchers in education debate what constitutes a significant question or contribution to the field and which methodological strategies are appropriate for achieving those answers or contributions (Pasque, Carducci, Kuntz, & Gildersleeve, 2012). There are legitimate concerns on both sides. On one hand, researchers are right to resist the temptation to allow external influences to decide what constitutes a significant problem to address or question to answer. In an era when researchers are expected to generate financial support to conduct their work, it can be tempting to adapt one's work to the priorities of funders. The natural consequence is that some issues and problems are privileged relative to others. On the other hand, educators, practitioners, and policymakers are wrestling with complex issues and challenges, and they need theory and research to inform their work. In their absence, decisions will be made based upon the best information available to those key constituent groups. If researchers are unable or unwilling to engage, then policies and practices will be implemented that at best are underinformed but at worst could be detrimental to the intended audiences.

We argue that researchers should be able to attend to both the theoretical and methodological significance valued by the research community and the practical significance for practitioners; this is discussed in more detail in the chapters by Esmeralda Hernandez-Hamed and Betty Overton. More important to this conversation, researchers must become more adept at translating their work for "practical" audiences, or institutions of higher education must value scholarship that translates between the two worlds.

Addressing Problems in Broad and Complex Ways

The academic community recognizes the value of interdisciplinary think-ing to address complex problems and generate new knowledge. Some of our best advancements in academic research are the result of applying theories or methodologies from one discipline to questions and problems in another discipline. In the organization of social change, collective impact provides a useful parallel. Communities recognize that problems are complex and inter-related and, as such, cannot be solved by educators or policymakers or civic leaders alone. Complex social problems like poverty or educational inequal-ity cannot be solved by educators or civic leaders or philanthropists alone. They require complex solutions that may draw upon social services, pub-lic health, nongovernmental organizations, and the business community to solve. Collective impact suggests that complex problems like these can be addressed effectively only when all of these partners come together, develop a shared agenda, and begin to move in a common direction.

The challenge for the academic community is that researchers and faculty are often trained to dig deep into a very small subset of problems rather than to look across multiple problems. As such, they may not be well equipped to address dimensions of the problem that fall outside their research areas. No single researcher will be able to speak to the complexities of a social change problem any more than a single agency will be able to develop comprehen-sive solutions to complex problems. The growth of interdisciplinary research within colleges and universities may help to close this gap. As Leavy (2011) asserts, truly meaningful interdisciplinary or transdisciplinary approaches to examining complex social problems require that researchers engage in new ways or train a new sort of professional who can think more broadly across the range of issues rather than delving more deeply into isolated questions. It may be that these new translators find their ways into organizations that routinely attempt to address complex social issues, including philanthropy, government agencies, and nonprofit organizations.

Integrating Theory, Research, and Context to Develop New Strategies and Solutions

Finally, social scientists might begin to embrace practices that are more com-monplace in the physical and biological sciences, such as engineering or medicine. Scientists commonly develop theories about, conduct research on, and develop new solutions to the problems they face. Medical researchers may develop new strategies to cure or prevent disease, or they might develop devices to improve quality of life. Engineers may develop new strategies to improve fuel efficiency in automobiles, develop stronger materials to prevent the collapse of buildings during earthquakes, or identify efficiencies for hospital management. The goals are all very different, but they require a common, systematic approach to developing theory, conducting research, and developing new strategies to solve complicated problems. In all of these cases, researchers also close the loop by testing those new strategies to see if they are effective and refining their models accordingly.

The state of Michigan has embarked upon an ambitious social change strategy designed to improve postsecondary opportunities for all of its residents. Its efforts to link locally developed grassroots strategies with state policy priorities have become a model for other states across the nation. Its experience also illustrates how complex a task it is to align agendas vertically and develop strong, sustainable relationships across community leadership to move collectively on an issue of public importance. The key to Michigan's success has been, and continues to be, the role various actors play to align agendas at multiple levels, from the linking structures of community foundations and the Council of Michigan Foundations to LCANs and the MCAN to the important, but frequently overlooked, role of engaged scholarship. All of these actors and relationships are critical in the Michigan context to help communities navigate the complex and, at times, contradictory pressures to differentiate strategies locally and attempt to adapt the constraints of best practices identified through laboratories of innovation. Any states or communities intending to address complex social problems will need to respond to a similar set of conditions and challenges, and their ability to strike a balance may have a significant effect on their chances for real and sustainable change.

References

Allensworth, E., Nomi, T., Montgomery, N., & Lee, V. E. (2009). College preparatory curriculum for all: Academic consequences of requiring algebra and English I for ninth graders in Chicago. *Educational Evaluation and Policy Analysis, 31*(4), 367–391. doi:10.3102/016237370934371

Avery, C., & Kane, T. (2004). Student perceptions of college opportunities: The Boston COACH program. In C. M. Hoxby (Ed.), *College choices: The economics of where to go, when to go, and how to pay for it* (pp. 355–391). Cambridge, MA: National Bureau of Economic Research.

Bettinger, E. P., Long, B. T., Oreopoulous, P., & Sanbonmatsu, L. (2009). *The role of information and simplification in college decisions: Results from the H&R Block FAFSA experiment (NBER Working Paper No, 15361)*. Cambridge, MA: National Bureau of Economic Research.

Cohen-Vogel, L., Ingle, W. K., Albee Levine, A., & Spence, M. (2008). The "spread" of merit-based college aid: Politics, policy consortia, and interstate competition. *Educational Policy, 22*(3), 339–362.

Conley, D. T. (2005). *College knowledge: What it really takes for students to succeed and what we can do to get them ready.* San Francisco, CA: Jossey-Bass.

Constantine, J., Seftor, N. S., Martin, E. S., Silva, T., & Myers, D. (2006). *A study of the effect of the talent search program on secondary and postsecondary outcomes in Florida, Indiana and Texas.* Washington, DC: Mathematica Policy Research, Inc.

Daun-Barnett, N. (2011). The Kalamazoo Promise: A new twist on tuition guarantees. *Journal of Student Financial Aid, 41*(1), 28–37.

Daun-Barnett, N., & Das, D. (2013). College access and the web-based college knowledge strategy: Analysis of the Know How 2 Go campaign. *Journal of Marketing for Higher Education, 23*(1), 113–134.

Daun-Barnett, N., & Holohan-Moyer, I. (2013). Local college access strategies: Examining the equitable distribution of postsecondary access in Michigan. In G. Sunderman (Ed.), *Charting reform, achieving equity in a diverse nation* (pp. 251–272). Charlotte, NC: Information Age Publishing.

Daun-Barnett, N., & Lamm, H. (2012). Investigating the roles of community foundations in the establishment and sustainability of local college access networks in Michigan. *Foundation Review, 4*(3), 65–76.

Daun-Barnett, N., & Mabry, B. (2013). Simplifying the FAFSA process: Local initiatives linking tax preparation with FAFSA completion. *Journal of Student Financial Aid, 42*(3), 25–45.

Daun-Barnett, N., Wangelin, J., & Lamm, H. (2013). Models of social change: Community foundations and agenda setting. *Foundation Review, 4*(4), 84–97.

Delaney, J. A., & Doyle, W. R. (2007). The role of higher education in state budgets. In K. Shaw & D. E. Heller (Eds.), *State postsecondary education research: New methods to inform policy and practice* (pp. 55–76). Sterling, VA: Stylus.

Doble, J. (1996). *Responding to the critics of deliberation* (p. 60). Englewood Cliffs, NJ: Kettering Foundation.

Forsyth, P. B., Adams, C. M., & Hoy, W. K. (2011). *Collective trust: Why schools can't improve without it.* New York, NY: Teachers College Press.

Frumkin, P. (2006). *Strategic giving: The art and science of philanthropy.* Chicago: University of Chicago Press.

Gandara, P., & Maxwell-Jolly, J. (1999). *Priming the pump: Strategies for increasing the achievement of underrepresented minority undergraduates.* New York, NY: The College Board.

Governor's Commission on Higher Education and Economic Growth. (2004). *Final report of the Lt. Governor's Commission on Higher Education & Economic Growth.* Author: Lansing, MI.

Hanleybrown, F., Kania, J., & Kramer, M. (2012). Channeling change: Making collective impact work. *Stanford Social Innovation Review,* 1–8. Retrieved from http://www.ssireview.org

Heller, D. E. (1999). The effects of tuition and state financial aid on public college enrollment. *The Review of Higher Education, 23*(1), 65–89.

I Have A Dream Foundation. (2008). *History of I Have A Dream Foundation.* Retrieved from http://www.ihaveadreamfoundation.org/html/history.htm

Institute for Higher Education Policy. (2007). *College Goal Sunday 2007: Evaluation report* (pp. 1–44). Washington, DC.

Kania, J., & Kramer, M. (2011). Collective Impact. *Stanford Social Innovation Review,* 36–41.

Kirst, M., & Venezia, A. (2004). *From high school to college: Improving opportunities for success in postsecondary education.* San Francisco, CA: Jossey-Bass.

Kitchens, R., Gross, D., & Smith, H. (2008). *Community capitalism: Lessons from Kalamazoo and beyond.* Bloomington, IN: AuthorHouse.

Kremers, A. (2011). Use of layering for effective partnership building: Leveraging positive impact in educational philanthropy. *Foundation Review, 3*(3), 36–44.

Leavy, P. (2011). *Essentials of transdisciplinary research: Using problem-centered methodologies* (Vol. 6). Walnut Creek, CA: Left Coast Press.

Long, B. T. (2007). The contributions of economics to the study of college access and success. *Teachers College Record, 109*(10), 2367–2443.

Mathews, D., & McAfee, N. (2003). *Making choices together: The power of public deliberation.* Dayton, OH: The Kettering Foundation.

McLendon, M., Heller, D. E., & Young, S. P. (2005). *State postsecondary policy innovation: Politics, competition, and the interstate migration of policy ideas. The Journal of Higher Education, 76*(4), 364–400.

Michigan Senate Fiscal Agency. (2008). *Michigan Promise Zone Act—Bill Analysis.* Retrieved from http://www.legislature.mi.gov/documents/2007-2008/billanalysis/Senate/pdf/2007-SFA-0861-F.pdf

Miller-Adams, M. (2008). *The Kalamazoo Promise: Building assets for community change.* Kalamazoo, MI: Upjohn Institute for Employment Research.

Miron, G., & Cullen, A. (2007). *Trends and patterns in student enrollment in Kalamazoo Public Schools: Evaluation of the Kalamazoo Promise* (working paper no. 4.) Kalamazoo, MI: Western Michigan University Evaluation Center.

Musoba, G. D. (2004). *The impact of school reform on college preparation: A multilevel analysis of the relationship between state policy and student achievement.* (Doctoral). Indiana University, Bloomington, IN.

National College Access Network. (2014). *History of NCAN.* Retrieved from http://www.collegeaccess.org/history

Ohio College Access Network. (2014). *About OCAN.* Retrieved from http://www.ohiocan.org/the-network-2/about-ocan/

Pasque, P. A., Carducci, R., Kuntz, A. K., & Gildersleeve, R. E. (2012). *Special issue: Qualitative inquiry for equity in higher education: Methodological innovations, implications, and interventions* (Vol. 37). San Francisco, CA: Jossey-Bass.

Perna, L. W. (2006). Studying college access and choice: A proposed conceptual model. In J. Smart & M. Paulsen (Eds.), *Higher education: Handbook of theory and research.* Memphis, TN: Springer.

Perna, L. W., Rowan-Kenyon, H., Bell, A., Thomas, S. L., & Li, C. (2008). A typology of federal and state programs designed to promote college enrollment. *Journal of Higher Education, 79*(3), 243–267.

Say Yes to Education. (2013). *Say Yes to Education—Our mission.* Retrieved from http://www.sayyestoeducation.org/our-mission

Seftor, N. S., Mamun, A., & Schirm, A. (2009). *The impacts of regular upward bound on postsecondary outcomes 7–9 years after scheduled high school graduation: Final report.* Washington, DC: Mathematica Policy Research Inc.

St. John, E. P., & Asker, E. H. (2003). *Refinancing the college dream: Access, equal opportunity, and justice for taxpayers.* Baltimore, MD: Johns Hopkins University Press.

St. John, E. P., Daun-Barnett, N., & Moronski, K. (2012). *Public policy in higher education.* New York, NY: Routledge.

Swail, W. S., & Perna, L. W. (2002). Pre-college outreach programs: A national perspective. In W. G. Tierney & L. S. Hagedorn (Eds.), *Increasing access to college: Extending possibilities for all students* (pp. 15–34). Albany, NY: State University of New York Press.

Tierney, W. G., Corwin, Z. B., & Colyar, J. E. (2005). *Preparing for college: Nine elements of effective outreach.* Albany, NY: State University of New York Press.

Tough, P. (2008). *Whatever it takes: Geoffrey Canada's quest to Change Harlem and America* (pp. xii, 310). Boston, MA: Mariner Books.

U.S. Department of Education. (2011). *College access challenge grant program.* Retrieved from http://www2.ed.gov/programs/cacg/awards.html

Vandeventer, P., & Mandell, M. (2007). *Networks that work.* Los Angeles, CA: Community Partners.

Vargas, J. H. (2004). *College knowledge: Addressing information barriers to college.* Boston, MA: The Education Resources Institute.

Venegas, K. M. (2006). Low-income urban high school students' use of the internet to access financial aid. *Journal of Student Financial Aid, 36*(3), 4–15.

W. K. Kellogg Foundation. (2004). *Logic model development guide* (p. 71). Battle Creek, MI: Author.

REFLECTIVE NARRATIVE
Ashley Smith's Journey
Ashley Smith

When I arrived on campus at the University of Michigan (UM), I was certain that I knew exactly what I was interested in studying based on what I had learned in high school. I had it all planned out—I was going to major in psychology in order to become a clinical psychologist. For this, of course, I would need to attend graduate school and that meant one thing: research.

Research played a key role in my decision to attend UM. I wanted an institution where I could receive research experience as an undergraduate. UM has a wonderful program called the Undergraduate Research Opportunity Program (UROP) that connects students with faculty members who are conducting research of their own. This program actually allows students to be a part of the research process. The students choose projects based on their interests. The undergraduates then interview for numerous research positions. If offered more than one position, the students have to decide which position they want to accept. It is important for students to find a project that interests them and take into consideration the faculty member with whom they will be working. This is important because, for some fortunate students, the research sponsor becomes a mentor who helps students excel in research and with academic plans in general.

Certainly, a mentor is a valuable asset to have during a college career. I know that Penny Pasque, my research sponsor, has helped me in countless ways and has provided me perspectives that have guided my plans for the future. This is why it is important when searching for a project that the undergraduate keep an open mind and consider not only the research topic but also the faculty sponsor as well. I have to say that I went into the program pretty closed-minded. I wanted to do psychology work, and I was not interested in much else. That was, until I had my interview with Pasque, who was working as a visiting scholar at UM at the time.

My interview with Pasque was the second interview of my life. Needless to say, I was nervous. I did not know much about the topic of injustices in higher education organizations. But as I heard more about the research project during the interview, the more excited I got about it. I had never explored this topic or even noticed the injustices before this project brought them to my attention. I just figured that people in high positions are usually White males and that is the way it was across institutions. I did not realize that there was something I could actually do about it to make change happen. Pasque's passion for the subject certainly inspired me to become passionate about educational equity as well.

After the interview, I knew that this was the project I wanted to work on, and Pasque was the person with whom I wished to work. When Pasque introduced the concept of "literature reviews" to me, I was confused to say the least. I could not imagine how one could translate important information from an article into the highly condensed form of a review.

When I started searching for of sources on our topic of critical advocacy perspectives on organizations in higher education (Pasque & Carducci, 2015), to be honest, it was a mess. I was looking up articles that had nothing to do with the project. Luckily, Pasque was patient with me and helped me narrow down my results, and I participated in a workshop offered by the university libraries. In no time at all, it felt like I was finding relevant articles. Then came the next problem: There were not many articles on this particular topic. There were plenty of articles about the injustices and inequities experienced by higher education faculty members and students, but not many about the people throughout the organizations (e.g., in the highest positions like deans, provosts, or presidents or in the entry-level positions like clerical, housekeeping, or maintenance). Clearly, more research needed to be conducted. At that point, it dawned on me that the whole purpose of the research project was to show that more research needed to be done and to explore methodologies regarding how to do it.

I started questioning this lack of sources about obvious injustices throughout higher education organizations. I realized that people were probably in the same boat as I was; they simply did not realize that this was a serious problem. To change the way things are, we must first bring attention to the current injustices and inequities within the system of higher education.

Participating in this research project opened my eyes to the world around me. It made me question things that otherwise I would not have noticed. I also realized that the glass ceiling for women—in and out of higher education—remains unbroken. I have been inspired to work for change and stand up for the people who do not have a voice. Looking through the advocacy articles made me aware of higher education leadership injustices and made me aware of many of the injustices that we live with in society every day. People are often judged and held back by the color of their skin, their gender, and/or their sexual orientation. It is a sad truth that I learned from this project, but I am glad that I learned it, because now I can try my best to do something about it throughout my own academic and professional career.

I hope that one day these injustices and inequities will cease to exist, but I know that is naïve. This journey will be a long process of change, but it must be continued. It will take work from every person, not just those affected by the injustices. We must work together to make our world a place where every human being can thrive and get the respect she or he deserves.

Reference

Pasque, P. A., & Carducci, R. (2015). Critical advocacy perspectives on organization in higher education. In M. B. Paulsen (Ed.), *Higher education: Handbook of theory and research. 29*(30). New York, NY: Springer.

REFLECTIVE NARRATIVE
Growing, Learning, and Bringing Back
Amicia Gomez Bowman

This is a narrative where theory trickles down to practice. Mine is a lived experience that, according to research, would be limited to a statistic—and one that many people do not know. It is a story that is my own and that I am proud to share in this book about engaged research and practice.

I identify as a first-generation, Latina college graduate who grew up in southwest Detroit, Michigan. I came from a single-parent, low-income household and a community that did not have (and still struggles to offer) quality education or other human services. I faced much adversity in pursuing an education because of Detroit's many funding issues and resultant lack of public services.

My story would be incomplete if I avoided the topic of my father and his friends, even though it is a difficult story to share. I did not have a father who loved and cared for his family. My father is an alcoholic and an aggressive man. He was incarcerated for sexual abuse from the time I was 7 until I turned 13. God gave us the ability to forgive, the strength to move on, and the perseverance to continue loving others and ourselves.

We came to live in Detroit to "start over," as my mother called it, when I was five years old. The Detroit public schools were where I started school and learned English in the classroom. Though I did well academically, life at home was still a struggle. My father kept drinking, and my older sister and mother fought all the time.

Before my teenage years, I was taught what not to do through the mistakes made by my parents and older sister. I saw firsthand the traumatic damage that a history of infidelity, drugs, alcohol, and sexual and domestic violence does to a family. Education was what helped me cope through all of the personal obstacles that encompassed my life. I had great teachers in school who believed in me and told me to always do my best. It was learning

265

that distracted me from the issues at home and my anger. For example, I always took advantage of being involved in something positive after school. Being involved in sports, social clubs, and counseling sessions with my psychologists kept me together emotionally. These experiences helped me move forward with my life. I was able to attend the University of Michigan (UM) because of the Hispanic College Fund and Horatio Alger Association scholarships; my economic family contribution was zero. As an undergraduate at UM, I continued to participate in social clubs such as the Michigan Research Community, Delta Tau Lambda Sorority Incorporated, and the Latino Students Organization, and I worked in university programs related to tutoring, mentorship, and education. Each of these experiences helped me gain additional professional and leadership skills. This active participation also helped me feel included in the university community. Learning inside and outside of academia motivated me to become a campus leader and a representative of higher education for my home community within Detroit. I learned the power that universities can have when they partner with communities like mine to address issues.

I learned through my sociology and Latino studies major, and African and Afro-American minor, that my Latin@ community and I face a lot of adversity in pursuing a quality education. When I realized that I was the only one—or one of two—persons of color in my lectures and discussions, I made a commitment to invest in having more Latin@ at the forefront of the educational community at UM. I promised to graduate from college, continue on to graduate school, and simultaneously teach my community to do the same.

The Chicano/a Educational Pipeline shows that out of 100 students, 8 will actually graduate with a bachelor's degree (Solórzano & Yosso, 2006). I am currently one of the eight students with a bachelor's degree. In studying the data in various journal articles, figures, and tables, I began to question why so many of us have been defeated by these challenges. Why have we not flipped the statistics so that it is 92 out of 100 who graduate with a bachelor's degree?

Through my research and experience, I learned that statistics could be changed and that more of us can be high school and college graduates if we speak up for ourselves and become the researchers, the grant writers, the teachers, and we sit at the table with people who hold these titles and make educational policies. Latin@ can be our own leaders. Schools and teachers across the United States invested in the well-being of their students need access to this research and these theories so they can implement them into academic practice. Soon after this realization, I began to search for opportunities to gain knowledge about the philanthropic structures of academic institutions so that I could bring it back to my community. My search led me to the National Forum on Higher Education for the Public Good.

I started working at the National Forum in 2012 as an office assistant and research associate when I was an undergraduate senior. After I graduated from UM, I was promoted to administrative assistant and was given the opportunity to become more involved with research projects and directly assist the director with external activities at the National Forum. When I learned about this organization and the goals it strives to promote, I knew this was a place that would help me practice my passion for community organizing, educational access and attainment for underrepresented people. I also knew that my experience here would open more doors for my future and would teach me, through practice, how independent nonprofit organizations become established and successful. This would enable me to teach my community resource centers how to achieve success as nonprofits. Today, I have become a stronger advocate and role model for my community by being a researcher and working in administrative services that are affiliated with expanding access to higher education for the public good.

Few people with stories like mine get this far in higher education, and this is why I tell my story. I want to make it known that people like me are enrolled in colleges and universities across the country and that we are capable of overcoming the obstacles that keep us from progressing. We can graduate from high school, graduate from college, and reverse the numbers on the charts that represent us. We have let the statistics speak for us without realizing it; now we speak for ourselves.

Reference

Solórzano, D. G., & Yosso, T. J. (2006, March). *Leaks in the Chicana and Chicanoeducational pipeline* (Latino Policy and Issues Brief No. 13). Los Angeles, CA: UCLA Chicano Studies. Retrieved from http://www.chicano.ucla.edu/files/LPIB_13March2006.pdf

REFLECTIVE NARRATIVE
Undocumented Students
Chengchen Zhu

A s an intern at the National Forum on Higher Education for the
Public Good (National Forum), I was assigned to a project about
undocumented students. As an international student, I understood
the importance of having appropriate documents to be able to travel and
study in the United States, but I had only a vague notion of what "undocumented" status meant.

I knew that American history is marked by waves of immigrants, and
their presence has resulted in a country of remarkable creativity. I wondered about the latest wave and its reception, learning from media accounts
and my research that immigration reform has become a more visible and
divisive issue in the last few years. But I had little knowledge about why people become unauthorized or undocumented and what obstacles they face in
receiving an education. But I soon learned.

In 2014, over 11.3 million immigrants lived in the United States. An
estimated 65,000 undocumented children graduate from high school each
year (Krogstad & Passel, 2015). After reading articles, policy briefs, and
information online, I found out that many of these young people entered the
country with their parents and now have to hide their identities or face the
possibility of being returned to countries that are in some ways more foreign
to them than their adopted homeland. Although many of these students
perform well academically in the American K–12 system, college attendance
is a hurdle; there is little financial aid for them, and some colleges are reluctant to accept them. Being undocumented means they do not have the same
economic, social, and educational opportunities as others. After I became
involved in the research, the problems of undocumented students in college
became my concern too.

I have been studying the educational experience of undocumented
students in higher education. Although federal law does not prohibit

undocumented students from attending colleges or universities, most states require that they pay out-of-state tuition, and they are not eligible for most federal loans, financial aid, and scholarships. The accompanying pressures and lack of prospects for attending college lead to these students dropping out of school to seek full-time employment and taking lower-paying jobs. Apart from tuition, the students have other obstacles to surmount in college, such as a lack of adequate advising and mentoring, concerns about family and deportation, limited information about career eligibility, and concerns about what happens after college. Undocumented students are now taking greater risks by going public with their status in an effort to gain public support. This worries me. I want to do something. Is the research enough? Is gathering data and providing the information to agencies, institutions, and policymakers helping to change the situation? Are the meetings and the sharing of student stories sponsored by the National Forum sufficient to move people to action?

Some state governments and other institutions have been trying to help undocumented students. Currently, at least 18 states have provisions allowing for in-state tuition rates for undocumented students. What might influence more states to adopt such policies, and is pushing for that part of our proper role as researchers? I am convinced that a concerted effort, such as that encouraged and facilitated by the National Forum, by supportive mentors, high school counselors, and higher education administrators can have an enormous impact for undocumented students as they navigate the educational system. The federal government, state governments, and individual colleges and universities should ensure undocumented students have the same opportunities to succeed as their peers.

At the National Forum we talk about helping people move from awareness to understanding to commitment and then to action. I have gone through these stages. Engaging in the research on undocumented students significantly increased my awareness; from that understanding, my commitment to sharing what I learned and my desire to help move others to commitment grew. What I learned through the research spurred me to want to help people take action on this issue. I like the fact that we talk to and involve many different people in this work. I imagine this is why engagement works. Our research let me understand how providing higher education to everyone in society, specifically underprivileged and minority groups, creates a stronger democracy.

Higher education helped shape this society, and expanding it will create opportunities for more people. Greater access will advance and improve the way the country operates. Providing college access to undocumented students should improve the quality of life in the United States. College access creates social uplift and serves as a public good, not simply a private benefit. Is coming to this type of understanding what generates passion for an issue? I wonder if this is what makes engaged research so powerful—that people really do care about issues, that the work they do is not just about getting a publication or a promotion. It is about making a difference.

Learning about undocumented students has helped me understand more about American education and culture. Undocumented students need our help, and all of us can benefit from helping them. Helping them pursue their dreams of higher education proves that the United States is still a country that values hard work and rewards it with earned opportunities. With college degrees, these students will be able to contribute substantially more to society. As for me, I will probably never lose sight of this issue. Engaged research has been a door into this topic, and my education at the University of Michigan has been enhanced because of it.

Reference

Krogstad, J. M., & Passel, J. S. (2015). *Five facts about illegal immigration in the U.S. Fact Tank*, Pew Research Center. Retrieved from http://www.pewresearch.org/fact-tank/2015/11/19/5-facts-about-illegal-immigration-in-the-u-s

Part Five

CONCLUDING THOUGHTS ON ENGAGED
RESEARCH AND PRACTICE

12

REFLECTIONS
Lessons Learned and Next Steps

Betty Overton

Compiling this book has been an opportunity for us at the National Forum on Higher Education for the Public Good (National Forum) to refresh the motivations and passions that brought many of us to this type of research; to examine the level and quality of our practice; and to question outcomes and impact with an eye to strengthening direction, focus, implementation, and results. In reviewing the eclectic collection of projects pursued by National Forum staff, students, and graduates—as well as individuals with two or three degrees of separation from the National Forum—we have seen how each is an attempt to engage a community, an institution, or a constituent in a search for answers to real and immediate problems. In describing organizations doing *action research*—a term akin to our concept of "engaged research"—and the learning that happens in organizations, Ortrun Zuber-Skerritt (1991) notes: "It is vital that such learning be both encouraged and shared and in this way the system is endowed with a dynamic learning milieu or culture" (p. 31). At the National Forum, we covet this culture for ourselves, and we also seek it in our partners. As we put this portrait of our efforts before a larger public, we encourage the work of engaged research by others.

These reflections give only our side of the story. We talk about the lessons *we* have learned from our work. We do not intend to speak for those with whom we have partnered.

Research, Medewar (1969) tells us, is learning with the intention of adding knowledge to the public sphere. Through research we explain and share both propositions and suppositions about what is happening around us. *Engaged research* is collaborative learning with the specific intent of addressing social and organizational issues and adding to public knowledge. Even though most of the projects described in this book were discrete activities pursued independently of one another, they all share this intent, and not just because of their connection to, or knowledge of, the National Forum. Additionally, they share two common denominators at the heart of engaged research.

Collaborative and Participatory Relationship With an External Community

Engaged research is not bench science that can be pursued in solitary laboratories. Collaboration is necessary. Successful and sustained engaged research is seeded in relationships that grow out of shared perspectives, information, and resources. It brings researchers and collaborating partners into relationships to ensure the questions being pursued are grounded not simply in empirical calculations but in addressing problems that impact people's lives. The National Forum's work has always been tied to its relationships and partnerships. One of the definitions of *leadership* used by the W.K. Kellogg Foundation is "getting good things done with the help of others." In many respects, this is a definition about engagement, and one we embrace.

In thinking about engaged research, we might use a similar description. Engaged research is partnering and collaborating with others to pursue shared questions. Scholars and practitioners work together around issues of interest (St. John, 2013). In the research presented in this book, the work has been, in most instances, cocreated. For example, the National Forum's long-term focus on undocumented students would not have happened except for the relationship of the National Forum's director with national Latino scholars and leaders who felt focusing the issue on a major campus, outside of states where immigration issues were more predictably front and center, was in the public good. The National Forum was not the only research organization interested in this issue, but it could, from its stance in a major Midwestern research university, bring a unique perspective. In working with the National Forum, Latino leaders and scholars were at the table ensuring that the voices of people who knew the reality of the lives of undocumented students would help shape the research agenda.

Our work on immigration and undocumented student issues could not have taken place without such partnership; the National Forum did not initially have the expertise or experience to understand the issues or know the players. In his book, *Engaged Scholarship*, Van de Ven (2007) writes the following in a chapter entitled "Practicing Engaged":

> A basic premise of engaged scholarship is that researchers can make more penetrating and insightful advances to science and practice by obtaining

the perspectives of relevant stakeholders in problem formulation, theory building, research design, and problem solving than when they perform these research activities alone. The more ambiguous and complex the problem the greater the need for engaging others who can provide different perspectives for revealing critical dimensions of the nature, context, and implications of the problem domain. Engagement provides a way of triangulating on a research question. (p. 284)

The type of engaged research we pursue goes even further than the sharing of perspectives. This cocreation process is fraught with difficulty, as many of the writers in this book have shared. Relationships are hard to develop and maintain; they take time and close involvement. So, while many institutions are vested in the concept of engagement, they are impatient with the relational investment that faculty and administrators must make to ensure the success of such endeavors. And this does take time. Anyone who undertakes engaged research must be ready to invest significant time beyond the campus to nurture and support the partner relationship. Additionally, there is ongoing need to support sustainable campus structures that can allow for these long-term relational investments.

At Marygrove College, for example, we maintained office hours, just to be present on the campus. In the work that Esmeralda Hernandez-Hamed led with Hope Village, there were times we showed up for meetings, and no one else came. But we went back. We have learned we need to be patient in dealing with multiple constituents and partners who are not vested in our particular types of engaged research.

Just as money is one of the major causes of marital conflict, issues of resource sharing and funding are potentially difficult areas in relationships for engaged research. The euphoria and passion of marching off together to do battle against the forces of social injustice can be exciting; however, managing ongoing relationships requires organizational conversations.

Elizabeth Hudson's Chapter 3 notes the tensions that can arise when community members perceive institutions as profiting from their involvement with them. She mentions that work sometimes diminishes or stops as grant funding ends. Further, as John C. Burkhardt notes in his historical overview of the National Forum (Chapter 2), the important role that funding plays in the ebb and flow of research activities is extremely relevant. Interest does not wane, but resources to pursue those interests are not always reliable. Much of the literature about engaged research focuses on its philosophical and structural components. Scholars sometimes mention issues of time, structure, or ideological conflicts in these partnerships. Few share the struggles over resources. And in times of scarce resources the relational aspects of engaged research are crucial. If engaged research is centered in shared concerns about issues, grant funding is not the reason for the partnership.

In addition, leadership is important to collaborative and participatory engaged research. In this book, where appropriate, we have intentionally used people's names. W.K. Kellogg is famous for the saying that some of us learned from our association with our founding funder, namely that "only people make a difference" (personal communication, Russell Mawby, CEO, W.K. Kellogg Foundation, 1992). Though this may seem obvious, many researchers work in the world of ideas and theories. Effective participation with communities and other institutions is work with people, and especially with their leaders. Scholars bring the power and influence of academic knowledge into these collaborative arrangements, but to work toward the social justice outcomes many of our projects intend to address, we have to remain "in service to," as described in Chapter 1. In some instances, that can mean accepting different leadership dynamics. In our classrooms we teach and model for students when it is time to step up and when it is time to step back in discussions. Engaged research is an exercise in finding these times for researchers and our partners. In their chapters, Nathan J. Daun-Barnett, Cassie L. Barnhardt, and Penny A. Pasque allude to these leadership dynamics that are part of research partnerships.

But collaborative and participatory relationships are only one part of the uniqueness of engaged research. Another essential element is sharing the ownership of a problem or question, not just as an objective onlooker, but as someone vested in the issue who cares about it and the people involved and who wants to help seek solutions.

Shared Problems and Needs Identification: Shared Work

The relational nature of engaged research includes the approaches we take to our work. Researchers and community members share a responsibility for identifying and defining the specific research problems for collaborative work. Solo scholars carrying out research projects entirely in an academic environment do not solve most of the problems of our society, such as how to increase college attendance in economically challenged communities or how to influence leadership development in a large urban community.

Sharing the identification of problems and needs does not mean abandoning the principles of trustworthiness, reliability, and/or validity that are essential elements of credible social science research. If we are vested in social justice issues, we ask the people most impacted by them for the questions and the problems—we do not make them up. The impacted parties ask, *How might we get more immigrant students into community colleges? What things might our community do to get more students into college? How might we restructure our curriculum to embed leadership development in such a way that it impacts leadership in our community? How might we build a state process that would support local communities to better prepare students for access to college? What can institutions do to promote better access for undocumented students?* It is important to begin this process with questions and dialogue. It is in such conversations that relational partners share what is most important, and that is what drives our research.

Because engaged research is collaborative and participatory, it can be more difficult than traditional social science research. But in the give-and-take of defining the focus of questions and methodologies lies the opportunity for issues to emerge that may not arise in other types of research endeavors. Magdalena Martinez's study (Chapter 10) began with questions from teachers struggling to understand the lives of their students. Their perceptions about their students' lives raised questions begging for the type of reality check that Martinez's study provided. The researchers engaged the student interview participants in ways that allowed for authentic sharing; it is in this shared framing of the research that the essence of engagement occurs.

The work on undocumented students began with concerned leaders trying to understand how to discuss the emerging issue and how to generate information that could open dialogue and policy change. Engaged research can be more complex than other types of research precisely because it does not rest solely on the knowledge of university researchers. There is a body of community knowing that always needs to be integral to the engaged process. This means this type of research can be more time consuming. People outside universities do not observe the academic calendar. They do not care about university spring breaks. The needs of families, economic realities, political pressures, and social stratifications drive the agenda. Esmeralda Hernandez-Hamed's work in Detroit is an example of ways the university had to adjust its calendars to the community's pace of work. Lara Kovacheff-Badke's description of the Marygrove partnership gives a different example. It is a case study in how our researchers had to not only understand and follow the clock of another institution, but also understand how the institution's time frames were also anchored to funding schedules, an accreditation process, and changing institutional personnel.

Shared problem identification brings complexity to research, as it often involves multimethod approaches to data collection and managing a network of relationships outside the university. The resulting types of research can also be riskier and more likely to be derailed because the researcher may have less control over events that may jeopardize the direction or completion of the work. The vagaries of community culture, politics, and resources complicate our planning and data collection processes. In our work with one inner-city community school, the principal changed three times in six months. Flexibility is called for when scholars and community collaborate to do research. The outcomes of successful collaboration are worth working for, but they are challenging to achieve.

We have found, in thinking about shared agenda building for research, especially with our work focused on educational access, that the advice given by Edward St. John (2013) is undoubtedly useful. He suggests that researchers should

1. Maintain a willingness to test their own claims about the links between interventions and outcomes and encourage practitioners to do the same (avoid advocating solutions and be willing to pilot)
2. Consider equity in access along with quality measures when assessing educational and social policies
3. Design and conduct studies that explore how alternative and diverse strategies can move schools, communities, colleges, states toward identified goals
4. Balance equity and quality outcomes with cost considerations including how desired changes can be sustained
5. Recognize that the quality of education and social services is seriously challenged by a decline in public funding. (p. 50)

Conclusion and Recommendations

Engaged research is a process as well as an outcome of intentional activities based on shared interests and issues. The National Forum intends this book to foster thinking about how scholarship and research can be in service to community. In real ways, we have not moved far from the original ideas of the Kellogg investment. The work assembled in this book is selective and not exhaustive of the projects we have undertaken, but we believe this collection of work is illustrative and might be useful to others engaged in this type of work.

We have three concluding recommendations. First, we recommend that other practitioners use these examples to generate their own dialogues about engaged research. Do these chapters meet the test of definitional clarity and help others to understand and imagine their own use of engaged research? Does any of the work featured here support or negate conceptualizations of engaged research, and, if so, how? We suggest that such a conversation among faculty colleagues, graduate students, research associates, or others would allow for more opportunity to think about what it means to do engaged research.

Second, we suggest that new scholars starting to think about their own careers as researchers consider some of the work offered here as examples of how to advance through the processes of academic scrutiny and reward. This is research that many, but not all, institutions advocate. Tenure and promotion guidelines vary, but engaged research is increasingly an accepted and welcomed avenue to pursue important work in the community and in the academy.

Finally, we recommend that institutions revisit and reexamine where this type of work is being done on their campuses, identify issues and challenges for persons pursuing this type of research-focused engagement, and find ways to build or improve supportive structures for sustaining the work over time.

References

Medewar, P. B. (1969). *Induction and intuition in scientific thought.* London, England: Methuen.

St. John, E. (2013). *Research, actionable knowledge, and social change.* Sterling, VA: Stylus.

Van de Ven, A. (2007). *Engaged scholarship: A guide for organizational and social research.* New York, NY: Oxford University Press.

Zuber-Skerritt, O. (1991). *Action research for change and development.* Aldershot, England: Avebury Gower Publishing.

CONTRIBUTORS

Briana Akani is a senior in the University of Michigan's College of Literature, Science, and the Arts, where she is majoring in psychology and minoring in Afroamerican and African studies and community action and social change. In the fall of 2013, Briana joined the National Forum on Higher Education for the Public Good as an undergraduate research assistant on the Historically Black Colleges and Universities project. She remains involved in this project. During her time at the university, Akani developed strong academic interests in issues pertaining to social justice and equity, particularly for underrepresented populations. Accordingly, her research and career interests revolve around breaking barriers to and resolving disparities in academic, social, and economic success for students and youth of color.

Cassie L. Barnhardt is an assistant professor of higher education at the University of Iowa. Barnhardt's research focuses on various aspects of civic and public engagement—addressing the multiple ways in which college students learn about and enact social responsibility, as well as the ways that universities contribute to democracy and civic life. Some of her specific studies have examined campus-based activism. Examples include the student antisweatshop movement, advocacy for undocumented immigrant students, campus organizing related to affirmative action policies, and contentions over campus labor conditions. Barnhardt's work has been published in *The Journal of Higher Education, Research in Higher Education,* and the *Journal of College Student Development,* among others. In 2015 she was named an Emerging Scholar of ACPA-College Student Educators International. Currently, she teaches courses on the administration of student affairs, organizational behavior and management in postsecondary institutions, and mixed-methods research design.

Amicia Gomez Bowman, former administrative assistant and research assistant at the National Forum on Higher Education for the Public Good, is now a resource teacher in the Ypsilanti Michigan School District. A graduate of the University of Michigan, with bachelor's degrees in sociology and Latino studies and a minor in Africa and African American studies, Bowman is pursuing a master's degree in social work.

John C. Burkhardt has directed the National Center for Institutional Diversity since 2013. He is also a professor of clinical practice in the Center for the Study of Higher and Postsecondary Education at the University of Michigan and serves as special assistant to the provost for university engagement. He was the founding director of the National Forum on Higher Education for the Public Good, which he led from 2000 to 2013. From 1993 to 2000 he was program director for leadership and higher education at the W.K. Kellogg Foundation, where he led several major initiatives focused on transformation and change in higher education and participated in a comprehensive effort to encourage leadership development among college students. Burkhardt's research focuses on leadership and transformation, organizational culture, and the role of philanthropy in U.S. society. He has authored several books and articles on leadership and on higher education.

Jessica L. Cañas earned a bachelor's in anthropology and environmental studies from Loyola University–Chicago in 2006. Upon graduating, she worked in Chicago with communities on the southeast side of the city as the community educator for the Southeast Environmental Task Force. Later, she worked in the Field Museum's Department of Environment, Culture and Conservation as an urban conservation educator. In 2014 she earned a master's degree in higher education at the University of Michigan–Ann Arbor. Prior to arriving at the University of Michigan she completed one year of graduate studies at Cornell University in international agriculture and rural development and served in the Peace Corps from 2010 to 2012 as a protected areas management volunteer in Honduras. Cañas's interests lie in the intersection of the conservation of natural areas and the peoples and cultures they sustain, social and environmental justice, and the disparity of underrepresented racial minority students in the sciences.

Jill Casner-Lotto is director of the Community College Consortium for Immigrant Education. She is also a writer and research consultant with over 20 years of experience in human resources and labor–management issues. Casner-Lotto has directed numerous national policy research projects, working in conjunction with business, labor, and academic leaders to anticipate workplace trends and undertake new fields of research aimed at improving both business results and employees' quality of working life. Her research has been funded by the Ford Foundation, Alfred P. Sloan Foundation, U.S.-Japan Foundation, and major corporations and labor unions. She earned a bachelor's degree in social sciences from Johns Hopkins University and a master's degree in journalism from the Medill School of Journalism, Northwestern University.

Tony Chambers is the chairperson for the Leadership, Higher and Adult Education Department; associate professor of higher education; and founding director of the Centre for the Study of Students in Postsecondary Education at the Ontario Institute for Studies in Education (OISE)/University of Toronto. He previously served as program coordinator of the Higher Education Program at OISE and associate vice provost of students at the University of Toronto. Chambers was formerly associate director of the National Forum on Higher Education for the Public Good and adjunct associate professor at the University of Michigan. He has served as an administrator and/or faculty member at several higher education institutions including Michigan State University, University of Iowa, University of Missouri–St. Louis, University of Florida, and Illinois State University. He researches and teaches in the areas of student learning, development, and success, as well as in the social purposes of postsecondary education. Chambers has been awarded several fellowships and served on several domestic and international boards focusing on education and learning. He has been invited to make major presentations at conferences and meetings internationally and has published widely in various professional journals and edited books. His publications include the coedited book *Higher Education for the Public Good: Emerging Voices From a National Movement* (Jossey-Bass, 2005).

Will Cherrin is an academic adviser for the CUNY Start program at the College of Staten Island in New York. Prior to his work at the college level, Cherrin spent seven years providing college access and success services for high school students in the Bronx, New York, and Richmond, California. Though he prefers the West coast (especially the hip-hop), he loves working with his New York students and learns from them every day. Cherrin graduated from the Center for the Study of Higher and Postsecondary Education (CSHPE) at the University of Michigan in 2014 with a concentration in diversity and social justice. During his time with CSHPE he served as a graduate student research assistant at the National Forum on Higher Education for the Public Good.

Nathan J. Daun-Barnett is an associate professor of higher education administration at the University at Buffalo. Daun-Barnett's work examines state financial aid and high school course requirement policies, the roles of community colleges as gateways to postsecondary opportunity, and the growing emphasis on community-based strategies to increase access to college. Currently, Daun-Barnett conducts a formative evaluation of the Florida College Access Network (FCAN), directs two College Success Centers in Buffalo Public Schools, and also oversees a GEAR UP grant that will expand the college success center model to five additional schools. For the past four years, he has partnered with Buffalo Public Schools and Say Yes to Education–Buffalo to coordinate the Buffalo FAFSA Completion Project, an initiative to increase FAFSA completion rates among Buffalo City and charter school students. Additionally, he is cochair of the postsecondary pathways taskforce for Say Yes to Education, which is charged with identifying strategies to address systemic barriers preventing students in Buffalo from transitioning from high school to college. His most recent book, *College Counseling for Admissions Professionals: Improving Access and Retention* (Routledge, 2013), challenges college admissions professionals to rethink their collective roles and responsibilities in the transition from high school to college as they help students become college and career ready.

Esmeralda Hernandez-Hamed is a doctoral candidate at the University of Michigan's Center for the Study of Higher and Postsecondary Education and a research associate at the National Forum on Higher Education for the Public Good. Prior to moving to Ann Arbor to join the doctoral program, she was a student at the University of California–Irvine, where she received her bachelor's degree in political science in 2012. Her current research interests include the role of university-community partnerships in increasing college-going culture in communities, understanding institutional decisions to improve or restrict access to higher education for underrepresented populations, and the role of institutional agents in facilitating access to higher education for underrepresented students in high school.

Elizabeth Hudson is a senior lecturer in the Irvin D. Reid Honors College at Wayne State University. She teaches seminars about urban structures and active citizenship. Her research emphasizes community-based deliberation and problem-solving related to education concerns. Hudson earned a doctorate at the Center for the Study of Higher and Postsecondary Education at the University of Michigan in 2013 and worked at the Charles F. Kettering Foundation before starting her position at Wayne State.

Aurora Kamimura is a doctoral candidate in the Center for the Study of Higher and Postsecondary Education at the University of Michigan, and a research associate at the National Forum on Higher Education for the Public Good. Kamimura has extensive administrative experience in statewide postsecondary access initiatives and multicultural affairs and most recently served as an associate dean of student services working with underserved and underprepared students in the K–20 pipeline. Her research agenda examines organizational resilience of postsecondary institutions, with a focus on minority-serving institutions.

Kamimura complements her research agenda with a specific emphasis in broadening access and success strategies for underserved and underprepared students. She earned her bachelor's in social sciences with a minor in public health from the University of California–Irvine, and her master's in administration, planning, and social policy from Harvard University.

Lena M. Khader received her master's degree in professional counseling at the University of Oklahoma and earned a bachelor's in psychology at Oklahoma City University as a Clara Luper Scholar. With the help of community members and Upward Bound students, Khader founded Making Herstory, a created safe space for young high school women of color and allies to participate in workshops regarding women of color feminism, ethnic studies, and members' personal narratives as a form of self, social, and political empowerment. In the future, she plans to work as a high school counselor with low-income and/or immigrant populations in her community of south Oklahoma City.

Lara Kovacheff-Badke is a doctoral candidate in higher education with a concentration in organizational behavior and management at the University of Michigan. Her research explores the negotiation of legal pressures and institutional interests as university decision makers construct responses to legal mandates. Specifically, she addresses ambiguities and paradoxes that affect institutional interests and societal goals of justice and fairness. As a senior research associate at the National Forum on Higher Education for the Public Good, she employs organizational and social justice frameworks to applied research and practice on issues of organizational transformation, strategic planning, institutional culture, assessment and accreditation, sustainable programming, urban leadership, and educational access and success. Kovacheff-Badke earned her juris doctor (1997) from the University of Windsor and holds a master of art in higher education leadership and administration (2008) from the University of Michigan.

Megan B. Lebre currently serves as an academic adviser in the Department of Molecular and Cell Biology (MCB) at the University of California–Berkeley. Her special areas are supervising the peer advisers program, counseling students on major probation, liaison to the faculty, and supporting event coordination for the MCB department. Previously, she served as an adviser/programming coordinator for student life and leadership programs at California State University–East Bay in Hayward, and has also worked at the University of Portland in Portland, Oregon, as a residence hall director. Lebre is a May 2011 graduate from the University of Oklahoma with a master's degree in adult and higher education administration with an emphasis in student affairs administration. She is also a May 2009 graduate of the University of Oklahoma with a bachelor's degree in communication with a minor in nonprofit organizational studies.

Estefanía López obtained a master's in higher education at the University of Michigan–Ann Arbor, where she worked as a research assistant for the National Forum on Higher Education for the Public Good and as a program assistant for the National Center for Institutional Diversity. Born in San Salvador, El Salvador, and raised in Los Angeles, California, she grew politically and socially aware of the issues affecting undocumented immigrants. Her research, professional, and service interests center on exploring empowerment perspectives that validate a multiplicity of cultural, linguistic, and racial-ethnic student backgrounds. She seeks to utilize research and policy tools to educate vulnerable communities and advance a social advocacy agenda for educational equity, and immigrant and workers' rights. She currently serves as an outreach coordinator for the Center for Educational Outreach at the University of Michigan.

Magdalena Martinez is an assistant professor for the Department of Educational Psychology and Higher Education and director of education programs at the Lincy Institute at the University of Nevada–Las Vegas (UNLV). Prior to UNLV, she served as the assistant vice chancellor for academic and student affairs for the Nevada System of Higher Education. Martinez also worked at the National Forum of Higher Education for the Public Good at the University of Michigan, where she served as a program evaluator for a leadership program to prepare individuals for the presidency at minority-serving institutions. Her research interests encompass student access and success for underrepresented students, the role of community colleges, and higher education leadership and public policy. Martinez holds a doctorate in education from the University of Michigan, a master's in education from Harvard University, and a bachelor's in business from UNLV.

Betty Overton is a professor of clinical practice in the Center for the Study of Higher and Postsecondary Education (CSHPE) and the director of the National Forum on Higher Education for the Public Good at the University of Michigan. She received her doctorate in educational leadership from George Peabody College of Vanderbilt University. Her undergraduate and master's degrees in English are from Tennessee State University, and she has done further study at Harvard University. In CSHPE, she teaches courses in the history of higher education, race and ethnicity, access and equity, and other areas. Overton is active in higher education, serving on the Higher Learning Commission of the North Central Association of Colleges and Universities, the board of the American Association of Higher Education & Accreditation, and the editorial board of *Liberal Education*, published by the Association of American Colleges and Universities. She has been a member of the board of the Council of Graduate Schools, the Fund for the Improvement of Postsecondary Education, and the advisory board of the Center for the Study of Higher Education at Pennsylvania State University. Overton served as provost at Spring Arbor University, Michigan, for a decade, where she was responsible for all aspects of the academic program.

Penny A. Pasque is the Brian E. & Sandra O'Brien Presidential Professor and program area coordinator of adult and higher education in the Department of Educational Leadership and Policy Studies at the University of Oklahoma. She is also an affiliate faculty with women's and gender studies and the Center for Social Justice. Currently, Pasque serves as the associate editor for *The Journal of Higher Education*. Her research addresses in/equities in higher education, dis/connections between higher education and society, and complexities in critical qualitative inquiry. She teaches diversity in higher education and qualitative research and has served as a keynote speaker and facilitator on diversity and social justice issues across the country. Her research has appeared in *The Journal of Higher Education, Qualitative Inquiry, Diversity in Higher Education,* and *The Review of Higher Education,* among others. She is author of *American Higher Education Leadership and Policy: Critical Issues and the Public Good* (Palgrave Macmillan, 2010); *Empowering Women in Higher Education and Student Affairs: Theory, Research, Narratives, and Practice From Feminist Perspectives* (edited with Errington Nicholson, Stylus, 2011); *Qualitative Inquiry for Equity in Higher Education: Methodological Innovations, Implications, and Interventions* (authored with Carducci, Kuntz & Gildersleeve, Jossey-Bass, 2012); and *Critical Qualitative Inquiry: Foundations and Futures* (edited with Cannella & Salazar Pérez, Left Coast Press, 2015).

Kimberly A. Reyes is currently pursuing a doctorate in higher education at the University of Michigan's (UM) Center for the Study of Higher and Postsecondary Education. Prior to entering the doctoral program, Reyes earned her master's degree in higher education from UM. Originally from Los Angeles, California, she graduated from Duke University in 2003. While at Duke, she became involved in *Mi Gente: Asociacion de Estudiantes Latinos* and *Latinas Promoviendo Comunidad*/Lambda Pi Chi Sorority, Inc. After working at Teach for America–Miami and the admissions staff at the University of Miami, she returned to UM in 2007 to work as an assistant director of admissions and coordinator of Latino student recruitment in the under-graduate admissions office. Reyes also continued to serve her sorority as the national vice president of expansion and southeastern regional director and currently sits on the executive board for the Duke University Latino Alumni Association.

Ashley Smith is a third year in the College of Literature, Science, and the Arts at the University of Michigan. She is concentrating in psychology with minors in cultural anthropology and Italian. Smith grew up in Midland, Michigan, and attended the Saginaw Arts and Sciences Academy in Saginaw, Michigan, for her secondary education. Her research focuses on the injustices faced by minorities, women, and the LGBTQ community. After graduating from the University of Michigan, she plans to pursue a doctorate in clinical psychology.

Kyle Southern is a doctoral student in public policy and postsecondary education at the University of Michigan. He also serves as a graduate student research assistant with the National Forum on Higher Education for the Public Good and the National Center for Institutional Diversity. Prior to pursuing his doctorate, Southern worked as a policy research associate with the Tennessee State Collaborative on Reforming Education and as an education research specialist for CAN, a nonprofit research and development corporation in suburban Washington, DC. He holds a master's in education policy and bachelor's in American studies from Vanderbilt University. Southern is a native of Winston-Salem, NC.

Edward P. St. John was Algo D. Henderson Collegiate Professor Emeritus at the University of Michigan's Center for the Study of Higher and Postsecondary Education (2005–2016). Now an emeritus professor, his scholarship focus is on education for a just society, an interest that stems from three decades of research on educational policy and practice. He is a Fellow of the American Educational Research Association and has received awards for leadership and research from the Association for the Study of Higher Education.

Teresita Wisell is associate dean of the Gateway Center at Westchester Community College in Valhalla, New York, and executive director of the Community College Consortium for Immigrant Education. Wisell has been in the field of higher education administration and enrollment management for over 24 years. From August 1994 through July 2008, she served as director of admissions at Westchester Community College. She was born in Camaguey, Cuba, and immigrated to the United States with her family as a child. Wisell regularly serves as a panelist and presenter on issues regarding access to education and the immigrant population. She holds a bachelor's degree in international relations and Spanish and a master's in marketing.

Chengchen Zhu comes from China and is in her first year as a master's student in teaching and learning in educational studies at the University of Michigan. Prior to moving to Ann Arbor, she received her bachelor's at Sichuan International Studies University, China, majoring in teaching Chinese as a foreign language. She had a one-year exchange experience at University of California–Riverside during her third year of college. She was involved in a project of the Department of Education in Southwest University, China, and participated in writing a research article ("Local Identity of No-Fee Preservice Students and Its Impact on Their Localized Professional Orientation" (*Chinese Education & Society*, 2014) In addition, she cowrote another essay, "The Balanced Development of Vocational Education: Case Study on Four Municipalities in China" (*Cross-cultural Communication*, 2015). She shows great interest in higher education in comparative perspectives related to China and hopes that all students, regardless of their culture, language, and religion, have equal chances to pursue academic success.

community engagement at, 167
community-university partnerships
    at, 157, 159, 166–67
demographic changes at, 154
Detroit helped by, 157
engaged research exemplified at, 173
engagement integrated by, 153
faculty engagement at, 171
FERA collaborating with, 166
fundraising for, 167
future direction of, 170–73
historical background of, 154–55
institutionalization stages at, 168
mission of, 154, 172
National Forum assisting, 166
as National Forum project, 15, 17
organizational transformation at,
    156, 157, 168–69, 172
resources for, 158
social change at, 160
social problems addressed by, 152
urban leadership development at,
    154–55, 156–61, 162
urban leadership supported by
    faculty at, 168–69
MCAN. See Michigan College Access
    Network
McClure, Gail, 5
MDC. See Miami Dade College
methods, WHEN analysis, 40–41
Miami Dade College (MDC), DACA
    collaborating with, 143–44
Michigan
    college access context in, 242–43
    community engagement in, 244
    community foundations in, 242–43
    community role elevated in, 236
    Gratz v. Bollinger affirmative action
        case in, 236
    Grutter v. Bollinger affirmative
        action case in, 236
    higher education as low priority in,
        243
    LCAN in, 240–41

social change strategized by, 258
university access strategies in, 236,
    242, 243
Michigan College Access Network
    (MCAN)
    community appreciating, 253
    grant levels of, 253
    LCAN of, 250–51
    and LCAN structure, 251–52
    models for, 250
    partnerships of, 251, 253–54
    social change accelerated by, 252
    as state college access network,
        249–55
    STRIVE partnering with, 251
Mi Hermana Mayor (My Older
    Sister), as mentoring program for
    immigrant students, 145–46
minoritization
    in community, 104–5
    in education, 186–87
    engaged research on, 187
movement, as research variable, 26

NACAC. See National Association for
    College Admission Counseling
NASFAA. See National Association
    of Student Financial Aid
    Administrators
National Association for College
    Admission Counseling (NACAC),
    203, 205–6
National Association of Student
    Financial Aid Administrators
    (NASFAA), 200, 201, 202, 204,
    205
National College Goal Sunday
    Initiative, 238
National Forum immigration initiative
    acknowledgments of, 192
    action-based research within, 211–12
    as engaged research, 211–12
    environmental influences on, 208–9
    focus shifted in, 206

team developed by, 63–64
urban leadership
BOLD connected to, 173
coaching of, 169
community embracing, 172
Marygrove College developing,
154–55, 156–61, 162
Marygrove College faculty
supporting, 168–69
organizational structures of, 162–64
principles of, 165
student skills in, 170
UROP. *See* Undergraduate Research
Opportunity Program
U.S. Department of Education (USED)
grants administered by, 241
local solutions recognized by, 241

Van de Ven, A. H., 8, 274–75

Walnut Hills Baptist Church (WHBC),
40, 49
Walnut Hills Coalition (WHC), 40, 49
Walnut Hills Community Schools
(WCS), 40, 47
Walnut Hills Education Network
(WHEN)
analysis methods of, 40–41
challenges of, 38, 47, 51
community as vision of, 47
community constructs in, 41
dynamic community need in, 45–46
findings of, 41–42
funding for, 49–51
goals of, 39, 48, 49

higher education supporting, 48–49
inclusive community need in, 42–45
National Forum working with,
37–39, 41, 43–44
partners of, 37–49
WBC as partner of, 40, 49
WCS as partner of, 40, 47
WHC as partner of, 40
WBC. *See* Walnut Baptist Church
WCC. *See* Westchester Community
College
WCS. *See* Walnut Hills Community
Schools
*We ARE Americans: Undocumented
Students Pursuing the American
Dream* (Perez), 217
Weerts, D. J., 85
Westchester Community College
(WCC), 145–46
WHC. *See* Walnut Hills Coalition
Wheatley, M. J., 88
WHEN. *See* Walnut Hills Education
Network
Wisell, Teresita, 17
W.K. Kellogg Foundation
belief of, 5–6
BOLD funded by, 160, 170–71
National Forum supported by, 5–6,
23
working the hyphen, 86

Yosso, T. J.
community culture model by, 217,
230
linguistic capital described by, 229

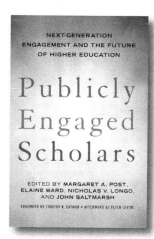

Publicly Engaged Scholars

Next-Generation Engagement and the Future of Higher Educations

Edited by Margaret A. Post, Elaine Ward, Nicholas V. Longo, and John Saltmarsh

Foreword by Timothy K. Eatman

Afterword by Peter Levine

"*Publicly Engaged Scholars* is both unflinching in its presentation of the challenges—personal, professional, political—facing those who seek to transform higher education for the greater good and hopeful in its demonstration of the persistence and adaptability of engaged scholarship. Anyone concerned about higher education's contribution to democracy should read it."—*Andrew J. Seligsohn, President, Campus Compact*

Sty/us

22883 Quicksilver Drive
Sterling, VA 20166-2102

Subscribe to our e-mail alerts: www.Styluspub.com

Also available from Stylus

Community-Based Research
Teaching for Community Impact
Edited by Mary Beckman and Joyce F. Long
Foreword by Timothy K. Eatman

"As a resource to assist scholars and practitioners who wish to effectively conduct [community-based research] CBR, this volume provides useful suggestions for facilitating the process and substantive examples of research projects within a range of disciplines and at different stages of development. Equally important is its potential to serve as an instrument to facilitate strategic thinking and a design for research undertakings that lead to ameliorative outcomes and impact in the communities where the work is done. As such, this book advances the field significantly and helps move us toward these purposes in a focused manner. The aims of this volume are needed to strengthen the field, but especially the second purpose—focus on CBR impact—helps us to attend to critical but often overlooked ethical issues of engagement research. This book likewise presents a powerful set of methodological choices to advance the mission and to provoke the kind of momentum needed to sustain the field."—*Timothy K. Eatman, Higher Education Department, School of Education, Syracuse University, and Faculty Codirector, Imagining America*

Engaging Higher Education
Purpose, Platforms and Programs for Community Engagement
Marshall Welch
Foreword by John Saltmarsh

"Rarely in a maturing scholarly field does a volume provide both breadth and depth of scholarship on community engagement, but Marshall Welch's volume accomplishes this feat masterfully. Welch provides an overview of the community engagement field in its current state, rooted in research and scholarly analysis. From its historical origins as a movement to the evolution of community engagement as a field, this volume extends an evidence-based synthesis of how higher education systems structure and implement community engagement, as well as a 'how-to' for higher education institutions. It will serve multiple purposes for higher education administrators, faculty, community engagement center directors, and graduate students in education."
—*Patrick M. Green, Founding Director, Center for Experiential Learning, Loyola University Chicago; Past Board Chair, International Association for Research on Service-Learning and Community Engagement*

(Continues on previous page)